Empty Nets

HOW GREED AND POLITICS WIPED OUT THE WORLD'S GREATEST FISHERY

Gus Etchegary

with Stephanie Porter

BOULDER
PUBLICATIONS

Library and Archives Canada Cataloguing in Publication

Etchegary, Augustine, 1926-, author
    Empty nets : how greed and politics wiped out the world's greatest
fishery / Augustine Etchegary.

Includes bibliographical references.
Issued in print and electronic formats
ISBN 978-1-927099-30-8 (pbk.).--ISBN 978-1-927099-33-9 (mobi).--
ISBN 978-1-927099-34-6 (epub)

    1. Atlantic cod fisheries--Closures--Atlantic Coast (Canada).
2. Atlantic cod fisheries--Government policy--Atlantic Coast (Canada).
3. Fishery policy--Atlantic Coast (Canada). 4. Fishery management--
Atlantic Coast (Canada). 5. Overfishing--Atlantic Coast (Canada).
6. Etchegary, Augustine, 1926-. 7. Fishery Products International.
I. Title.

Published by Boulder Publications
Portugal Cove-St. Philip's, Newfoundland and Labrador
www.boulderpublications.ca

© 2013 Gus Etchegary

Co-writer: Stephanie Porter
Copy editor: Iona Bulgin
Design and layout: John Andrews

Printed in Canada

 We acknowledge the financial support of the Government of
Newfoundland and Labrador through the Department of Tourism,
Culture and Recreation.

We acknowledge the financial support for our publishing program by the Government
of Canada and the Department of Canadian Heritage through the Canada Book Fund.

To my wife, Kay, and family, without whose
love, affection, and support this book
would not have been written

ABOUT THE AUTHOR

Gus Etchegary accepted a job with Fishery Products Limited in 1947 and worked his way up through the company over the next decades, finally serving as its president from 1976 to 1984. In 1984, FPL was dissolved and rebuilt as Fishery Products International as part of a government-led restructuring of the east-coast fishery; Etchegary served as executive vice-president of the new enterprise until his retirement in 1988.

Etchegary is a former Canadian commissioner to the International Commission of the Northwest Atlantic Fisheries (ICNAF) and the North Atlantic Fishery Organization (NAFO). He participated in various international fishery negotiations, including the signing of a bi-lateral agreement between the USSR and Canada with Romeo LeBlanc. He was president of the Fisheries Association of Newfoundland, chair of the Fisheries Council of Canada, and an advisor to the Coalition of Churches, which formed in the wake of the cod moratorium in 1992. Since retiring, Etchegary has been an active fisheries consultant and a passionate advocate for a sustainable fishery. In 2007, he became the first Newfoundlander to be inducted into the Canadian Soccer Association Hall of Fame.

Etchegary was born in the mining town of St. Lawrence, Newfoundland, in 1924. He lives in Portugal Cove-St. Philip's.

TABLE OF CONTENTS

Part 4: Advocacy

PREFACE

At the heart of this story are the fish. The fish in the waters off Newfoundland and Labrador are a common property resource, owned by all Canadians. Fishermen and fishing companies are licensed to catch quotas of fish, each of which is a portion of a total allowable catch (TAC) determined by scientific assessment.

The federal government's responsibility is to provide science-based fisheries management and, through appropriate regulations and enforcement, to conservatively manage the resource on behalf of Canadians.

It is a responsibility they have never met. Through mismanagement by political leaders, bureaucrats, and internationally controlled fisheries commissions such as the International Convention for the Northwest Atlantic Fisheries (ICNAF) and the Northwest Atlantic Fisheries Organization (NAFO), uncontrolled and unrestricted fishing has led to the demise of most of Newfoundland's fisheries.

When Newfoundland joined Canada in 1949, Canada was elevated from fourteenth to sixth place in the world as a fish-exporting nation ("The famed Newfoundland fisheries add 50% to the total Canadian catch," the *Financial Post* proclaimed in 1950 in an article entitled "Canada Now Top Atlantic Fisher"). That's how valuable the resource was. Newfoundland presented Canada with the golden gift of her fisheries. Documented scientific data illustrates that all groundfish, pelagic fish, and shellfish stocks adjacent to Newfoundland and Labrador were in a strong, healthy condition in 1949. Within 10 years, that changed. Within 20 years, many of these stocks were in serious trouble.

This book traces the transition in Newfoundland's fishing industry from salt fish to fresh-frozen fish. It details the rapid expansion of the frozen-fish industry and the challenges of harvesting, processing, marketing, managing thousands of workers, and dealing with Canadian governments and ICNAF, NAFO, and other international bodies. It tells the tale of a lucrative family-owned fishing business, built with great ingenuity and hard work, torn apart by backroom politics and Canada's reluctance to take a stand and protect her resources.

I have had a front-row seat for it all. Good science has been ignored, short-sighted deals have been signed, and vote-getting has obstructed conservation. Time after time, opportunities to save the fish stocks were missed. I watched them go by, I have argued for change, I have fought for the fish—and I did not do enough.

This book is also my story: how a young man who accepted a job to electrify the province's first fish plants in the 1940s became the impassioned president of a major fish and seafood corporation and then a self-appointed watchdog and fisheries advocate. Throughout the decades I spent on the fish-plant floor and in the boardroom, I knew that the success of Fishery Products Limited (FPL) depended upon having healthy, sustainable fish stocks to harvest. Without the fish, we would fail—and we knew never to take these resources for granted. That hasn't changed.

I wrote this book because I, like a few others, refuse to accept that this once huge, renewable resource cannot be rebuilt to play a role in the economy of Newfoundland and Labrador and provide a source of food for an increasing world population.

The state of the fisheries could determine the long-term prosperity of the province of Newfoundland and Labrador. In the waters around the province lies the potential for a sustainable resource that could serve this province well into the future. Norway, Alaska, Iceland, and Russia have fisheries that are alive, thriving, and contributing to their national economies. Newfoundland does not—but it could. I still believe it could.

Those responsible for the management of Newfoundland and Labrador's fisheries have been driven not by the desire to ensure long-term sustainability but by short-term political gain and greed.

Attempting to manage the Newfoundland fisheries from Ottawa, 2,000 kilometres away, has resulted in a lack of understanding, consideration, and communication. A poorly informed and apathetic public has only made it easier for the abuse to continue.

No one in Newfoundland and Labrador is paying enough attention to the state of the renewable fisheries. Politicians, industry players, and fishermen are fighting one another. Poor decisions are being made. Whole fish are being shipped to other countries for processing, displacing this province from a market that has taken 70 years to develop. Long-term planning is ignored. Other nations continue to heavily fish outside the 200-mile limit, while Canadians stand by and watch.

The east-coast fisheries are not rebounding or rebuilding. They are dying. This book begs Canadians to notice and care and do something about it.

PART 1: EARLY YEARS

The best policy for Newfoundland is to cherish and develop her cod fishery, for in it her people have a reliable mainstay.

—Rev. Dr. Moses Harvey, 1900

Chapter 1
State of the resource 1:
Moses Harvey, 1900

Moses Harvey's enlightened advice has been ignored by those managing Newfoundland and Labrador's fisheries for the past half century or longer.

Born in Northern Ireland in 1820, Harvey emigrated to Newfoundland in 1852. He was the respected and renowned leader of St. Andrews Presbyterian Church in St. John's and a prolific writer, naturalist, historian, and champion of Newfoundland. He wrote books, essays, and articles (over 900 of which were published in the *Montreal Gazette*) and served as secretary of the Newfoundland Fisheries Commission starting in 1887. Harvey was also one of the first to complain about foreign nations fishing on the Grand Banks: "They [the Grand Banks] are most esteemed for their codfish and are in consequence the general fishing grounds of all European nations."[1]

In 1900, the Newfoundland fishery was already more than 400 years old. There was no reason to believe it wouldn't continue for another 400. "The fisheries of Newfoundland constitute the staple industry of the country," Harvey wrote. "The gathering in of the great sea harvest has been and will long continue to be the main employment of the people" (41).[2]

Newfoundland in 1900, Harvey's overview of the geography,

---

1   F.A. Aldrich, "Harvey, Moses," *Dictionary of Canadian Biography*, vol. 13 (University of Toronto/Université Laval, 2003–), http://www.biographi.ca/en/bio/harvey_moses_13E.html, accessed July 10, 2013.

2   Moses Harvey, *Newfoundland in 1900: A treatise of the geography, natural resources and history of the island, embracing an account of recent and present large material movements* (New York: The South Publishing Co., 1900).

natural resources, and history of the island, includes statistics high-lighting the importance of the fisheries: of 210,000 Newfoundland residents in 1900, about 56,000 were "engaged in catching and cur-ing fish." All other occupations together employed only an addition-al 12,000 individuals.

Harvey placed the total value of fish caught at the turn of the century at $7 million a year—$6,600,000 in exports and $400,000 consumed by residents (41). In 2013 dollars, that would be about $203 million a year.

One chapter of *Newfoundland in 1900* is devoted to the "largest cod fishery in the world" (44), encompassing the Newfoundland inshore, Labrador coast, and Grand Banks fisheries. Most New-foundlanders fished off Labrador and in Newfoundland's inshore waters; their presence on the Grand Banks was relatively small, only 48 vessels, leaving the majority of the offshore fishing effort to fishermen from the French island of St. Pierre (off Newfoundland's southeast coast), American fishing centres such as Gloucester and Boston, and overseas nations.

The harvested cod were put to good use: cod liver oil was ex-tracted and sold. Codfish skin was made into glue. The bones and head were turned into fertilizer. New products were developed, in-cluding strips of cured boneless and skinless cod, and dried codfish, which was ground into a fine meal and packed into tins. As well, Harvey wrote, "[a]n experiment is soon to be tried on a large scale by which the cold storage system is to be used in conveying the fish fresh to market" (49).

Harvey mentioned other fisheries, including the "neglected" her-ring fishery (worth about $250,000), and the $100,000 salmon fishery, which suffered the results of "reckless and destructive practices in connection with it, which have gone unchecked" (58). Those practices included closing off the mouths of rivers with nets during spawning season, building traps and dams, and using seine nets to sweep salm-on pools. He spoke about the importance of fisheries management and the dangers of overfishing, warnings echoed by many fisheries scientists—to no great avail—in the century after his death:

The danger lies in over-fishing any locality and taking immature fish before they have reached the reproductive stage. Implements of a deadly and destructive nature are too often used, such as bultows, and also nets with small meshes which destroy the young fish. Close seasons also are not carefully observed. All these injure the cod fishing, so that now, although many more than formerly are engaged in it, the catch is stationary or declining. (46)

In 1900, well over a century ago, Harvey—a distinguished member of Newfoundland society—publicly warned that the fisheries must be managed in a more responsible fashion. Yet no one listened. Consequently, one of the world's greatest fisheries has collapsed completely because fishing boats from Europe and elsewhere caught immense quantities of fish, especially small, undersized fish, without any protest from Canada.

In 1890, the Newfoundland government created a Fisheries Department and hired a fisheries superintendent. The first fisheries regulations were developed and enforced. With advances in processing and an increased vigilance over the resource by the government, Harvey was optimistic about the future of the fisheries in Newfoundland:

[I]t may be reasonably hoped that under this more enlightened plan, the decline in the fisheries will be arrested and a gradual restoration to former productiveness will be secured. With a vigilant and skillful supervision and a greater care in curing, these fisheries have a brighter future before them and will become increasingly a source of wealth for the country. (46)

Harvey's optimism was, sadly, misplaced. For over a century, Harvey and others—including Dr. Wilfred Templeman in the 1960s, the Save Our Fisheries Association (SOFA) in 1971-72, Dr.

Leslie Harris in the 1990s, a dedicated coalition of churches in the mid-1990s, and countless scientists both in- and outside of the Department of Fisheries and Oceans (DFO)—have made governments aware of the declining fisheries, all without success.

As Harvey so succinctly wrote about the struggling salmon fishery, words that can be applied in broader terms: "Human ignorance and greed of immediate gain have wasted and partially destroyed what might be, at this time, one of the most valuable resources of the colony" (58).

Chapter 2
The Basque beginning

Where else to start my part of this story but at the beginning—the Basque beginning—and how the Etchegarys came to be planted in Newfoundland?

The first Etchegary to settle on this side of the North Atlantic was Michel Etchegary, my grandfather, in the 1880s. Cod lured him across the Atlantic for summers of fishing on the Grand Banks. But it wasn't the rich fisheries that convinced him to stay—but a young girl from Lamaline, on the Burin Peninsula.

According to family lore, my grandfather was a young but seasoned Basque fisherman when he traversed the Atlantic, one of a legendary breed of men from the border region of France and Spain. It is possible that Basque fishermen had been visiting the Grand Banks as early as the 1400s, long before John Cabot lowered a basket into the teeming waters off Newfoundland. There are no photos of my grandfather, but I can picture him, an elderly man who had great difficulty speaking English, sitting in our kitchen, stocky, still powerful, with leathery, wind-weathered skin.

It is said that when Christopher Columbus recruited his sailing crew for the New World, Basques made up the largest nationality of the group, and they continued to participate in voyages across the Atlantic during the earliest years of European exploration of North America. They may also have been among the first to perfect the salting of cod.

The Basques were sailors, whalers, and expert fishermen. Drawn first by the cod-fishing grounds around Newfoundland and Labrador, Basque mariners stayed on to hunt the even more lucrative bowhead and right whales. In the early 1500s, Basque whalers set up seasonal whale-processing facilities in Red Bay, on the south coast of Labrador. Each spring a fleet of vessels would arrive in Red Bay to process whales. On the return to the Basque country in the late fall, each vessel was loaded with barrels of whale oil, which was in great demand in Europe for medical and industrial use.

But before and after oil, there would be fish.

By the 1800s, Basque schooners were long-time participants in the fisheries off Newfoundland. Two or three times during the fishing season, these schooners landed at St. Pierre for provisions, water, and recreation. There Michel Etchegary of St. Jean De Luz, a fishing port in southwestern France, met Katherine Fleming of Lamaline, a small community on Newfoundland's Burin Peninsula. Katherine, like many young Newfoundland women at the time, had been recruited to work in the home of a well-to-do French family.

One year, in the late 1800s, as Michel's schooner departed St. Pierre for the final time that season, he made a decision. Choosing to follow his heart over financial stability, adventure in a new land over a return to the old, my grandfather dove overboard into the mouth of the harbour and swam to nearby Dog Island. He wasn't alone. Another lovesick sailor was by his side for every stroke.

The skipper didn't turn the schooner around. The fishing season was over and fishermen were to be paid a share of the catch; he was probably only too pleased to keep the profits the deserters had left behind. The Basque boat headed back across the Atlantic, and Michel headed for Katherine. He started his life in the New World with little more than the shirt on his back and a love for the sea.

Michel Etchegary and Katherine Fleming soon married. They lived in St. Pierre for a few years before relocating first to Lamaline to be closer to Katherine's family and then to nearby St. Lawrence, where they would stay. Michel and Katherine had five children: Louis, Michael, Anthony, John, and Laura. Michel provided for his family as an inshore fisherman. Fishing was practically the only career in outport communities around the coast of Newfoundland, many of which were built in the most inhospitable places with not much connecting them and not much to celebrate except their proximity to productive fishing grounds.

Years passed, from one fishing season to the next.

On January 9, 1909, Michel and Katherine Etchegary's eldest son, Louis, married Philomena Slaney of St. Lawrence at the local Roman Catholic church. According to the wedding announcement published in the local paper, the bride "looked charming in a costume of cream silk with flowing veil and orange blossoms." The next night, a ball was held at a local hall with about 200 invited guests. "The presents were numerous and costly, which showed the esteem and respect in which the bride and groom were held." [3]

Louis, an inshore fisherman like his father, settled in St. Lawrence with his bride. He owned a fishing skiff, flake, dory, stage, and a dry store for the fish. His was one of the thousands of small salt-fish operations at the heart of most Newfoundland communities. He would also periodically take part in the deep-sea bank fisheries on vessels out of Fortune, Grand Bank, or Nova Scotia.

Louis and Philomena built a home in St. Lawrence and had five children—Theophilus, Kathleen, Florence, Louis, and Augustine. The youngest surviving child, I was born Augustine Alexander Etchegary on May 28, 1924. My younger sister lived just long enough to be baptized.

My mother died of tuberculosis three years after I was born. I have vague memories of her working with my aunt on the fish flakes and toiling in the kitchen at the daily household chores. I have heard enough throughout my life to know that she was a fine woman.

After her death, my father stayed close to home, focusing on the inshore fishery with my older brothers, salting and drying their catch to sell to Burin Peninsula fish merchants for export in the fall. He ran a small cod-liver-oil plant to augment his earnings and provide for his growing family. My care was entrusted to my two older sisters and the extended Etchegary clan. We were a tight-knit family; we couldn't be otherwise.

My first vivid memory is of a major event that shaped not only my youth but also my family and community—the 1929 tsunami.

---

3 "Wedding Bells: Etchegary & Slaney," *Daily News*, January 10, 1909.

•••

It was early evening, November 18, 1929. I was in the warm kitchen of our St. Lawrence home, watching a plate of sliced potatoes warming in a cast-iron pot. Suddenly the earth around me rumbled and groaned and the potatoes and plate clattered on the stove. The strange commotion lasted several minutes. I was transfixed.

My sisters, Kay, 18, and Flo, 13, were with me in the house. The next thing I knew, they grabbed my hands and we ran out of the house toward town. I was only five years old, bewildered and afraid because of the death grip my sisters had on me.

Our home was built on a hill about a half a kilometre from St. Lawrence (*Etchegary*, in fact, means *house on a hill*). Partway down the hill we ran into a crowd of people running the opposite way, toward our home. An earthquake had struck, someone said, and water surges or tidal waves were possible. The wide eyes of everyone in the crowd mirrored those of my terrified sisters. Earthquakes were practically unheard of in Newfoundland, and no one knew what could come next.

Measuring 7.2 on the Richter scale, the underwater quake had originated along two fault planes about 260 kilometres south of the Burin Peninsula. It was felt as far west as New York and Montreal, and as far east as Portugal. The subterranean quake triggered an underwater landslide, which, as predicted, forced a series of large waves across the ocean surface. As we stood there, the tsunami raced toward Newfoundland at speeds of up to 140 kilometres an hour, slowing to 40 kilometres an hour in the shallower water close to shore.

The elders in the crowd advised us to retreat to higher ground. My sisters and I did an about-face and headed back up the hill, followed by dozens of others. The crowd gathered on the wide verandah that wrapped around our home. Most in the group were Catholic, and if there was ever a time they were going to show it, that was it, down on bended knee praying the Rosary and pleading with God for mercy.

My two older brothers, Theo and Louis Jr., weren't home from school when the quake hit. Our father was also out, likely down on his stage or in the cod-liver plant.

It was a beautiful moonlit evening, almost as bright as day. We watched as more and more people trickled up the road to our house on the hill. They gathered on and around the porch and joined in prayer. To our great relief, my brothers and father soon made their way home. As a family and community we huddled together, waiting for whatever was coming next.

At about 7:30 p.m., the inner part of St. Lawrence harbour suddenly receded to expose the sea floor. Boats that had been docked tumbled over on their sides.

Then came the first of three waves.

In most places the tsunami caused the sea level to swell 3 to 7 metres above normal, but in some of the Burin Peninsula's long, narrow bays, including St. Lawrence, the water rose by 13 to 27 metres. A wave seemed to form at the entrance of the harbour and, as it came in, it got higher and higher. I can still see it. The moonlight caught the wave and illuminated it: tall and foaming white at the tip, charging over everything close to shore, bigger than anything I had ever seen or imagined. The wave's roar drowned out our prayers and the counting and clicking of the rosary beads. Just as fast as a wave rose up, it receded, to be followed a few minutes later by another. And then another.

Some residents of St. Lawrence lived close to the harbour's edge, but most of the homes were well away from the water and high enough, like ours, to escape damage. But the waves took with them stages, stores, flakes, and fishing boats, depositing some inland, as much as a kilometre above the high-water mark. The tsunami caused 28 deaths on the Burin Peninsula. Luckily not a life was lost in St. Lawrence.

Still, the destruction of fishing gear and infrastructure was devastating to our community. St. Lawrence lost every flake, stage, and boat. Total losses were tallied at just over $81,000, a fortune in those days, considering an average stage cost $100 and the going rate for a dory was $40.

The Newfoundland government was in terrible financial shape at the time, exacerbated by ongoing internal political turmoil. Leftover expenses from World War I, the cost of maintaining the Newfoundland Railway, and attempts to diversify Newfoundland's economy—funded by borrowing from foreign investors—combined for a massive national debt by 1929. Nevertheless, the government eventually paid out an estimated $32,000 in compensation to more than 100 fishermen in St. Lawrence. It was far less than the replacement value of everything that was lost, but it was a start.

My father's livelihood was literally in splinters. The cod-liver plant was heavily damaged, as was his personal property. According to government records, my father lost a fishing boat, stage, flake, store, three cod nets, and a cement tank used to clean fish. His total loss was valued at $415; he was eventually awarded $270 in compensation.[4]

He also had $200 in the bank, making him more fortunate than most—codfish, not cash, was the general currency of the day. My father quickly rebuilt, as did many of the other industrious, self-reliant outporters.

Recovery wasn't as simple as getting new flakes and stages. The tsunami had another, less obvious, effect on the communities of the Burin Peninsula. The waters around the Burin Peninsula had always been known for good fishing, but that changed after the tsunami swept through. The 1930 inshore cod fishery, the most important part of the economy, was a total failure. Scientists later determined that changes in the sea floor likely affected the migratory pattern of fish moving from the outer banks to the inshore region; whatever the reason, catch levels remained low for years. It would take some years for the resource to recover.

The timing could not have been worse. The tsunami hit just as the Great Depression was beginning. When the worldwide economy started its downturn in 1929 and 1930, Newfoundland's export

---

4   Garry Cranford, *Tidal Wave, A List of Victims and Survivors, Newfoundland, 1929* (St. John's: Flanker Press, 2000), 195.

economy, which depended almost completely on fish, was extremely vulnerable. Newfoundland's national government teetered on the verge of bankruptcy. The price of dried cod plummeted to half its previous worth, as did the value of fish exports. The few fish left in the waters off the Burin Peninsula were practically worthless.

•••

An estimated 60,000 Newfoundlanders were forced on able-bodied relief during the Depression. Most depended on money from the government as their primary income, and, even then, they lived on a mere six cents a day—the dreaded dole.

Whether from stubbornness or pride, Louis Etchegary didn't take handouts from the government or elsewhere, not even with five children. With no inshore fishery to turn to and a family to take care of, he headed offshore, fishing for cod on the Grand Banks for six or seven months each year.

The Bank fishery was a major industry conducted out of various ports on Newfoundland's ice-free south coast, as well as ports in Nova Scotia and New England. The Bank fishery vessels varied in size and carried from 10 to 20 dories. The fishermen, two to a dory, started early in the morning, setting out baited hooks to catch cod. They stayed out on the water until late in the evening, when they would return to the schooner, discharge, split, and salt the catch, which was then stored in the schooner's hold. Before turning in to their bunks for a few hours' sleep, they would bait their gear with capelin, herring, squid, or mackerel in preparation for the next day. The salted fish was eventually landed on shore and sun-dried. The Bank fishery kept participants away from home for weeks, sometimes months, at a time, but it provided practically year-round work and a steady income.

The absence of my father hit us all hard. We pulled together, out of necessity, as many other families did. My eldest sister gave up her schooling to look after the rest of us and make sure we could all go to school. One way or another, our father always managed to send money home when he was away; he always made sure we were well looked after. Times were hard, but no one starved, and we all had boots on our feet and clothes on our backs. It was a difficult and lonely period in our lives, especially for my father.

Louis Etchegary did, however, find opportunity beyond the banking schooners. There was more work to be had at sea than in the fisheries, and there was money to be made in rum-running.

The 1920s and early 1930s were Prohibition years in the United States. American gangsters such as Al Capone and Jack "Legs" Diamond used the French islands of St. Pierre and Miquelon as a launching pad for smuggling liquor into the United States. The boom to the French islands lasted until 1933 and the end of Prohibition.

My father was a rum-runner in 1931 and 1932. He worked on schooners that delivered St. Pierre alcohol, under cover of darkness, to boats waiting 12 miles off the American coast, considered then to be international waters. It was a risk he took out of sheer determination to keep his family safe from poverty. A love for life on the sea and a taste for adventure didn't hurt. His voyages on the other side of the law were not always smooth. My father got caught once while serving as a mate aboard a liquor-laden ship called the *Whichone*. The vessel was seized and the crew arrested by the American Coast Guard for allegedly drifting inside the 12-mile limit. It was towed to New York harbour and the Newfoundland crew, my father included, thrown in jail.

When news reached St. Lawrence, my brothers and sisters and I were paralyzed with worry. Jail? It seemed impossible that my father could be behind bars. We spent the next three weeks in church, all five siblings and our aunts, praying for my father and the rest of the crew.

The owner of the *Whichone* and its liquid cargo was a New York businessman named Vanny Higgins. Fortunately, Higgins was able to afford a first-class lawyer to defend the crew. The lawyer successfully argued that, contrary to the allegations, the rum-runners were not actually inside American territorial waters when they were arrested. The crew and vessel were eventually released and returned home to the Burin Peninsula, arriving with great fanfare.

Although technically smugglers, rum-runners were regarded as heroes who did what they had to do—at least that's how it was in St. Lawrence. Fifteen or 20 men from the area were on various boats, and they all took part in the illegal trade because it was good money, the biggest kind of money, and in that day and age, there was not much cash to be had. It was too good to miss out on.

There were other benefits. My father brought home a radio from one trip, only the second radio in St. Lawrence. The town had electric power in the early 1930s, generated at a hydro plant a mile away in Little St. Lawrence. My brothers set up an antenna between two poles 30 feet apart. Radio reception was excellent from the US and Canadian mainland radio stations and from Europe through short-wave reception.

The first song we heard on that radio was on the BBC and it was called "The Garden Where the Praties Grow." We listened to boxing matches between Joe Louis and Max Schmeling, Jack Dempsey and Gene Tunney. We were already being dominated by American culture—CBS and NBC radio stations were much clearer than local radio stations like VONF in St. John's, and Lowell Thomas and Gabriel Heatter, well-known news anchors for the big US networks in the 1930s were as familiar to us as Peter Mansbridge or Rex Murphy are today. The connection between St. Lawrence and the US was being forged over the airways; it would only become stronger in the coming decade.

When my father was released from the New York jail, his days of rum-running were done. As fate would have it, St. Lawrence was about to experience an economic resurgence, temporarily leaving behind its status as a fishing community. And for the first time in at least several generations—maybe several centuries—the Etchegarys got out of the fishing business.

Chapter 3
War and rescue: The end of childhood

In 1933, still at the height of the Great Depression, economic hope came to St. Lawrence in the person of American entrepreneur Walter Seibert. He hired local men to mine deposits of fluorspar, a non-metallic ore used as a flux for smelting, and to make aluminum, glass, and Freon, a refrigerant. The demand for Freon was escalating, particularly in the US, because of the home-freezer market and the fledgling fresh-frozen-fish industry. St. Lawrence, it turned out, was the location of one of the biggest fluorspar deposits in North America.

The men of St. Lawrence responded to the call to the mines with enthusiasm, even though the work was back-breaking and, for a while, unpaid. Seibert's company, the St. Lawrence Corporation of Newfoundland, started developing the mine without much in the way of startup cash; some of the first workers toiled six months without compensation to get the mines up and running. The promise of steady work and a regular paycheque kept them focused.

The original open-cut mine operated by the St. Lawrence Corporation was developed at Black Duck, a place quite close to town. Later, operations were moved to a new site, Iron Springs, a mile and half from Chambers Cove, the site of the 1942 USS *Truxtun*'s sinking. Iron Springs became the main source of ore for export by the Corporation until its closure in 1957.

My father was one of the first men hired by the Corporation, in 1933. He was fortunate to be working above ground at the mill where the fluorspar went through the first refining process before being shipped to the US. Later he was appointed mill superintendent, a position he held until his retirement.

The new job meant our family were back together and financially stable. Although the fish eventually returned, by that time St. Lawrence was a prosperous mining community. Workers came from surrounding towns on the Burin Peninsula to join the St. Lawrence miners.

The rest of the country was not faring so well. The Newfoundland government was so crippled by unsustainable debt, political unrest, and the Depression that it turned overseas for help. Great Britain agreed to support Newfoundland and provide financial relief, but only in exchange for political control. Newfoundland surrendered her responsible government in 1933 in favour of a government by commission.

But times were booming in St. Lawrence. In 1937, the community's fluorspar industry grew yet again as a second company, the Aluminum Company of Canada (ALCAN), set up. Both companies developed into major operations, employing close to 700 people. With the latest technology, the mines could be expanded from open-cut mining to deep vertical shafts and underground horizontal drifts.

The two companies operated side by side for many years without issue, perhaps because the St. Lawrence Corporation of Newfoundland exported its product to the US and ALCAN supplied its operations in Quebec and other parts of Canada.

Although fishing was in my history and in my blood, I always felt that I grew up in a mining community, and we did well by it. My family, along with the other residents of St. Lawrence and the area, thrived during those decades.

It was not until the late stages of the mining operations that it was discovered that those who had worked in the fluorspar mines had been exposed to high levels of silica dust and radon gas. Many of them developed industrial diseases, including cancer and silicosis, and far too many, many of my friends and neighbours, died prematurely. Much has been written about the tragedy that eventually resulted in improved working conditions in Canada's mining industry.

In the 1930s, before illness and tragedy descended, St. Lawrence developed its new industry with optimism and determination.

•••

Maybe because of my mother's unexpected death, and my father's extended absences, I remember a childhood centred around my siblings and extended family. My world was my family, the ocean, school, and the Catholic church.

And then there was the soccer field. If anything could compete with the church for the bodies and minds of the youth of St. Lawrence, it was soccer.[5] The pitches we played on were by no means regulation-sized soccer fields. A match could be played on any patch of grass or field within running distance of the community. I always felt that in St. Lawrence, when you got out of the cradle, you started to look for a ball. It was almost instinct. We'd head for the meadows at the break of dawn, running late into the evening.

Except during senior games, regulation store-bought balls were unheard of. When we were youngsters, our soccer balls were sometimes made of rags tied together in a knot, but the best ball was one made from a "ram's purse." There were several sheep farmers near St. Lawrence in the 1930s and, in the fall of the year, when the animals were gathered for slaughter, we would contact the owners to ask for the scrotum or "the purse-y." The scrotum would be cut up into the animal's stomach as far as possible and then pickled, which made the skin tough and hard, and also allowed the hair to be easily removed. The skin was stuffed with hay and then sewn together to make a great ball.

St. Lawrence later became known as the soccer capital of Newfoundland, thanks to the passion and skill for the sport that persist today. For us, soccer was more than a sport—it was all-consuming. Our passion was not at all discouraged by our coach, the local Catholic priest.

Father Augustine Thorne was originally from Torbay, near

---

5   It was always "football" to us, as it was across the province until the Newfoundland Football Association joined the Canadian Soccer Association in the 1970s.

St. John's, but he had learned the finer art of soccer while training in the seminary in Ireland. The first organized game, so the story goes, was played in Patty's Farm in Little St. Lawrence in 1903 between St. Lawrence and a group of young men from Scotland and England who worked at the whaling factory in Little St. Lawrence. A rivalry grew between teams from St. Lawrence and surrounding communities such as Lawn, Grand Bank, Fortune, and Burin.

We built our days around the games. In the early 1940s, we would often play Grand Bank, about 80 kilometres away. We'd have to leave St. Lawrence by truck at 4 p.m. in order to arrive and get a game in before dark. The young miners, all good friends, came out from underground after an eight-hour shift, got in the back of the truck, put on their soccer boots, and went to Grand Bank to play. Occasionally, we would use a trap skiff to take the team to Burin for a match. Those games, when we would go to Grand Bank, Lawn, Fortune, or Burin or their teams would come to us, were great occasions. Transportation and communication between the communities were limited and it was a rare opportunity to connect.

Our fiercest rivalry was with St. Pierre. Rumours circulated that St. Pierre brought in soccer coaches from France, which only added to our determination to win, and we'd have major matches on holiday weekends. The weekend of June 24, the feast day of St. John the Baptist, was always a good game and a major event. Players, wearing rubber inner tubes for life jackets, would travel the 40 kilometres from St. Lawrence to St. Pierre in a trap skiff. Occasionally, a government coastal passenger vessel would be chartered and as many as 100 or more fans would travel to St. Pierre for a soccer tournament.

Soccer had our hearts, but it did not get in the way of schooling—my father made sure of that. We were educated by Catholic nuns, the Sisters of Mercy, at St. Augustine's, a three-room schoolhouse in St. Lawrence. Beyond the regular school curriculum, the nuns taught music, drama, and elocution. Every Saturday morning, my friends and I—Father's orders—would spend two hours at school for elocution class. As part of the class we would have to stand up on chairs or stools and give speeches on subjects chosen by the nuns.

Newfoundland has hundreds of outports, many with distinctive accents, but we didn't seem to have a strong accent in St. Lawrence, probably because many of the young people were taught elocution by the nuns. St. Lawrence may have been isolated, but it was not cut off from the world—not in speech, not in industry, and certainly not from major world events such as the world wars.

•••

World War I ended half a dozen years before I was born, but it deeply affected the Etchegarys of St. Lawrence. Two of Michel Etchegary's sons, my uncles Michael and John, enlisted with the Newfoundland Regiment and fought overseas.

Michael died in Europe in 1917. There was no publicly available record of when or where he was killed, which was one of my family's greatest disappointments.[6] A picture of a fresh-faced Michael, looking as young as he was—just over 16, underage when he enlisted—but sophisticated in his army uniform and carrying his walking stick, was on display in our home for decades, and still hangs in my den.

John was seriously wounded during the war but made a good recovery. He married Florence Tarry from Cheshire, England, after the war ended. The newlyweds moved to St. Lawrence for a while, but Aunt Florence didn't take to outport life and they soon moved on to Halifax, then Montreal, and finally settled in Torrington, Connecticut. Their son, Frank, continued to live there and he raised a family of Etchegarys that are now living in various parts of the United States.

As was the case in communities across the western world, the scars and memories of World War I were still fresh in St. Lawrence when World War II broke out in September 1939. At school the

---

6   In 2012, I learned that Michael had been buried at Vimy Ridge in 1916. Uncle Michael, underage when he joined the Navy, quickly determined he didn't like the sea—in fact, he hated it. He deserted, changed his name to William McGrath, and joined the Army. He received three awards for bravery before he was killed.

nuns read the news bulletins as part of our studies. The radio my father had brought home from his rum-running adventures sat on the table in the parlour, our front room. We gathered around it to follow the news, our ears practically stuck to it. Even today, I can hear the sound of Adolph Hitler's voice, yelling like a hyena, booming through our home. I was 15 years old and, frankly, frightened as I listened to him.

It wasn't just Hitler on the air. I remember hearing Joseph Goebbels, Hitler's propaganda minister; Hermann Goring, Hitler's right-hand man; and Neville Chamberlain, who was prime minister of England for the first eight months of World War II. We listened with great interest to Chamberlain in the days preceding the declaration of war, when he returned to England after meeting with Hitler, whose German army had just invaded Czechoslovakia. Hitler promised Chamberlain that it would be the last aggressive action by the Germans; Chamberlain's policy of appeasement obviously did not work out, as war was declared and raged for six years. The names of Hitler, Goebbels, Winston Churchill, and the others still come to me as if they lived next door.

Everyone was concerned about the war and the possibility of someone belonging to them becoming involved. Newfoundlanders were as patriotic, if not more so, than the residents of any other Commonwealth country, and they joined the war effort in droves.

My oldest brother, Louis, along with many others from St. Lawrence and elsewhere in Newfoundland, enlisted. Louis trained with the Royal Canadian Air Force in Winnipeg, Manitoba, and Mont-Joli, Quebec, and made quite an impression when he returned home in his uniform, cap, and medals. I adored the ground Louis walked on and, though I was too young, I thought seriously about signing up for the war myself. Louis forbade it. "Under no circumstances are you to join," he told me. "And if you ever give it a single thought, I'll desert and punish you accordingly."

He had a second piece of life advice: "Whatever you do, don't go down into the mines." Louis had worked in the mines for a year after high school, before war broke out. Several times during that year he confided in me that he didn't see himself continuing as a miner. Neither did his close friends Clyde and Robert Fitzpatrick. No one was surprised when the three took off, leaving their jobs in the mines for Halifax and a few months of work in road construction. Then Louis and Robert joined the Royal Canadian Air Force and Clyde took off for British Columbia, where he became a fishing skipper and did quite well for the rest of his life. Whether Louis and the others had a premonition regarding the tragic experiences of many of the miners or simply didn't like the work, no one can say. I do know Louis and his friends were intent on following other pursuits, for which I am grateful.

I took Louis's advice. In 1940, I continued to work for the St. Lawrence Corporation of Newfoundland above ground at the Iron Springs fluorspar mine as I had during summer vacations. I shovelled my share of fluorspar onto the conveyor belts during those months and carried out odd jobs at the mine mill.

Frequently, I would walk to and from work at the mill with Jim Creed, an engineer employed as head of the electrical department at the site. Originally from Ontario, Creed was responsible for the installation and maintenance of electrical services at the mill and the mines. As we walked together, we discussed his work and, one day, Jim offered me the job of helper in his department. I quickly accepted.

Occasionally, being employed in the electrical department meant venturing 500 or 600 feet underground. After being exposed to these working conditions I could understand why Louis and his friends had decided on other occupations. I took every opportunity to absorb as much as I could from Creed's expertise as an electrical engineer. His genuine interest in training and mentoring me had a profound impact on my future.

•••

World War II came directly to the shores of St. Lawrence in the early morning of Ash Wednesday, February 18, 1942. Two American destroyers, the USS *Wilkes* and USS *Truxtun*, and the supply ship

USS *Pollux* went off course and ran aground in a blinding snow-storm, less than 3 kilometres apart off the Burin Peninsula between St. Lawrence and Lawn.

The flagship *Wilkes* was refloated within three hours, and it sailed on to Argentia as planned with all hands safe on board. But the *Pollux* and the *Truxtun* were not so fortunate. The *Pollux* had run aground near Lawn Point. The *Truxtun* had struck bottom in Chambers Cove, a crescent-shaped cove near St. Lawrence, and was practically leaning against a great rock on her starboard side. About 100 yards from her starboard bow was a cliff sloping to the sea, buried in white water. Known as Pinnacle Head, the cliff's 300-foot rock was a landmark for fishermen.

Freezing cold, soaking wet, and covered in a thick coating of congealed oil that had escaped from his ship, 18-year-old Edward L. Burgeron, seaman second class, climbed the face of Pinnacle Head, using a knife to hack handholds in the ice. When he got to the top, he ran roughly 3 kilometres to the site of the Iron Springs mine and alerted the first group of people he saw, including my father, that his warship was on the rocks in a cove under cliffs. The miners knew it had to be Chambers Cove.

Along with many others, three members of my family were in-volved in that day's rescue effort: my father, then superintendent of the mine mill; my brother Theo, a strapping 28-year-old chemist at the mill; and me, 17, not long out of high school and working as an apprentice electrician.

Theo received news of the disaster in a telephone call from the mine. He and others quickly spread the news through St. Lawrence, and then he commandeered a company-owned pickup driven by Alan Farrell. Alan, Theo, and I collected as much rope as we could and headed for Iron Springs mine, which had been shut down so that all workers could take part in the rescue. From there, we went straight to Chambers Cove. Imagine the sight: the three of us stand-ing on the cliff in a snowstorm, looking 250 or 300 feet below us at a warship lying on her side, partly submerged. There were men in the water, and more hanging desperately to the superstructure of the ship that was above water. I had never confronted anything like it and will always remember the desperate situation these sailors faced.

The snow was driving horizontally in the howling winds. The seas, blackened by oil, crashed on the rocks of Chambers Cove. Some of the sailors had managed, somehow, to make it to shore aboard life rafts. We could see many more bodies bobbing in the raging sea. We used the ropes we had brought to climb down to the shore. We had no clear plan but to get down and do what we could. The sailors aboard the *Truxtun* had attempted to link a heavy cable from that ship to the shore as a means to ferry more rafts to safety, but the line got tangled in the rocks on the bottom and the plan had to be abandoned.

The only chance the sailors had was to jump overboard. After landing in the frigid water, they needed to swim to the centre of the cove, against the natural undertow, hoping the tide would help sweep them toward the safety of a narrow spit of beach where rescuers had gathered. Each time the waves receded, the men would claw their hands into the beach rocks in an effort to try to hold on so they could be rescued before the waves sucked them back into the ocean. In some cases they made it. In others they didn't; they just couldn't hold on. Many sailors couldn't, or didn't, jump, waiting and clinging to that part of the *Truxtun*'s hull that remained above water, praying for some means of survival other than attempting to swim in the frigid water.

My brother, father, and other men from St. Lawrence tied ropes around their waists and, with a companion holding tight to the other end, waded out into the oily water between the breaking waves to try and save sailors close to shore. My father shouted instructions to me to gather wood for a fire on the beach. It seemed to take forever, but eventually I got the fire to catch and come to life. The flames seemed to give off next to no heat, but the sight of the small flickering light drew the survivors and seemed to raise their spirits.

A young man about my age lay on the beach, unable to move. I went over, picked him up, and helped him walk around and around the fire. Cassie Brown included our interaction in her book, *Standing into Danger*, about the disaster and rescue:

> "What's your name?" Gus asked.
> "Butterworth. Bill Butterworth," the youth mumbled, his body shaking with weakness and cold.
> It struck Gus that this was no mere adventure; this was stark truth, life and death, and total involvement in it.
> Heedless of the wind and sleet on his own body, Gus took off the old jacket with a sheepskin lining that he was wearing and put it around Butterworth. "It'll keep you warm," he said. Presently he had to leave the youth to search the shoreline for more wood for the fire….
> Gus had scrounged the shoreline for more firewood and when he returned he discovered young Butterworth lying dead on the beach.[7]

It was blowing like hell, and snow, wet snow, everywhere. It was pretty damned miserable and then, if it could be worse for them, everyone was saturated in salt water and oil. It was a horrible place for those sailors to meet their end. Words cannot adequately describe what happened on the deck of that warship. The men, 18, 19, and 20 years old, had to decide whether to stay with the ship and hope for the best or to jump overboard. Many almost made it to the beach, only to be sucked down by the undertow or up and into the jagged cliffs by the high waves.

Forty-six sailors survived from the *Truxtun*. I can't say how many we had a hand in rescuing; it wasn't anything we did so much as the luck and the agility of those sailors who survived. Whether a sailor was saved really came down to his ability to get himself in a position to be rescued. We couldn't go out in a boat to help. We

---

7   Cassie Brown, *Standing into Danger* (Toronto: Doubleday Canada, 1985), 166, 168.

thought of getting a plane to drop a rope to the men on the boat, but that wasn't possible, not in that weather.

There were many heroes that day. I do not consider myself among them. But I am absolutely certain that if the disaster had occurred in any other community near the sea in Newfoundland and Labrador the local people would have done the same. At the end of the day, we counted about 79 bodies pulled up over the hill and laid out in a row on top of Chambers Cove. There's a photograph of that tragic scene in Brown's book.

One hundred and ten sailors were lost from the *Truxtun*. Down the coast, near Lawn Point, the *Pollux* faced a similar fate: of 233 officers and enlisted men on board, 93 were lost. The grounded *Pollux* had been first sighted by two young people from the Lawn area, who alerted the residents of that community. Men rushed to Lawn Point; they were joined by men from St. Lawrence and American sailors who had arrived in St. Lawrence on naval vessels from the nearby Argentia base.

The *Pollux* survivors were transported by horse and sleigh to the Iron Springs mine site, where the women of St. Lawrence had already gathered to care for the *Truxtun* survivors. The unsung heroes of the tragedy were the women of St. Lawrence, who went all out to ease the pain and losses suffered by the young sailors. They prepared meals and tended to the injured and oil-soaked men. They continued to care for them in their own homes until US authorities sent more ships to St. Lawrence and transported the sailors to the nearby base at Argentia.

The *Truxtun* and *Pollux* rescuers were almost all fishermen or former fishermen, from a long line of fishermen. Like so many who live on the east coast of Canada, they were familiar with the perils of the sea and the fears and anxieties of trying to wrest a living for themselves and their families from it. Even though they knew the dangers of a raging ocean, they were prepared to challenge it. I watched rescuers wade chest-deep into these seas to try and recover the lost lifeline from the stricken *Truxtun*. The people of St. Lawrence and Lawn responded to the monumental task of saving lives under the most difficult circumstances with the skill, courage, and instinct of those who live and work by the sea.

The world was in the midst of a major war; many family members and friends were overseas participating in the conflict. Every day we listened to news about the thousands of victims of war and, then, right in front of us came the reality. We watched people matted in oil, helplessly digging into the beach for dear life as the water surged and receded. We saw many young American men die in the water and on the beach of Chambers Cove and on Lawn Point, thousands of miles from their homes. We could not help but think of our own relatives in the armed forces who might be facing a similar fate in another part of the world.

That tragic event had a lasting impact on me, the rescuers, the rescued, and the community.

Billy Butterworth, in particular, stuck with me. It took me 40 years to track down the young sailor's relatives, who lived in Lawrence, Massachusetts. I visited them when I was in the area in 1980 and spoke at length to his cousin. It was the first time I had the opportunity to talk to anyone who knew Billy, who had become almost a legend in my mind. The meeting was a poignant event.

Closure? Maybe. I did come away with a feeling of peace.

Chapter 4
Mining, military, Monroe: Settling on a career

Even though the *Truxtun* and *Pollux* disaster made the war more tangible for me—and for the rest of the Burin Peninsula—I stuck by my promise not to enlist. It was, however, time for me to set off on an adventure of my own.

In the spring of 1942, three months after the *Truxtun* ran aground, the St. Lawrence Corporation organized a mining expedition to Labrador. Fifteen or so miners from St. Lawrence were to be transported to Saglek Bay in the Torngat Mountains to mine graphite. I begged my father to let me go. I was certainly not a miner, nor did I have ambitions to be one, but I was ready for an adventure, and I succeeded in persuading the Corporation that I could do the odd jobs that would be necessary from time to time.

In St. Lawrence we boarded a 120-foot two-masted schooner, the *E.M.A. Frampton*, and loaded on our supplies. The captain was Ralph Smith from Hodges Cove, Trinity Bay; he and most of his crew were from Trinity Bay, but the cook was from Ladle Cove. Built by the renowned builders of Trinity Bay, the sturdy schooner served us well over the next few months. Without a doubt, it was the first time the sturdy vessel had a tractor, a pre-fabricated bunkhouse, and an assortment of mining equipment lashed to her deck.

It was a first for me too. I had never been away from my family, except for short trips to play soccer, and I had prepared for this journey with great anticipation. It wasn't until the *Frampton* left the wharf and sailed out through St. Lawrence harbour that I realized the long trip that was ahead. If not for my Basque pride I would have jumped overboard and swum ashore then and there. With time as I became familiar with the schooner's crew and the miners, I regained my enthusiasm.

On the way to Saglek Bay, where we would spend three and a half months, we stopped at St. John's for supplies, as well as at Port Union, St. Anthony, and several Labrador coastal fishing communities. Because of the prevalence of small and large icebergs on the Labrador coast, Captain Smith preferred, when possible, to sail during daylight hours. This added to our travel time.

In Port Union, we picked up Lewis Little, a former member of the Newfoundland government and a representative of the firm that had staked the claim of ownership on the Saglek Bay graphite deposit. Little seemed to be well respected by everyone along the coast; he was warmly greeted in every port we entered.

We stopped in Hebron, Labrador, to pick up two Inuit guides who were familiar with the site of the graphite deposit in the Torngat Mountains. I went ashore in a boat with two others. It was the first occasion I had to interact with Newfoundland and Labrador's native population. One of the guides, Julius Nathaniel, and his family had just returned to the coast from their winter hunting grounds in the country. As was their custom, they fished during the summer months and moved to their more permanent quarters in the backcountry for the longer winter period. Nathaniel, a wonderfully friendly individual, and his wife and six children lived in a large tent during the summer.

In 1942, Hebron was the most northerly populated community on the Labrador coast. During our short time there I also met Newfoundland Ranger Frank Mercer of Bay Roberts, who was in charge of the Hebron detachment of the Ranger Force.[8] Finally we departed for Saglek.

Our arrival in Saglek started with a busy period of preparation to get our equipment ashore and moved to the mine site, about 25 kilometres inland. There was no big wharf, no roads, no infrastructure of any kind. To my surprise, I was asked to drive the tractor from the vessel's deck, down a reinforced gangway, and onto a float-

---

8   The Newfoundland Ranger Force was the predecessor of the Royal Canadian Mounted Police (RCMP), which came to Newfoundland after Confederation in 1949.

ing wooden platform (supported by 22 empty oil drums) that was to be towed to shore. We were all anxious—Captain Smith, his crew, the miners, and me—as the tractor settled on the floating platform, sinking it within inches of the water's surface. Luckily, Saglek is a sheltered bay, and we reached the shore.

Several days later, it was time to transport the pre-fabricated bunkhouse to the mine site. The terrain, however, was uneven and included several miles of slope. The bunkhouse was loaded onto a sled made of three large logs, chained together so it could be towed by tractor to the site. We trundled along the side of the 3,000-foot mountain. The miners stayed in front, moving the large boulders aside as needed, when suddenly one of the runners of the sled went over a large rock. The bunkhouse parts that had supposedly been securely fastened to the sled broke loose, capsized, rolled down the mountainside for several hundred feet, and were converted to a pile of matchsticks.

Fortunately, expedition planners had had the foresight to pack canvas tents, which we lived in for the next three months.

The Saglek mine site was well north of the treeline, and we saw few wild animals other than an occasional fox. As anyone who has been fortunate to visit the area knows, the Torngat Mountains are beautiful. One of the great attractions is the Northern Lights, and almost every night there was a magnificent display of bright, colourful lights dancing across the northern sky.

The three months of mining were uneventful. I settled into a routine of transporting graphite from the mine to the vessel by tractor. There was no telephone, no radio, and no communication with the outside world for the entire time we were there. With no news and no interaction with people other than those on the ship or working in the mine, the war receded into the distance.

Given my constant journeys back and forth from the campsite to the vessel, I alternated between living at the campsite and on the vessel. I looked forward to having a day and night on board because, after I was done with the chores of moving the graphite and loading it, I would have the pleasure of a few hours of char fishing in the

Getting a haircut from Captain Smith aboard the *Frampton*, summer 1942.

bay with Captain Smith. He became a good friend and looked after my best interests. I still treasure a picture of Captain Smith's giving me a haircut on the stern deck of the *Frampton* in Saglek Bay that summer.

Isolated as were in Saglek, little did we know that we were playing a role in the faraway war. The graphite we extracted was returned to St. Lawrence, and then shipped to Delaware, Maryland, and onward. We were told—but we can never know for certain—it was eventually used in the construction of the atomic bombs that were dropped on the Japanese cities of Hiroshima and Nagasaki.

I did learn, many years later, that we had set up camp just 50 kilometres south of where the Germans had established a weather office on the Labrador coast. It was no coincidence that just as our schooner was leaving Saglek Bay for home—loaded with graphite and a bunch of homesick miners—we observed a massive vessel on the horizon. The *Bremen*, as Captain Smith read through his binoculars, was a German troopship. It was only publicized in the 1990s that the Germans had established a weather station in Labrador; the *Bremen* must have been there to set up the post or to drop off supplies to the Germans onshore.

On our return trip to St. Lawrence, we stopped in St. Anthony. Some of us wandered over to the Grenfell Mission to use their telephone to contact our families for news from home. "Oh Gus, we've been desperate to reach you," said my sister Kathleen, who was the telephone operator in St. Lawrence. "Louis was on the *Caribou*."

The passenger ferry *Caribou*, which sailed between Port aux Basques and North Sydney, Nova Scotia, had been torpedoed early in the morning of October 14, 1942, by a German U-boat. My brother Louis and an air force friend from St. Georges were on the ferry returning home from Mont-Joli, where they had been training with the Royal Canadian Air Force. Both on "embarkation leave" prior to being shipped to Europe for duty in the war, they had been in their cabin when the torpedo struck. The explosion jammed the cabin door, but they used a fire axe near the door to smash it and get out. They both reached the deck and jumped overboard. Louis injured one foot in the incident but managed to make his way to a raft, and he was brought to hospital in Sydney. He never saw his friend and enlistment buddy, who was listed as one of the missing persons, again.

This telephone conversation with Kathleen about Louis affected me deeply. I was extremely close to Louis and, standing in the offices of the Grenfell Mission in St. Anthony, I was badly shaken. Of 237 aboard the *Caribou*, only 101 survived. I was happy to know Louis was one of them, particularly in light of the loss of so many lives. After he recovered, Louis went overseas as a pilot, flying 43 missions with the Royal Canadian Air Force over Europe.

Robert Fitzpatrick, who had originally left St. Lawrence with Louis, joined the Royal Canadian Air Force and flew numerous missions over Europe. He was shot down over Belgium during the last year of war. He is buried in Arnheim; I had the honour of visiting his grave on several occasions in the 1960s.

•••

When I returned to St. Lawrence in late October 1942 it was time to make another life decision. If I wasn't going to enlist, and if I wasn't going to work in the mines, then I had to do something else.

My brief experience as an electrician's helper had been positive. I heard through a friend that the Americans, who had established a large base at Fort Pepperrell in St. John's, were advertising a training program in accordance with an agreement between Newfoundland's Commission of Government and the United States military. The Americans were prepared to employ Newfoundlanders at their military bases in Newfoundland and Labrador to replace some American civilians working on their bases, and also to train local civilians to work with their military maintenance personnel. I applied and was accepted for an electrical course at Fort Pepperrell.

After completing the program, and fully enjoying my time in the capital city, I was offered a job at the American base of my choosing in Newfoundland. I selected Argentia because it was the closest to home.

I was the first Newfoundland civilian to work in the American

Navy marine maintenance division repairing and maintaining electrical equipment aboard surface ships and submarines. While American servicemen were paid more than $1 an hour, tradesmen from Newfoundland were paid 21 cents an hour. This inequity resulted from the agreement the Commission of Government had made: the rate of pay for Newfoundland civilians on the American bases could only match the salaries paid by commercial operators in Newfoundland. Presumably, the goal was to avoid the possibility of labour unrest or ill feelings between those working for Newfoundland-owned commercial companies and those working at the American military bases.

No matter the pay discrepancy, I was getting a regular paycheque, I wasn't working in the mines, and my years in Argentia were good ones. I worked hard, took advantage of ongoing training, and gained experience and confidence as an electrician. It was a great, at times glamorous, time. I was the first Newfoundlander to make the American softball team at Argentia. It was big stuff, on a base of 8,000 to 10,000 people. We would fly to New England or Goose Bay to play against teams from all over. The days of hopping on a fishing boat with an inner tube looped around me or riding in the back of a truck to play a game of soccer seemed far away.

Every night the cinema at the base played a different movie. Big-name entertainers such as Frank Sinatra and Bob Hope and movie stars such as Betty Grable came to visit. The military personnel were well entertained by visiting celebrities, and those of us living on the base were given passes to visiting United Service Organizations (USO) shows. On weekends my buddies and I would head to St. John's for fun.

Above all, I loved my job, whether it was working in the bowels of a submarine or on the radar of a warship. I was always treated well and, even after the war ended with big celebrations in 1945, I didn't intend to leave. I was young and enjoying life.

•••

While I was working and living on the American base, my

brother-in-law, Don Poynter, had struck up a friendship with Arthur Monroe, a fish merchant and the son of former Newfoundland prime minister, Walter Monroe.[9] Poynter, who had married my sister Florence, was manager of the St. Lawrence Corporation mine.

Avid salmon fishermen, Poynter and Arthur Monroe often met at Cape Rogers River in Placentia Bay. During one of their fishing trips, Monroe mused aloud about his upcoming plan to build new fresh-frozen-fish plants in Newfoundland. The trouble was, Monroe said, the ideal location of the fish-processing plants with respect to the resource—places like Isle aux Morts, Burgeo, and Burin, which were ice-free year-round and strategically located near the Grand Banks, Gulf of St. Lawrence, and St. Pierre Bank fisheries—were isolated. There were no roads to Isle aux Morts or Burgeo and, while a road did connect communities on the Burin Peninsula, there was no road to St. John's or any other part of the island. There were no roads for land transportation and virtually no communications but, above all, there was no electrical power supply in any of the three ideal locations for fish-processing plants.

Poynter perked up. "My brother-in-law is a trained electrician," he said. "A young and capable one at that."

And so it happened that one day in the middle of 1947 I got a telephone call at the Navy marine maintenance building at the Argentia base from Monroe. "I'm in the fish business and this is a very important time in our history," he said. "And your brother-in-law says that you might be the man I'm looking for."

•••

It wasn't unusual for me to head to St. John's on a weekend, but this time I ignored my usual good-time haunts there and headed straight down to the harbourfront. The pier belonging to the Monroe Export Company was easy to find and teeming with activity. Salted dried fish was being wheeled in and out of the buildings as I made my way down the alleyway from Water Street west to the offices.

---

9   Monroe served as prime minister of Newfoundland from 1924 to 1928.

Arthur Monroe was waiting. "I've got a job for you, if you're interested," he said. Monroe always got straight to the point.

"I'm interested in anything," I said.

Monroe asked if I knew anything about the fish business. I admitted I didn't. At that moment, I remembered being on my father's trap skiff when I was six years old. One of the crewmen decided to have some fun and, just as the cod trap was drawn up to bail the catch out into the boat, he lowered me down into the writhing mass of fish. *That's* what I knew about fishing.

Monroe sketched out his plans and my place in them. He had small operations in Isle aux Morts, Burgeo, and Burin. Using the limited premises available in the communities, he was processing and freezing fresh fish for sale to the US and Europe. Isle aux Morts did not have electricity; Burin and Burgeo had some power but not enough to run a plant. Small diesel engines were being used to power the equipment, but this was a temporary setup: Monroe was expanding all frozen-fish operations and needed a proper, reliable power source to do so.

Monroe's plan was to acquire 500-horsepower diesel engines for each plant and commission General Electric Company (located in Peterborough, Ontario) to build generators to fit the engines. During wartime and well into the post-war period, it was difficult to find new diesel engines, since all the manufacturers had been focused on the war efforts. After considerable searching, three second-hand engines had been located in the US. These engines would power new fish-processing plants and fish-meal-production facilities, including all of the equipment required to freeze fresh fillets and process fish offal into fishmeal. The new plants would be large, capable of employing hundreds of individuals, and productive. The world's markets were looking for Newfoundland fish, Monroe said, and he had plans to supply them.

But first, Monroe needed someone to complete the installation of the new power plants in the three communities. Also on the job list: completing the electrification of the new plants and establishing a preventative maintenance system for fishing trawlers and freezer ("reefer") vessels that would transport the finished product to market. He needed that person immediately. His proposition sounded intriguing, even if I did not grasp the full scope of what he had laid out in front of me.

Monroe asked what I'd like to be paid. Without thinking, I said, "$250 a month."

"Let's make it $300," he countered. "And I hear you're getting married."

"I'm not getting married yet, but I am going with a girl," I said, surprised again.

"I'll give you a place to live."

The deal was sealed. I gave two weeks' notice at the base and, at 23, got ready to start what would be a lifelong career in the Newfoundland and Labrador fisheries.

PART 2: ON THE FISH-PLANT FLOOR

While exact figures for comparison are lacking, the supply of cod in the Newfoundland and Labrador inshore and bank areas, and the total catch by all countries, probably have not declined since the early part of the 19th century.

—Walsh Report, 1953

Chapter 5
State of the resource 2: The Walsh Report, 1953

The *Newfoundland Fisheries Development Committee Report* is one of the best and most accurate reports ever done on the Newfoundland fisheries. It is the one document I have read that spells out exactly what the fisheries of Newfoundland was at the time of Confederation, how it worked, and what needed to be done to move it forward.

When Newfoundland joined Canada in 1949, provisions were made in the Terms of Union that the Newfoundland Fisheries Board, which had been set up in 1936, could continue to operate for five years. The goal: a smooth transition in fisheries management. Newfoundland brought with her into Canada a huge and pristine resource—the fishery—but it was an industry facing great changes and huge challenges, the living standards of fishermen not the least among them.

In 1951, by joint agreement, the governments of Canada and Newfoundland established the Newfoundland Fisheries Development Committee. This committee was asked to research and write an exhaustive report on the state of the fisheries of Newfoundland and offer a program for the future best use of these resources.

Chaired by Chief Justice Albert Walsh, the committee was made up of fishermen, fish processors, and exporters, and federal and provincial government representatives. Dozens of fishing communities were visited and many more surveyed. The final report, commonly known as the Walsh Report, published in 1953, is accurate in its portrayal of an industry in transition.

The scope of the study was three-fold: to examine the fisheries resources available and the possible development of others, the economics of existing methods of harvesting and recommendations of new techniques, and processing methods in use and new methods that could be applicable:

> These undertakings are for the purpose of recommending increased utilization of fishery resources through methods of fishing and processing based on sound scientific, economic and social considerations, and, in particular, of recommending a programme capable of implementation by both the Federal and Provincial Governments and those engaged in the fishing industry and outlining the respective responsibilities of each ... (7)[10]

From this statement of purpose through to the conclusions, the Walsh Report confirms that the governments of Canada and Newfoundland agreed to joint management of the fisheries. That intention was never acted on.

Walsh achieved something important in his description of the 1950 Newfoundland fisheries. Before the publication of his report, the scope and the workings of the fisheries of Canada's newest province were not well understood because of the isolation of many of its participants (and the province itself), the sparse distribution of population, and lack of communication. Those who read the report were given a solid background.

•••

The introduction of the fish plant and the frozen-fish industry completely changed the Newfoundland fisheries and fishing culture. A giant step from ingrained traditions, it presented a possible solution to the sharply falling standard of living among those involved in producing salt fish.

---

10   A.J. Walsh, chair, *Newfoundland Fisheries Development Committee Report* (St. John's: Department of Fisheries, 1953) (cited in text as *WR*).

The traditional salt-fish industry was composed of thousands of individual producers around the coast of Newfoundland and Labrador, and had been for decades, if not centuries. At the time of World War I, there were some 40,000 fishermen on the island; by the end of World War II, and the time I was getting involved in the fishing industry, this had declined to about 28,000 (WR, 9). At the time of the Walsh Report, this had declined further. Still, an estimated 25 per cent of the adult (15 years and older) male population of Newfoundland and Labrador were fishermen.

These fishermen were sprinkled all along the island's coast—small communities and outports were built in coves and on headlands. The main reason for the "wide scatter and low degree of concentration" of the population was "the predominance of primitive methods of fishing which have led fishermen to select their places of residence mainly so as to be in immediate proximity to their fishing grounds." The presence of fish stocks, considered a common property resource, assured fishermen of a source of income to support themselves and their families. Many of these isolated communities would have been poor choices for settlement if not for their adjacency to fishing grounds—consequently, there was little in the way of employment options other than fishing (WR, 10).

Each fishing family had its own full production facility, which generally consisted of a 30-35-foot-long trap skiff powered by a 5- or 7-horsepower engine; a small dory; two or three cod traps; a stage, which included a salt supply, splitting table, and storage; flakes for drying; and a store in which to keep the dried fish. About 15,000 or 20,000 of these little factories were scattered throughout hundreds of communities.[11]

In all my travels around the world, I have never seen anything that came close to the enormous number of these operations, which, together, produced a huge amount of salt fish. When the fishing was good, and the family-run factories were operating successfully, the

---

11   In 1949, at the time of Confederation, Newfoundland and Labrador had about 1,450 communities; in 2012, about 700.

process was a sight to behold.

A trap skiff would come home to its harbour, and nine times out of 10 it was so full of fish it bivvered at the gunnels. The skiff was probably also towing a dory-load of fish. The boat tied up at the dock and the fishermen pronged the fish from the skiff and dory to the stagehead. From there the fish were taken to the splitting table, where three men were waiting. The first split and gutted the fish, the second removed the head, and the third removed the soundbone, or backbone. The fish was washed, laid out, and packed in salt. After a few days the fish was "fully struck," meaning it had absorbed the right amount of salt. The excess salt was washed off and the fish brought to the flakes to dry. The women generally took over at this point, managing the drying and storing of the finished salt fish, leaving the men to catch, clean, and salt it.

Salting and drying fish required expertise and vigilance. The drying process needed six to eight days of good weather. Every fish had to be laid out in the morning and brought in at night or if the weather changed. It could take three months for a fisherman and his family to properly cure all of his catch (WR, 101).

The problem was that a season's worth of fish was generally caught in six or eight weeks in the summer, when temperatures were high, often affecting the quality of the product, especially if it took weeks before curing was completed. Differences in weather, skill, and standards meant that the quality of cured cod could vary wildly between family operators and communities. This discrepancy affected the markets for Newfoundland cod. The colony's chief competitors in the salt-cod business, Iceland and Norway, were known to produce consistently higher-quality product and sell to the rich markets of Brazil, Portugal, and Greece. Newfoundland's uneven salt cod tended to go to the lower-end markets, fetching a lower price in places like the Caribbean.

At the end of a Newfoundland summer, the dried salted cod was picked up by merchants and traded for credit, supplies, or, least frequently, cash. Although some communities had bank branches in the early 20th century, most fish producers had no access to financial institutions. In the 1940s, the majority of fishermen still operated on credit, virtually bound to the merchant who had brought them their supplies at the beginning of a season (*WR*, 14).

Unfortunately for Newfoundland and Labrador families, there never was any real profit in the production of salt fish; most were lucky to get enough supplies to carry them through to the next season. They simply could not produce enough salt fish to allow for any extras. As the standard of living increased in North America, the economic discrepancy between families in Newfoundland and those in Canada and the US grew. Newfoundland fishing families survived, but times were tough, due to the price of cod, as well as the difficulty in producing consistently high-quality product. By the 1930s, roughly one-third of Newfoundland fishing families were on government welfare.

According to the Walsh Report, "It is because of their extremely low productivity, and for no other reason, that fishermen involved in the traditional inshore enterprise are poor" (17). In fact, "for a good many families, income from fishing is insufficient to sustain even the low standard of living to which they are accustomed" (21).

There was little means of escape from the traditional way of life. While other, more lucrative, occupations attracted some younger men, their "isolation and ties, material and other, to their native places tend to immobilize them to a certain extent and thus prevent their taking full advantage of opportunities outside the fisheries" (*WR*, 11). It would be well into the 1950s and 1960s before transportation, communication, and educational facilities improved enough to make a difference in the lives of these fishermen. This is not to say the fishermen did not work hard. It took the considerable skill and perseverance of all involved to develop and maintain the salt-fish industry, considering an almost complete lack of communication and road transportation and a reliance on merchant sailing vessels to bring the product to an international market.

There were valid criticisms about salt-fish quality and controversies about the role and power of merchants, but great credit is due to the fishermen and their families who risked lives and capital to create the industry that provided the foundation of the economy of Newfoundland and Labrador.

But change was coming. The long-established "equilibrium of the resource, the industry (including the population depending on it or involved in it) and the market [was] breaking down." It was time to establish a new, modern industry, "an increase in the size of fishing craft, in the efficiency of gear, and in the extent and variety of processing facilities." Old standards would no longer hold up: "With an increase in fixed 'plant' expenses comes a greater urgency to eliminate variability in the supply of raw material" (*WR*, 24).

To survive, those engaged in fishing had to catch more fish, with greater consistency throughout the year, and production methods had to change and quality improve. With the advent of freezing technology, processing plants, and an increasing demand for the final product, the time for the modernization of the Newfoundland cod fishery had arrived.

This was the situation of the fishing industry into which I stepped in 1947.

•••

Walsh explored the health of Newfoundland's fisheries using the best information available at the time. Two dozen commercial species of fish, shellfish, and marine mammals were identified and examined for their possible economic contribution. The report's section on cod supports the importance of a winter cod fishery along some parts of the Newfoundland coast. It also highlights the health and stability of cod stocks, noting that the numbers of cod in the waters off Newfoundland and Labrador "probably have not declined since the early part of the 19th century" (27).

Newfoundland exported over 1 million quintals (a *quintal* equals 50 kilograms/112 pounds) of salt cod annually from 1815 until the 1940s; in many years it neared 2 million quintals (*WR*, 27). But by 1953, "Newfoundland's share of the cod fishery [had] declined considerably: to less than a million quintals. The growing fleets of European vessels [had] been increasing their captures of cod as our catch ... decreased." Foreign nations were heavily fishing near Newfoundland; Walsh suggested that the Newfoundland fishing industry could likely increase its catch by three- or fourfold without harming the stocks, if and when it became profitable to do so (28).

Acknowledging "present limited knowledge," the report encouraged the expanded exploitation of cod, redfish, flatfish, and herring; other species, including salmon, yellowtail flounder, and lobster, were judged "incapable of much greater exploitation" (37). Walsh recommended further study in all cases. The report concluded with a Programme of Development and acknowledged that the production of salt fish was on the decline, though the "cod fishery continues to be the most important branch of the fisheries" (90).

The fishing industry had been plagued by a lack of technological advancement, research, training, and investment. Participants were leaving the fisheries when they could—and, if they couldn't, they were often left in their home communities, struggling to make a living. The report stressed the importance of research, advocating the establishment of "extensive research facilities" (94), which would include both biological and technological laboratories and research stations. Research was required to ensure conservation and maximum exploitation without depletion:

> Experience elsewhere and, in respect of species such as lobster, in Newfoundland has shown that the assets of the sea may be depleted by over-fishing or by taking large quantities of immature fishes or by taking certain species at certain times. In view of the large quantities of different species taken on the nearby international fishing grounds, modification of a programme of development of the industry may become necessary in the light of new data as to the continuance of adequate stocks. (WR, 93)

Walsh advocated that new vessels and equipment had to be

adopted if the industry was to survive; the days of sun-curing fish and expecting to make a living from that were over. Some limited centralization was recommended. The frozen-fish industry offered a welcome solution: "The establishment of filleting plants strategically placed for diversified production and year-round operation at large centres of production along the south coast from St. John's to Isle-aux-Morts ... has gone a long way towards modernization of the fishing industry on that coast" (*WR*, 103).

The Walsh Report's far-reaching Programme of Development, designed to improve the lot of fishing families and the industry, suggested a division of responsibility among the provincial government, federal government, and private industry. It also proposed the implementation of a standing joint committee "to secure coordination of the activities of the governments and their respective departments, and of the departments of each government amongst themselves, and coordination of the activities of those engaged in the industry with governments" (122). This committee should be made up of senior officers from the federal and provincial governments and be presided over by an executive secretary and a joint chair from each. The responsibility and cost of the committee were to be shared equally between the governments of Newfoundland and Canada.

The Walsh Report was authorized by and agreed to by the governments of Canada and Newfoundland. Both governments participated equally in the extensive discussions leading up to and after the report's publication. This is an important historical document, filled with sensible advice. My strong feeling is that, despite the report's clarity, it was not absorbed by those who commissioned it. Federal politicians and senior bureaucrats did not recognize the vast difference in the structure, size, and diversification of the Newfoundland and Labrador fisheries compared to those of Canada's mainland fishing provinces. The background and understanding offered by a shared history was never present.

Had Walsh's recommendations been implemented instead of ignored—especially the call for a stable joint management structure—I believe the result would have been greater cooperation between industry and both levels of government. Joint management could have helped keep the Newfoundland and Labrador fishing industry on track, perhaps in a position to rival those in Norway, Iceland, and even Alaska.

Chapter 6
Arthur Monroe and the first fish plants

I t wasn't just the promise of a good salary and a house that solidified my commitment to Arthur Monroe, although these were
important to a young man of 23. Monroe's vision caught my
imagination and his enthusiasm for the future was contagious. It
was easy for me to believe that following him would give me a front-
row seat for major events in Newfoundland's business and cultural
evolution.

Monroe was a leader in, if not the driver of, the biggest reset in
500 years of New World fishing history: the switch from traditional
salt-fish operations to the modern frozen-fish industry. Throughout
the 40 years I knew and worked with Arthur Monroe, he had a
profound influence on my attitude, performance, and dedication to
building success in the frozen-fish industry. He was an inspiration,
a mentor, and a friend.

The Monroe Export Company, a salt-fish firm, was founded by
Walter Monroe in 1909. When he stepped into politics in the 1920s,
his son, Arthur, took over management of the successful business.
Born in St. John's and educated in England and St. John's, the younger Monroe had been working with the company for years and was
even more entrenched in the world of fisheries at that point, both
within Newfoundland and internationally, than his father.

A natural leader, Arthur Monroe had gathered a long list of
prominent contacts throughout the international fishing world. He
had lived in Spain and travelled through England and continental
Europe for years, marketing salt fish for his father's company. He
returned to Newfoundland in the 1930s and became equally well
known through mainland Canada and the northeastern US.

Monroe's return to the northwest Atlantic coincided with a new and exciting trend: the home freezer was fast becoming a household appliance, especially in the US. Demand for salted fish in many regions was still strong—particularly in Italy, Spain, Portugal, Brazil, and the Caribbean—but there was no doubt in Monroe's mind that appetite for the new frozen product was growing and would soon overtake that for salt fish.

Starting in the late 1930s, Arthur Monroe spent considerable time in New England, particularly the Boston area, which was developing into a hub for this new industry. He and his wife left Newfoundland each winter to live in New England for three or four months. His extended stays gave him a deep understanding of the market potential in that region and allowed him to cultivate important connections within the New England seafood industry and academic community. By the time World War II began in 1939, Monroe was ready to lead his traditional family operation into the cutting-edge fresh-frozen-fish business.

A crucial step in the transition was adopting a new brand. Monroe formally incorporated Fishery Products Limited (FPL) in 1941 as a fresh-frozen-fish company. The largest investor in FPL was the Monroe Export Company, allowing it to remain a family-owned and -operated enterprise. Five years later, in 1946, FPL purchased the assets of the Monroe Export Company, bringing the two companies—the frozen-fish and salt-fish operations—together under one banner. FPL was the largest producer of frozen fish in Newfoundland and among the largest exporters of salt fish, by volume, for the next decade.[12]

In 1941, Monroe also incorporated Fishery Products Inc., a wholly owned subsidiary of FPL, based in the eastern US but with (over time) satellite offices throughout the US and Europe. It was the official marketing arm of FPL, and the one and only organization available to market Newfoundland fish products stateside. Monroe knew there was no point in developing a fresh-frozen-fish

---

12   Miriam White, *A Fishery for Modern Times: The State and the Industrialization of the Newfoundland Fishery, 1934-1968* (Don Mills, ON: Oxford University Press, 2001), 29.

industry, particularly on the heels of 400 years of the salt-fish industry, without a way to market and sell the product. Fishery Products Inc. also built and operated a secondary seafood processing plant in Cleveland, Ohio, the first of its kind in the US, operated by another subsidiary, Blue Water Seafood. This was Monroe's great vision: to set up an effective vertically integrated company capable of managing every step of the fish and seafood production process, from ocean to dinner plate—harvesting operations, fish plants, transportation, secondary processing plants, product development, and marketing. It was an effective business model, one no other Canadian seafood company ever managed to successfully emulate.

Monroe's many contacts helped him considerably. Bob Gruber, an official with a large grocery chain and purchaser of Monroe's products, became a close friend and colleague. He was instrumental in starting Fishery Products Inc. and Blue Water Seafood, and he was president of the latter company for years.

The collaboration extended to product development. When the production of frozen fish began, cod and other groundfish (including haddock, flounder, and redfish) were processed and sold in 1-, 5-, and 10-pound packages. These products came from medium to large fish, which were generally caught offshore. The small cod from the inshore cod-trap fishery produced smaller fillets, which were unsuitable for the premium packs. This fish had to be marketed at a lower price, until Gruber and Monroe found a solution. The two worked together to develop the "cod block" in the early 1950s; cod blocks could be composed of smaller, less marketable cod fillets. The cod was generally frozen in 16.5-pound cubes, which could be shipped, ready to be further processed. In most cases, they were mechanically cut into smaller sizes and processed in the US-based secondary plant as fish sticks, burgers, and other neatly sized portions.[13]

Gruber continued to experiment and became known as a

---

13   Anneka Wright and William Folsom, *Neptune's Table: A View of America's Ocean Fisheries* (Silver Spring, MD: National Marine Fisheries Service, 2002), 33.

pioneer in developing and marketing innovative fish products. He was the first person from the seafood industry to be inducted into the Frozen Food Hall of Fame, a honour he received in 2003, after 60 years in the business, two years before his death.[14]

FPL's product development group, comprised of production and marketing personnel, was monitored by Monroe, his son Denis, and Gruber in the US. In the early days, Denis was involved in market development and secondary processing operations in the US and between them they oversaw the development of hundreds of seafood products. Denis, after years of involvement in the market development and secondary processing operations in the US, moved to St. John's in 1971. He succeeded his father as president of the company from 1971 until 1976.

Julia Child, noted nutritionist (later cookbook author and television personality), was an outspoken proponent of the benefits of seafood consumption to the American public and a major contributor to promotional programs directed toward increasing fish consumption. She was also a close friend and associate of Bob Gruber and Monroe.

The first board of Fishery Products Inc., in the 1940s, included the dean of engineering at MIT, David Clinkenberg (a vice-president of American Express), Ted Sorenson (later a member of President John F. Kennedy's cabinet), and others of equal prominence. They may not all have known much about fishing, but their influence, connections, and general knowledge of American business and its economy were integral to the expanding market for frozen seafood. These contacts were key components of Monroe's market development plan for the US. They also made him aware that the US and some European countries were already far ahead of Newfoundland in the frozen-food industry. In order to be competitive, Newfoundland businesses had to catch up. Monroe was determined to do just that.

---

14   "Frozen Food Hall of Fame (People in the News)," *Seafood Business*, February 1, 2003.

When Monroe died in 1985, Gruber contributed to a newspaper obituary, characterizing him as "a brilliant and aggressive leader" who had made "a very lasting contribution to Newfoundland's progress and development in the fishery."[15] FPL broke new ground in Newfoundland, and Monroe was always determined to elevate its place in the international marketplace. Under Monroe's leadership, FPL became one of the largest employers in Newfoundland and marketed and sold its broad range of fish products in the US, Europe, and Asia.

At its height, the company employed over 6,500 men and women in its workforce and management. FPL operated fish plants in Isle aux Morts, Burgeo, Burin, Harbour Breton, St. Lawrence, Burin, Marystown, Trepassey, Port Union, Greenspond, Joe Batts Arm, Change Islands, Twillingate, St. Anthony, and Port au Choix; and up to 800 men worked aboard FPL trawlers. After the federal and provincial public service, FPL was the largest employer in the province.

Monroe constantly strove for growth, at times pushing beyond the comfort level of many politicians and other industry leaders. He applied for a $100,000 loan from the Commission of Government in 1945; he was turned down over concerns about his disregard for risk and his "penchant for overexpansion."[16] Monroe's thirst for innovation, the latest technology, and improvement in all areas of the fishing industry ran deep. Product quality, continuity of supply to the market, improving productivity, and bringing an ever-changing variety of seafood products to market were priorities for him and those who worked with him.[17] Demands for innovative fish products by the food service and retail sectors were loud and Monroe was always ready to respond.

---

15   "Arthur Monroe Is Dead at 85," *Evening Telegram*, December 19, 1985.

16   White, 31.

17   Research scientist Dr. Wilfred Templeman, who served with Monroe on the Fisheries Research Board of Canada, called him "a brilliant and remarkable man who continually kept abreast of technological advances" ("Arthur Monroe Is Dead at 85" [*Evening Telegram*, December 19, 1985]).

Arthur Monroe's contribution went far beyond new product launches. He built the first processing plants in isolated communities, necessitating the provision of electric power. The salt-fish industry was generally limited to cod, whereas the advent of fresh-frozen technology created a demand for redfish, haddock, turbot, flounder, and other species.

The residents of Newfoundland fishing communities were not familiar with any fish production other than salting; training on a major scale was a priority. When I was manager of the fish plant in Burin, Monroe encouraged me to recruit experts in such disciplines as fishmeal production, fish oil extraction, and the development and production of liquid plant food. We brought in individuals from the US, UK, Iceland, Germany, Denmark, Norway, and elsewhere. They lived in our staff house in Burin, some for four or five years and others who became permanent employees. The in-house experiments were successful: the plant food was used in the sugar-cane industry in Barbados; preserving the freshness of cod offal resulted in higher-quality fish meal; oil from cod, redfish, halibut, and other species was sold for industrial and medicinal use (in particular, our experiments with halibut liver oil enabled the preservation of higher levels of vitamin A).

Monroe found new ways to improve quality. When trap-fished cod were heavily glutted with capelin, for example, he experimented with holding them in pens in the ocean until the cod naturally rid themselves of the capelin. The result was a firmer fish, a higher finished product yield, and better returns from the market.

All of that would follow. In the early years FPL set up its first freezing plants in St. John's and Holyrood. Small plants in Isle aux Morts, Burin, Burgeo, and elsewhere soon followed. By the time the war ended in 1945, FPL could count among its assets four trawlers, many smaller boats, and its first two reefer vessels.

When I came on board in 1947, FPL was poised, under Monroe's leadership, to be the largest fresh-frozen-fish company in Newfoundland and Labrador.

•••

Getting ready for the first day of my new job wasn't as simple as packing a lunch and pressing my best shirt. One day in August 1947 I took the train across the island to Port aux Basques, where I met the longliner Monroe had sent to take me 25 kilometres down the coast to Isle aux Morts. Isle aux Morts looked like many small Newfoundland fishing communities I had seen: wooden houses built close to the rocky shoreline and flakes and stages perched along the coast. Typical of small Newfoundland fishing communities, it was isolated, with little in the way of communication infrastructure, and had rough gravel roads that went no farther than Margaree and Foxroost, the adjacent settlements. The new fish plant, prominent at the centre of Isle aux Morts, however, was not so typical.

I disembarked and took my belongings up the hill to the boarding house, eager to meet up with Monroe and find out what was to happen next. The owner of the boarding house pointed me to the fish plant. It didn't take long to find the two men working inside, high up on a scaffold: Monroe and his chief engineer, George Tucker. It was 4 p.m. on a Sunday and the two senior executives were busily connecting a liquid line in the refrigeration plant. I took that display of energy and dedication to heart and tried to apply it in my own work with FPL in the days, months, and years that followed.

When Monroe and Tucker finished their work, we went back to the boarding house and had a long discussion that went on well into the night. The reality and scope of my job began to sink in.

The next morning I started early. There was work to be done. While the installation of the diesel-electric power plant was nearly complete, the filleting plant needed to be electrified and the equipment, which had been driven by small diesel engines, had to be converted so it could operate by electric motors. I was also responsible for a preventative maintenance system of the company-owned plant and trawlers. Monroe and Tucker returned to St. John's. They kept in touch with me and my progress.

It was a new community and a new business for me, but I

quickly felt at home. I enjoyed working beside the local people and getting the plant ready for operation. I don't think I experienced an unpleasant day in Isle aux Morts. The plant workforce and fishermen supplying fish to the plant were dedicated to making it a successful operation.

Abe Seeley from Bareneed in Conception Bay was appointed plant manager, and he became a close friend. One evening Abe and I were out for a walk and I witnessed for the first time the presence of foreign fishing vessels in Newfoundland's waters. (There wasn't even a 12-mile fishing limit around Newfoundland in 1947.) We saw many vessels close to shore and among the baited gear belonging to the Isle aux Morts fishermen. The next morning local fishermen found their hook-and-line gear either missing or in a mess, and the foreign fleet had retreated to 20 or 30 kilometres off the coast, only to return again during the night. Over the next few weeks we gathered information from fishermen in communities between Rose Blanche and Margaree about the number of foreign vessels fishing on those traditional fishing grounds.

One night 180 masthead lights were visible. The next morning we sent the trawler *Mustang*, which was discharging at the Isle aux Morts plant, out to see what the fleet was up to. The *Mustang*'s crew confirmed the fleet was about 25 kilometres off the coast and looked ready to resume fishing close to shore at nightfall. There was nothing we could do.

In 1962, 15 years later, I spent a day on a federal DFO surveillance plane based in Halifax—we had to refuel twice in Gander—flying over foreign fleets off Labrador, the Grand Banks, and the Scotian Shelf. We didn't have time to survey foreign presence in the Gulf of St. Lawrence, but that day we counted 925 foreign fishing vessels. During my time as a commissioner with ICNAF through the 1960s and 1970s, we were aware that up to 1,400 foreign ships with an estimated 60,000 crew were fishing on our continental shelf. It had been happening for a long time—little did I know, back in Isle aux Morts, that I was seeing the earliest signs of a terrible trend of foreign overfishing.

It took us seven or eight months to finish electrifying the Isle aux Morts plant, working morning, noon, and night. Monroe knew he was facing competition in the industry. National Sea Products in Halifax and H.B. Nickerson & Sons in North Sydney were our primary Canadian competitors; there were also local players: John Penny and Sons in nearby Ramea, the long-established merchant firm of Job Brothers, and Hazen Russell's Bonavista Cold Storage Company. Others would soon join in. It was a period of transition and it was important to keep up. Or, better, stay ahead of the crowd.

•••

Monroe selected Isle aux Morts as one of his first fish plants for two reasons: there were sufficient fish harvesters to provide a steady supply of fresh fish, and there were enough other potential employees in the community and surrounding area to work in the plant.

The fish supply in Isle aux Morts, as would be the case in Burin and Burgeo, came from both local inshore fishermen and trawlers that fished farther offshore. The Burgeo Bank and the St. Pierre Bank, no more than 60 to 90 kilometres from the plants, were easily accessible.

Cod migrated out from the Gulf of St. Lawrence in front of ice movement in winter and returned to the Gulf in the spring, providing coastal fishermen from Burgeo to Port aux Basques with excellent opportunities to catch them. This ensured a high-quality winter fishery, as well as good catches during the lucrative Lenten season. The catch per unit of effort in those days was high—a vessel could go out and return to port with 100,000 or 150,000 pounds of fish in two or three days. This productivity, plus the supply of winter fish, allowed the Isle aux Morts plant to be active all year.

The fish-plant employees were paid each Friday by cheque or cash. Men and women were employed at the plant, but there was a general division of labour. The male workforce received the fish from the harvester at the wharf, weighed it, and put it on ice or in holding tanks. The fish was then delivered to the production line for filleting and skinning. From there, the fish went to the (generally) female workforce. They selected fillets, wrapped them in cellophane, and placed them in packages, depending on size. The packages were inspected by quality control personnel, overwrapped by machine, frozen at -30° to -35°C, packed into larger corrugated boxes, and then placed into cold storage to await transport to market. Because there were no roads or railways from Isle aux Morts to market, a large reefer vessel would pick up the frozen fish from the plant and transport it to the US, generally Cleveland or New England.

The opening of the first major fresh-frozen-fish plants offered Newfoundlanders a doorway into the future and a way out of long-term relationships—good and bad—with St. John's merchants. Fishermen in the Isle aux Morts area began to sell fish directly from their boats to the plant and concentrated on maximizing their harvesting capabilities and landed catches. They were full-time fishermen who no longer had to worry about processing and salting or the whims of merchants. The year-round plant operations enabled workers to have a regular paycheque, the company to maintain reasonable profits, and the industry to take root and grow.

When it opened in 1948, the fish plant in Isle aux Morts employed about 200 people, but that grew as more fish was brought in; greater supply required more processors. It was just the beginning.

•••

After we finished readying the Isle aux Morts plant for production, I moved on to Burgeo and repeated the process of electrifying its plant and providing maintenance services for the fishing and reefer vessels.

Burgeo, a larger community than Isle aux Morts, had a longer history of inshore fishing and it was also once a port for banking schooners. The first settlers came to the Burgeo area in the late 1700s, drawn by the fishing grounds of the St. Pierre Bank, Burgeo Bank, the Gulf of St. Lawrence, and even the Grand Banks. Just a few miles away lay Ramea, the island community where the Penny family had long since established a significant salt-fish operation, which was also in the midst of a full transition to fresh-frozen product.

Prior to 1941, Burgeo depended almost entirely on salt fish. Fish was salted, dried, and exported to markets in Spain, Portugal, and the West Indies by local schooners operated by families such as the Clements (from England) and the Moultons. In 1941, Monroe established a floating fish plant, moored permanently in Burgeo Harbour, and began small-scale fresh-frozen-fish processing. This floating plant, converted freighter *The Netherton*, processed and froze fish fillets using brine freezing—not the Birdseye plate freezers[18] which later became the accepted method of freezing. Fillets from *The Netherton* were exported to the US until the vessel was destroyed by fire on November 5, 1942. Two men, Joseph Dicks and Gerald Mercer, were lost in the blaze.

Almost immediately after the fire, Monroe began constructing a land-based plant in Burgeo. Built from local wood and by local labour, the plant, one of the first fresh-fish processing plants in Newfoundland, opened in 1943 and remained in operation until 1976. Arnold (Arnie) Johnson was hired as plant manager. A forward thinker, Johnson also installed a fish-meal production plant, researched processing glue from fish skins, and initiated municipal government in the community. The Town of Burgeo was officially incorporated in 1950 and Johnson its first mayor. In spite of its isolation, Burgeo was a bustling and successful community. There was no road connecting it to other communities until 1979, but the town and its people prospered.

I enjoyed my days in this new community, and it was a great learning experience. Many people in Burgeo were dedicated to making the plant successful and ensuring the continued prosperity of their community. Monroe, his son Denis, and I grew close through these years of fast-paced expansion and transition, even as challenge after challenge was thrown our way.

Transportation remained a constant battle. There were few

---

18   American inventor Clarence Birdseye (1886-1956), considered the founder of the frozen-food industry, invented methods for freezing food, in particular a quick-freeze method that involved packaging fish and freezing the cartons, pressed between two refrigerated surfaces.

roads, of course, and certainly none to the Burin or Great Northern peninsulas. The ferry system, too, could be unreliable. FPL tried to sell unfrozen fillets to the burgeoning markets in New England and New York, especially during the Lenten season. This required us to get the fresh product from Isle aux Morts to Port aux Basques by boat, then to Cape Breton by ferry, and finally to market by reefer truck. Too often FPL's top-quality product was stuck in Port aux Basques due to weather, negligence, overbooking by mainland-based plants, or some other reason. After seeking and securing customers in the US, we were unable to deliver our fish consistently, and sometimes we weren't able to deliver an edible product at all.

Time after time we lost out to competitors from Maine, Massachusetts, and particularly Nova Scotia, suppliers with the advantage of geography: they were on the spot and able to meet market demand. As a result they secured precedence for shipment to market over us and other Newfoundland and Labrador fish firms. Our Maritime competitors enjoyed other advantages, particularly in the early days of the frozen-fish industry. Nova Scotia, Prince Edward Island, and New Brunswick had immediate access to rail and freezer truck transport. Their educational institutions, training facilities, and communications were more advanced than those in Newfoundland. To compete internationally in the new fresh-fish industry, FPL needed a concentration of well-trained men and women in the harvesting, processing, and marketing sectors. At that time, there was no Fisheries College or Marine Institute to provide assistance in any training programs in Newfoundland.

FPL found the best solutions under the circumstances. More than once, we hired experienced instructors from outside institutions, such as the Nova Scotia Technical College, for a few weeks at a time to come to the Burin Vocational School and conduct training programs for plant managers, supervisors, quality-control inspectors, and other jobs. It was an expensive and time-consuming exercise but the training did lead to improved productivity and handling procedures and helped us implement quality-control programs.

By 1949, plants like that in Burgeo employed 300 to 350

people and processed 200,000 to 250,000 pounds of fish per day. Communities around the fish plants grew slowly, attracting people with the promise of year-round, steady work. World markets for frozen fish were growing, just as Monroe had predicted.

Eight months after I went to Burgeo, my job was done. Even more than I had in Isle aux Morts, I regretted my departure from Burgeo. But it was onward to the last plant Monroe had originally hired me to upgrade and electrify. It was August 1948, and I was off to Burin, about 30 kilometres from my hometown of St. Lawrence.

•••

In 1955, FPL concentrated on other operations and sold the Burgeo plant to fish merchant Spencer Lake of the Lake Group of Companies, who operated it under the name Burgeo Fish Industries Ltd. Lake came to Burgeo at the behest of the Smallwood government—he was promised substantial support if he took over the failing fish plant. In 1956, Lake married Margaret Penny (whose family owned the fish plant in nearby Ramea), and they combined their fishing operations, making Lake a major player in the local fish industry. For the next 16 years, Lake ran the plant and transformed the town—even serving as its mayor.

Burgeo didn't have telephones or electricity in 1955 when FPL left. Everyone burned coal and wood. A decade later, telephones and electricity had been installed, and everyone had switched to oil. The town had a modern supermarket, laundromat, dry cleaners, beauty parlour, and barbershop, most of which were owned by Lake. Boats that picked up fish from the fish plant for export to the US returned with fruit, vegetables, and other supplies. A dairy farm was established, and a man delivered milk every morning by horse and cart. Water and sewer came next. Lake didn't act alone, but he was credited as the force behind many of the changes.

In 1971, Richard Cashin and Father Des McGrath held public meetings in Burgeo about organizing a union. This union would become the foundation of the Newfoundland Fisheries, Food, and Allied Workers Union (NFFAWU, later the Fish, Food and Allied

Workers Union or FFAW). It was their first foray into union organization. Cashin and McGrath gave convincing speeches, telling rapt audiences that people in other fish plants, including Burin, were earning more than those in Burgeo and that organizing could improve their wages and working conditions. From day one, Lake refused to sit down with Cashin; he said he would be done with Burgeo if a union was certified. Cashin told the people of Burgeo that Lake was bluffing.

Burgeo native Allister Hann, who worked as town manager under Mayor Spencer Lake during that contentious time, remembers how the topic of unionization caused a rift in the town: "I was town manager and trying to stay in the middle of it all," he said, "and not stand on either side of the debate. It tore families apart, even my own: I had one brother who was pro-union and one who was anti-union, one who was ready to take down Spencer Lake and one who was loyal to him. They were at each others' throats. It blew the town apart." Hann, who served as mayor from 1997 to 2005, says Burgeo never recovered.

When the time came to vote to form a union, the "yes" side narrowly won (105 out of 205 workers signed union cards). The union's first attempts at negotiations were shut down, however, when Lake rejected their demands. In June 1971, the fish-plant workers went on strike. Lake brought in non-unionized scab workers—some were said to be schoolchildren as young as 11. The union set up a picket line on the road; Lake brought the workers in by boat. A floating picket line was put up. Confrontations, sometimes violent, were regular occurrences.

Ten and a half months after the strike had begun Progressive Conservative Frank Moores managed a narrow victory, ousting Smallwood from the premier's chair. To fulfill an election promise, his government purchased the troubled plant from the Lake Group for $1 million.

The government sent managers in to run the Burgeo plant, but operations were often hampered by wildcat strikes. In 1976, the province sold it to National Sea Products of Nova Scotia. The union was still militant and fought against downsizing or other operational changes. In 1990, Bill Barry and SeaFreeze took over the plant. Barry was not known as a friend of the unions—the NFFAWU tried unsuccessfully to organize his operations in Corner Brook. The plant closed in 1992, before the cod moratorium was called, following a controversy between the Town of Burgeo, Barry, the union, and both levels of government. Burgeo, one of the province's earliest and most productive plants, was one of the first freezer plants to be closed in that era; it has remained closed, except for brief periods, such as in 1999 when crab was processed there.

Chapter 7
The post-war years:
Matters of equipment and supply

The conclusion of the war in 1945 left the fleets of many of the world's major fishing nations in shambles. The leading industrial nations had dedicated their manufacturing capacity and any available machinery and equipment to the war effort. All resources were directed to winning. Very few, if any, fishing vessels were constructed during those years; in fact, thousands of existing fishing vessels had been seconded for military use and had been damaged, sunk, or rendered obsolete by the time the war concluded. Countless industrial and manufacturing plants were destroyed and these needed to be rebuilt. Vast amounts of agricultural land had been rendered unusable. Years would pass before normal production could resume in Britain, France, Germany, Belgium, the Netherlands, the USSR, and Eastern Bloc countries.

The need for an alternative source of protein rose steadily throughout the war years, as the supplies of food millions had once counted on were cut off or destroyed. It didn't stop when the war ended; nations were left reeling and desperate to find ways to provide food for their people. European fishing nations, which had abandoned fishing during the war, focused on returning to the industry.

Europe was hungry, and the waters off Newfoundland and Labrador were teeming with virtually untouched fish stocks. Fish from the Grand Banks and elsewhere on the continental shelf were identified as preferred sources of protein. European nations had been fishing near Newfoundland for five centuries, but what was different in the late-1940s was the intensity of the effort. The decision made by European nations to engage heavily in fishing the northwest Atlantic in the years following World War II would dramatically influence the Newfoundland and Labrador population, both socially and economically.

As demand for fish increased, the challenges for Newfoundland fish processors to fill this increased proportionally.

Monroe desperately wanted to build up the FPL trawler fleet to provide a continuous, year-round flow of fish to capture and maintain a share of the market. But he ran up against another indirect effect of the war: shipbuilding yards everywhere were blocked with orders for freighters, and building fishing vessels was not a high priority.

During the war, there had been no way to get fishing vessels built in the naval shipyards in Canada, the US, or Europe—they were busy meeting the needs of the armed forces. Monroe managed to have some smaller, 100-foot wooden side trawlers built in Bay d'Espoir and other shipyards in Newfoundland. He also located, bought, and refitted—perhaps *rescued* would be a more appropriate word—three older steel trawlers out of New England.

In the years immediately after the war, the situation wasn't much better. Most shipyards were busy rebuilding and replacing mercantile vessels lost in the conflict. European shipyards began building freezer and factory-freezer trawlers, many of which would fish near the Grand Banks to supply their own needs. On a freezer trawler, the crew catch fish, remove the gut, and freeze the gutted fish for on-shore processing. A factory-freezer trawler can go one step further: the crew includes fish processors who fillet the fresh fish at sea and freeze the fillets.

Monroe searched internationally for vessels, and eventually found second-hand trawlers in England and the Netherlands to help him maintain a supply of fish to the busy plants. Finally, thanks to his New England connections, Monroe negotiated the building of two trawlers in Groton, Connecticut. Groton had been officially commissioned as a submarine base during World War I; the Electric Boat Division of General Dynamics delivered 54 submarines from its facility in Groton during World War II.[19] After the war, the operators of Groton's shipyard found they had enough submarine steel left over to construct two trawlers. And so, in the fall of 1946, two new 93-foot FPL side trawlers were launched, fitted with Enterprise engines, and christened *Zebu* and *Zebit*.

These trawlers began serving the Burin plant at about the time I arrived in Isle aux Morts. I made my first trip on one of them when I was in Burgeo. The *Zebu* was fishing on the St. Pierre Bank when FPL's chief engineer, George Tucker, asked me to travel aboard it to make some repairs and adjustments that needed to be done under actual working conditions. That trip was an eye-opener for me, and the first of many times I travelled with some of the best fishing skippers and crews in the business.

In 1948 Monroe called on his connections again and arranged for the construction of the wooden trawler *Zerda*, approximately the same size as the *Zebu* and *Zebit*, by the Bristol Yacht Company in South Bristol, Maine. A fishing company in New Bedford, Massachusetts, had sold him a second-hand, 95-foot steel trawler, which was named *Zebroid*. These four trawlers joined the growing side-trawler fleet of new and old vessels serving the plants in Burin, Burgeo, and Isle aux Morts.

Nearly all of the trawlers and reefer vessels in the FPL fleet had names beginning with the letter "Z." Monroe said he did it that way because it would be easier to locate FPL vessels in the Department of Transportation's registry if they were all together, at the end of the list. We searched far and wide for suitable "Z" names, beginning with place names from around the world. There were a few departures from the normal sources, and so it was that the trawler *Zaandam*, named for a town in Holland, was on the same page as the *Zimdowney*, named after Jim Downey of Greenspond, a fisherman friend of Monroe.

---

19   Town of Groton, Connecticut, http://www.groton-ct.gov/about/history.asp, accessed November 28, 2012. Groton is still home to the Naval Submarine Base, the Navy's Submarine School, and the Electric Boat Corporation, which provides submarines to the US Navy.

FPL wasn't just desperate for ships. Immediately after the war, neither Canada nor the US was making the machinery and equipment used in modern trawlers, and European manufacturing capability was on a long road to recovery. There were shortages of almost everything we looked for, from winches to electronics to main and auxiliary engines. Our company, like others, scrambled to provide a year-round supply of high-quality frozen fish to our customers.

FPL owed its survival in those early days—and many times in subsequent decades—to dedicated, creative employees at every level who were as interested in the growth, expansion, and viability of the company as its owners and management. There could not have been a more difficult period to expand fishing operations and undertake development of the new fresh-frozen fishery than the war and immediate post-war years, but finding a loyal workforce was not one of our challenges.

•••

The electrical power supply to most rural areas on the island of Newfoundland in the 1940s was, to put it mildly, scarce. Of the first three fish plants I worked on, there was no power available in Isle aux Morts or Burgeo, and only sufficient electrical power for domestic use in the Burin area.

To enable these plants to operate, three large diesel engines had to be located and combined with matching electric generator units. The generators were built to order by General Electric in Peterborough, Ontario. Securing large diesel engines for each unit, however, was not an easy task. New engines were completely out of the question, since production had gone directly to the war effort, and post-war demand was great. After considerable hunting, Monroe and Tucker eventually located two older engines in the US, which he had refitted for use with the GE generators in Isle aux Morts and Burgeo. It was a different story in Burin: despite the best efforts of Tucker and his staff, a suitable large diesel engine for the third generator simply could not be found.

After innumerable dead ends, one of the younger engineers

came forward with an idea.

While awaiting construction of a new fish plant, FPL had set up temporary processing operations in 1942 in the Burin Cold Storage facility. Burin Cold Storage was publicly owned and had been designed to freeze and store bait for fishermen; we had converted part of it into a makeshift fresh-frozen-fish plant supplied by inshore fishermen using cod traps, baited gear, and hand lines. A few small schooners took ice to preserve their catch and fished for four to five days at a time at Cape St. Mary's and on the St. Pierre Bank; several wooden side trawlers also contributed catch to the Burin plant.

One side trawler, the 90-foot *Coyote*, was equipped with a 450-horsepower Enterprise diesel engine, manufactured in San Francisco before the US entered the war. As the *Coyote* returned from her maiden voyage in 1946, fully loaded with cod, she grounded on Corbin Island at the entrance to Burin and went to the bottom. It was fairly shallow water, but there the *Coyote* remained for two years, buffeted by winter storms and high seas.

The young Burin engineer suggested that the engine from the *Coyote* be retrieved and combined with the GE generator to provide electricity for the plant. It wouldn't be an easy job with our limited facilities—in fact we weren't even sure it was possible—but we didn't have any options other than to use multiple small diesels as power supplies, and so we decided to give it a try.

A month later, a small group, led by Willis Mayo,[20] a veteran diver and long-time employee of FPL, was ready to go. Mayo and his team managed to release all of the fastenings holding the undersea engine in place. Then, using two trawlers equipped with heavy trawl winches, they hoisted it to the surface, secured it on a barge between the trawlers, and brought it to the Burin Marine Railway in Ship Cove. Maintenance workers overhauled and reclaimed the engine. This was a huge asset to the company and enabled us to get

---

20   Willis Mayo developed a reputation for the fast removal of trawl wires from Fishery Products trawler propellers over the years. The diving suit Mayo wore so many times doing difficult underwater jobs through the 1940s, 1950s, and 1960s is displayed in the Burin Heritage Museum.

the Burin plant up and running according to plan. *Coyote*'s engine, put in operation in 1949, functioned without a break for 15 years, providing the only source of industrial power for the Burin plant during that time. Sixty years later, it was still there, in impeccable condition. It's a testament to the dedicated men and women who contributed—improvising where necessary—to building a new and modern industry.

•••

With no roads out of Isle aux Morts, Burgeo, or Burin to transport our seafood products to markets in the US or mainland Canada, no Trans-Canada Highway across Newfoundland, and an inadequate ferry service to Nova Scotia, everything had to be transported from our fish plants by reefers.

In the summer months, our products would be shipped up the St. Lawrence River and Great Lakes to the US and then to the secondary processing plant in Cleveland; during the winter the processed product would go down the eastern seaboard to Boston or Providence and then transported by land to Cleveland or directly to market.

Meeting the need for marine refrigerated carriers was certainly no easier than locating or building fishing vessels. FPL did not have access to any suppliers or builders of modern reefer vessels suitable to operate year-round in the boisterous North Atlantic between Newfoundland and New England. *Not* having the vessels was not an option; the company needed them to get their fish products to market. Monroe was on the hunt for boats suitable to provide a dependable service.

Through one of his American contacts, Monroe learned that the Navy was decommissioning vessels, which were located at the naval station in Norfolk, Virginia. It was May 1945, the war in Europe was over, and several ships were done with active service. Monroe arranged to purchase a former Navy buoy tender which had been used to service buoys in the coastal area of the US. A Newfoundland crew sailed the vessel to Halifax, where it underwent complete

The *Swivel*.

mechanical and equipment reconditioning. The boat was in good condition but required an enormous amount of work to convert it into a first-class sea-going freezer. A refrigeration plant was added, the hold space was insulated, and the vessel became our first reefer vessel, which we christened the *Zebrula*.

The *Zebrula* transported chilled and frozen seafood products from Newfoundland to the US and Canada for years. During the lobster season, lobsters were held in pools in various communities along Newfoundland's east and south coasts until the *Zebrula* came to collect them. When the vessel, temporarily fitted with a temperature-controlled sea-water spray system, was filled to capacity, it delivered its carefully cooled load to New England. Under the command of Captain Hubert Grandy of Garnish, the *Zebrula* and its Newfoundland crew were busy 12 months of the year. As expansion continued, by 1948 the company's one and only reefer vessel proved insufficient.

I had almost finished installing the power supply in Burin when I was asked to accompany Tucker on a trip to Norfolk. On behalf of FPL, we bought three more Navy vessels: another buoy tender, which we called the *Zebrinney*; an ocean-going tug called the *Swivel*; and a minesweeper that we christened *Zipper*. The vessels had been out of service and were about to be decommissioned and sent to the scrapyard.

Our three "new" boats sailed to Canada and were successfully converted into reefer vessels at shipyards in Pictou and Sydney, Nova Scotia, and in St. John's. Once again, it was an expensive and time-consuming process, but we considered ourselves lucky, given the reasonable price we had paid for the vessels. They were soon on a regular schedule of picking up loads of seafood from around Newfoundland, not only from FPL plants but also from plants owned by other companies.

When paved roads were extended across the island and to the Great Northern and Burin peninsulas, finally connecting the plants in Isle aux Morts, Burin, Trepassey, and elsewhere, the *Swivel* was sold to the Lake Group. The Lake Group needed the boat to service the plant in Burgeo, which it had purchased from FPL in 1955.

•••

The habit of purchasing second-hand trawlers eventually caught up with FPL. The company had an ageing fleet of side trawlers that were not only expensive to maintain but also put FPL at a technological disadvantage.

Fishing technology, which had been virtually the same for hundreds of years, changed quickly after World War II. Warring nations had invested substantially in maritime and communications technologies for military use, much of it adaptable to the fishing industry. The world's top shipyards that had expanded to construct naval vessels for wartime, especially in Europe and Scandinavia, were not building traditional side trawlers. Instead, they started to produce, on a massive scale, the newest and largest kind of fishing vessel: the freezer stern trawler and factory-freezer stern trawler. Their new vessels were extremely well equipped, with the latest electronic devices, trawl winches, and propulsion and auxiliary engines.

These nations had not only the technology to build larger, more seaworthy fishing boats with advanced fish-finding capability, communications, and navigation technology but also the motivation to deploy it. The almost-virgin groundfisheries offshore Newfoundland—haddock, redfish, flounder, turbot, and especially cod—offered a way to feed their hungry populations.

Technical Institutes, such as the Torry Institute (later named the Fisheries Research Laboratory) in Aberdeen, Scotland, developed techniques that contributed greatly to the care and handling of fish at all stages—from harvest to arrival in the marketplace—and product of the highest quality. In contrast, the fishing procedures in use in Newfoundland were based on experiences of the past. Newfoundland's fishing companies were about to face stiff competition for both the offshore fish and a share of the marketplace.

For many decades (continuing through the 1940s, 1950s, and 1960s) the Newfoundland and Labrador inshore fishery used traditional cod traps and, to a lesser extent, baited gear, handlines, and cod nets to target cod.

The cod trap, the most productive method of fishing, captured some of the huge volume of cod, of all sizes, which pursued the annual migration of spawning capelin. Traditionally, capelin would arrive inshore between May (on the south coast and Burin Peninsula) and as late as August (on the Great Northern Peninsula and Labrador). The cod-trap fishery was traditionally conducted by family-owned enterprises; for a period of five to six weeks of the trapfishery all family members were involved in harvesting, processing, salting, and drying the fish for export.

As fish plants were constructed, many fishermen who lived close to them began selling their total catches to the plants. In certain areas during the trap season, it was not unusual to see as many as 10 to 20 skiffs and dories loaded with cod waiting line at a fish plant to discharge their catches. Fully exposed to the sun on a summer day, the quality of the product was, at times, compromised. With great volumes of cod being harvested in traps in a relatively short time, the problem of "trapfish glut," when the quantity of fish being landed surpassed the plant's processing capacity, arose. At those times, maintaining a standard of high quality was difficult.

Starting in the mid-1800s and continuing for nearly a century, the offshore fishery had been conducted by large- and medium-sized banking schooners, carrying salt and 10 to 20 two-man dories, which were deployed daily from the schooner to catch cod using baited gear. This fishery, based mainly in ports on the ice-free south coast of Newfoundland, was conducted year-round on the Grand Banks and St. Pierre Bank, and in the Gulf of St. Lawrence when ice conditions permitted.

During the ice-free months on the east coast, many fishermen from that area were involved in the Labrador fishery, either as land-based fishermen (stationers) or operating from vessels located in various harbours on the coast (floaters). Into this traditional fishery came the new trawling fleet from the other side of the Atlantic. Times and technology in the fishing industry were changing. FPL and other new entrants had to adapt quickly—any remaining schooners and dories had to be replaced by trawlers—in order to compete.

Local players worked fiercely to lay the foundations for the fresh-frozen-fish industry in Newfoundland and Labrador. All the major fish companies—FPL, John Penny and Sons, Job Brothers merchant firm, Hazen Russell's Bonavista Cold Storage Company, and the Lake Group—were building plants, constructing or purchasing otter trawlers, and selling products internationally. These companies and their owners took the initiative to invest and build strong businesses, all rising to overcome the same challenges.

Much of the development by these Newfoundland-based companies took place before Confederation with Canada and was accomplished without public money or government assistance or interference. There was little cash in the treasury of the Newfoundland government, which was still being run by the Commission of Government. An entrepreneurial spirit and thirst for progress propelled these companies forward in spite of all the challenges.

Chapter 8
From the west, Canada;
from the east, the European fishing armada

In 1948, my contract with Monroe to electrify his three fish plants had been completed. My time in the three communities had exposed me to every aspect of FPL's fishing and harvesting operations. When the Burin plant was fully electrified and all the small diesel engines replaced, Monroe asked me to stay on as manager of Burin's fish-plant operations and maintenance manager of the company's rapidly expanding trawler and reefer vessel fleet.

I welcomed the opportunity to set up a stable home in Burin, not far from my family in St. Lawrence, and focus on making the company a leader in the emerging frozen-fish industry. As my experience deepened, along with my connection with Monroe, my interest in the company's success and continued viability grew. The Burin plant offered many challenges but, thanks to the excellent staff, it became a major contributor to the economy in the area and a strong part of FPL.

I was 24, looking forward to a rewarding future, and optimistic about working with a progressive company and a dedicated workforce. It was time to admit that I should be serious about life.

Nora Fitzpatrick and I had met at a dance in St. Lawrence in 1944, about a year before I went to the Argentia base. Originally from Marystown, Nora had graduated from St. Bride's College, at Littledale in St. John's. Her first teaching assignment brought her to St. Lawrence shortly after I graduated from high school. We saw each other when we could through the years I worked at Argentia, Isle aux Morts, and Burgeo. When it was time for me to move to Burin, I knew it was the right time to get married. Our courtship had gone on for at least three years, plenty long enough.

Nora and I married in St. John's in January 1948. We moved into a company-owned house in Burin—the home Arthur Monroe had offered me at our first meeting. Our life together in Burin was happy, and we delighted in being so close to our hometowns and families. That proximity to family provided a haven for Nora and a comfort to me when I travelled on company business. Nora and I lived in Burin for the next nine years. We welcomed two sons: Glenn in 1955, and Grant in 1959.

The Burin years were exciting and challenging. My job as fish-plant manager expanded as Monroe gave me additional responsibilities, which I was eager to accept. I did not, however, know or grasp that crucial events in politics and industry were occurring—events that would forever change Newfoundland's fishing industry.

•••

Chief among these crucial events was Newfoundland's entry into Confederation. I was in Burin when the Confederation vote was held.

A certain percentage of the local population, I remember, was passionately aware of the ongoing political debate. They tuned in through the Newfoundland Broadcasting Corporation's VONF to hear Joey Smallwood and others discuss the virtues of a union with Canada. A large segment of the population had only a passing interest in it all—Burin, like so many places, was isolated from St. John's and many were too busy making a living and contributing to the economy to think about anything else.

Of those who *were* interested in the goings-on leading up to the Confederation vote, quite a few thought highly of Smallwood and the promises being made. Joining Canada would bring roads, financial assistance, better communication … there were many promises.

Others were suspicious, proud of their heritage and the fact that Newfoundland had been, at least until 1934, an independent nation. There was general agreement, however, that something had to change: the phrase "Commission of Government" was embarrassing, an admission to the world that Newfoundlanders were poor and needed help. I wasn't alone in believing Newfoundland would be best to go back to responsible government, at the very least, before joining another nation. I believed this even more strongly later in life.

I admit I wasn't very involved in the lead-up to Confederation. I was more inclined to put any spare time—not that I had much—into sports, especially the development of soccer in Newfoundland.

As was the case with many men my age, I would have preferred to join the US over Canada, simply because we were more familiar with the Americans through the Argentia air base, radio, and business. I knew the US was an emerging market for FPL, and even though the company's marketing arm was in that country, FPL always had to deal with tariffs and other inconveniences at the border. At the same time, many of my contemporaries didn't care too much for Canadians. The proposal to form an economic union with the US was popular for a while, and it seemed to gather some momentum with the support of broadcaster Don Jamieson. As the date of the referendum approached, however, the proposal to join the US was removed from the ballot.

Although it was barely cause for discussion between us, Arthur Monroe voted for Confederation and I voted against it. Monroe was close to Smallwood, in that Smallwood often held up FPL as a company that would lead the expansion of the fisheries in Newfoundland. Monroe's long-term business strategy could have included attaching himself to Smallwood and letting it be known that FPL was pro-Confederation.

The 1949 vote was close, in spite of all the goodies Smallwood offered on behalf of Canada. No matter how close the vote or how much debate about how it all unfolded, the fact is, Newfoundland joined Canada. I don't remember feeling too strongly about it at the time. Newfoundland brought with it a huge, healthy resource in one of the largest and most diversified fisheries in the world. Newfoundland turned over to Ottawa the responsibility for managing its fisheries, conservatively and sustainably. A five-year interim committee was set up under the direction of the Newfoundland Fisheries Board to ease the transition to federal management.

It was not a smooth transition. The federal Department of Fisheries did not have bureaucrats or politicians with the experience or knowledge necessary to manage the unique Newfoundland fishery. The recommendations of the Walsh Report, commissioned by both governments to examine the state of the Newfoundland and Labrador fisheries, were largely ignored; the blueprint it offered for joint management between industry and federal and provincial governments was put on a shelf to gather dust.

Newfoundland's late entry into Confederation left the province at a severe disadvantage in negotiating anything to do with resource management. The players in the Newfoundland fisheries were not experienced lobbyists like the Sobeys, McCains, Irvings, Morrows, Nickersons, and others in Nova Scotia and New Brunswick—business families with decades of participation in Confederation and who knew precisely how to gain the ear of politicians. Newfoundland had relatively few political representatives in the House of Commons and, as such, the province's representatives were never able to stress our unique situation or dissuade Ottawa from placing our fisheries in the same category as those of the Maritime provinces and Quebec—in spite of the fact there was no comparison in size, variety, or value.

Canadian fishing interests, particularly those in Nova Scotia, were not pleased about the newest member of Canada; to some extent Newfoundland was replacing them as the major contributor to the fishery sector of the Canadian economy. The Maritime provinces would not allow joint management or any special treatment of the new province. Time after time in subsequent years, Nova Scotia's interests prevailed in lobbying the federal government in areas of mutual interest.

In 1949 I had no idea how the outcome of the Confederation vote would affect the business I was becoming entrenched in. I was so consumed with the job in front of me that there was little time for reflection. Confederation had little immediate effect on our day-to-day operations. Was I ever wrong not to look at the long-term picture—federal fisheries policies and their implementation by remote politicians and bureaucrats effectively destroyed our once-huge resource.

•••

Just as Newfoundland joined Canada and turned its political control over to a country to the west, change was also coming from the east. What had been since the 1400s a relatively small presence of foreign fishing boats off Newfoundland became much more than that. Beginning in the early 1950s and ramping up through that decade and the next, a fishing armada descended on the coast of Labrador, the Grand Banks of Newfoundland, the Gulf of St. Lawrence, and the other prime fishing areas of the northwest Atlantic. Vessels from France, Portugal, Spain, the USSR, Norway, Iceland, other European countries, and even from Asia and the Caribbean, were on a mission to gather as much fish as possible.

Those of us who were involved in the Newfoundland offshore trawler fishery were aware of the arrival of the foreign fleets; our skippers and crews kept us informed. They let us know, for example, when they observed foreign trawlers "gang" fishing. Gang fishing involved four to seven massive, usually from the USSR, facto-ry-freezer trawlers operating as a unit, about half a mile from each other, sweeping through schools of fish in areas of heavy concentration. This fishing was regularly observed, especially when haddock appeared in large numbers during the 1950s and early 1960s. These trawlers remained over the Grand Banks' haddock grounds, month after month. The fish didn't have a way out or a chance to survive. Even so, we were unprepared for the number of vessels or the size of the foreign fleets that concentrated on the continental shelf. What was once a relatively limited foreign fishery was replaced by a mas-sive sustained fishing effort, starting about 1950.

The increasing fishing effort did not go unnoticed, but the Canadian government did little but watch. Some of the European countries that owned the boats which enthusiastically fished off Newfoundland and Labrador had been war allies; it's possible that Canada did not want to offend these nations during difficult times—

though their inaction applied equally to every nation present.

There were no quotas, no restrictions to the uncontrolled and unrestricted growth of foreign fishing, and no monitoring by any organization anywhere, certainly not by the Canadian government. Few federal politicians or bureaucrats demonstrated any understanding of the importance of the fisheries to Newfoundland and Labrador, or of the need to take action to preserve them.

There was, however, a slow recognition among the countries fishing the world's oceans that unless there was some form of management, the rich food resources of the sea would eventually be destroyed. A formal conference about this issue was convened in Washington DC from January 26 to February 8, 1949. It was attended by delegations of fisheries administrators, scientists, and industry representatives from Canada, Denmark, France, Iceland, Italy, Newfoundland (just before Newfoundland officially became part of Canada), Norway, Portugal, Spain, the UK, and the US. The Food and Agriculture Organization of the United Nations and the International Council for the Exploration of the Sea attended as observers. That meeting led to the establishment of ICNAF, which was ratified and came into effect in July 1950.

Although ICNAF is recognized as one of the first regional fisheries management bodies, and a leader in research and management techniques, its power was limited by its widespread lack of understanding about the effects of fisheries exploitation and limited control in international waters. The shortcomings of ICNAF, as well as those of its 1979 successor, NAFO—which I observed, first-hand, as a Canadian commissioner to its annual meetings—would become evident over the years ahead.

In the early 1950s no one knew how deeply the foreign fleets would affect our homegrown Newfoundland and Labrador fishing industry. Monroe and I *did* know that our competition had arrived and that somehow we had to keep up.

•••

The modern stern trawlers that led the fishing armada to

Newfoundland waters were derived from Antarctic whaling vessels. From the early1920s, whaling ships used deck winches to pull the whales up a stern ramp or chute and right onto the ship's afterdeck, where they were processed.

The first known use of this style of boat for harvesting fish was by a Norwegian captain in about 1925. Not long after, the whaling company of Christian Salvesen of Leith, Scotland, built the first all-purpose stern trawler. The traditional side-trawler layout was changed so that the trawl net, which was dragged behind the boat, could be retrieved through a ramp constructed as part of the stern section. The captured fish were directed to a protected area under the afterdeck for processing. Stern trawling offered a greater degree of safety and comfort for the crew than side trawling, as well as being efficient in terms of deploying and retrieving the trawl net. Although stern trawling was a major advance, side trawlers remained in use for decades.

In the early 1950s, the first European factory-freezer stern trawler appeared offshore Newfoundland. Christened *Felicity*, the boat was originally a 225-foot minesweeper built in Canada in 1944 and transferred to the British Royal Navy. *Felicity* was converted to a factory-freezer vessel in 1947; during renovations a stern ramp was added, making it the world's first combined freezer/stern trawler.

Following extensive trawling experiments on Scottish fishing grounds, *Felicity* was declared a resounding success. Salveson purchased the vessel, renamed it *Fairfree*, and sent it on its maiden fishing voyage to the Faroe Islands, Iceland, and the Grand Banks, a round trip of 8,000 kilometres. This, too, was a success, and *Fairfree* returned with a full load of frozen fish. Salveson had all the information he needed to proceed with the construction of an even larger version of the *Fairfree*.

The first of three new stern vessels built was the *Fairtry I* (3,500 tons and 280 feet long) in 1954, followed by *Fairtry II* (1959), and *Fairtry III* (1960). The captain of the *Fairtry I* was a British war hero named Leo Roymn and his first mate was Jim Cheater, who also served in the British Navy and was the son of a Twillingate fisher-

Inside the *Fairtry I* factory-freezer trawler, c. 1960.

man. Cheater later became the skipper of one of the *Fairtry* stern trawlers operating on Canadian fishing banks.

By the mid-1960s, the number of freezer trawlers and factory-freezer trawlers from eastern and western Europe, Scandinavia, Asia, and even Central America exceeded 1,400, with over 60,000 crewmen. The Canadian trawler fleet, like a flea on the rump of an elephant compared to the huge, combined foreign fleet, was scattered and confined to the Gulf region, the Grand Banks, the Scotian Shelf, and St. Pierre Bank. Included in the foreign armada was a benchmark-setting 10,000-ton East German factory vessel, the *Junge Garde*. In addition to its operating crew, it carried dozens of processing personnel. Five 100-foot trawlers provided the factory-freezer vessel with a continuous supply of cod from the Hamilton Inlet Bank, a prolific cod-spawning area. That massive factory trawler fished in heavy ice conditions on the Hamilton Inlet Bank for many years.

Coincidence or not, it was in 1968—the year of peak record-ed cod catches—that this notice appeared in the St. John's *Evening Telegram*:

> A fleet of four East German ships are steaming out of the Labrador Sea today for St. John's, after being trapped in the icefield off Labrador.
>
> Two of the ships, the 10,000-ton factory vessel *Junge Garde* and the trawler *Erfurt*, were damaged when the ice closed in on the fishing fleet Sunday off Hamilton Inlet on the frozen Labrador coast.
>
> The factory ship, which carries a crew of 170, re-ported she was taking on water and her engine room was flooded. However, later Sunday all four ships made it to open water. The *Junge Garde* was being towed by either the factory ship *Junge Walt* or the trawler *Elvira Eisenshreder*.[21]

The *Junge Garde* was the largest of 50 or more large East German vessels fishing off Newfoundand's coast for that country's ICNAF northern cod allocation. As the mother ship, it was supplied with fish by six or seven 120-foot otter trawlers. Its mechanized processing lines, fish-meal reduction plant, and workers operated around the clock.

That large factory-freezer vessel and its fleet of trawlers could remain on the fishing grounds until the factory vessel's hold was filled with finished product. Food and fuel were supplied from the factory-freezer vessel; it was, in turn, serviced by a large supply vessel from East Germany. This operation was so large and well planned that the vessels did not need to come to port on the east side of the Atlantic for fuel or provisions. In fact, the *Junge Garde* had been operating unnoticed by Canadian vessels offshore for four

---

21   "Four East German Ships Heading for St. John's," *Evening Telegram*, March 11, 1968.

or five years fishing groundfish and probably would not have been noticed at if it had not been damaged and needed assistance.[22]

The unsustainable fishing of Newfoundland's offshore resources had begun.

---

22   The *Junge Garde* was the largest foreign vessel involved in groundfishing off Newfoundland and Labrador; however, a much larger vessel was involved in the capelin fishery. The *Nordglobal* was a 27,000-tonne factory-freezer vessel, with the capacity to reduce 3,000 tonnes of capelin to fishmeal in 24 hours. Up to nine trawlers supplied capelin to the *Nordglobal*. Capelin is a primary source of food for cod and was overfished for many years.

Chapter 9
The Burin years

FPL's Burin operations expanded steadily throughout the 1950s while I was plant manager. FPL added additional trawlers to its fleet and, thanks to excellent catch rates, ran two full production shifts, employing close to 550 men and women.

For plant workers in Burin, as in Isle aux Morts and Burgeo, there was year-round employment and, as a result, unemployment insurance was practically unheard of. In fact, there was a labour shortage in that area for years, until several families from the islands in Placentia Bay transferred to the Burin area under the Smallwood government's 1960s resettlement program.

My daily routine included reporting the details of Burin's harvesting and processing activities to FPL's head office in St. John's. Because of its excellent workforce, the Burin plant steadily improved its performance over the decade I served as manager.

FPL built a new staff house, which included a general office, stockroom, and space for the federal Department of Transport to house ship-to-shore radio facilities and operators. It also provided accommodation for new employees and the consultants FPL brought in to provide expertise that wasn't available locally. Over the years we welcomed an electronics engineer from Telefunken Co. in Hamburg to maintain and improve the electronics equipment on our trawlers; fish-meal engineers from England and Denmark; fisheries experts from Iceland and Norway; and a German scientist who established a laboratory and, with local assistants, researched ways to improve the quality of fish meal, fish oils, and other potential fish products.

For three years, the staff house was home to four steam engineers from Hull, England. Because we were always desperate for more vessels, Monroe purchased two steam trawlers from Hull, and since there were no steam engineers available in Newfoundland or even in eastern Canada, we had to bring them from Europe. British engineers were hired to train Newfoundlanders to operate and maintain steam-trawler engines, boilers, and other equipment. The vessels operated satisfactorily for a decade and were eventually sold to National Sea Products of Nova Scotia.

Communication, transportation, and access to supplies were improving, but we still had to rely on ingenuity to meet our growing needs. The steam trawlers, for example, required bunker C oil. The local Imperial Oil supplier didn't carry bunker C, so we had to provide our own storage tanks and arrange for Imperial to replenish supplies as required. An FPL employee, while visiting Fishery Products Inc., our marketing company, discovered some discarded caissons that had been used in the construction of a bridge across the Delaware River. These cylindrical metal caissons were 10 metres high and 5 metres in diameter; they had been removed from the bridge columns and were sitting on the riverbank. They were exactly what we needed. We purchased eight caissons, transported them to Burin on the reefer vessel *Zebrula*, and installed them at the Burin plant as storage for bunker C and for fish oils from our processing plant.

•••

Monroe and his son Denis visited Burin and the other FPL plants often. Fish were plentiful, there was a continuous supply of quality raw material, and the plant was profitable. Managing it was a matter of responding to market requirements in a satisfactory manner, operating and maintaining the plant and vessels, and maintaining good relations with the growing workforce.

As was the case in most fishing communities, few of the Burin plant workers were immediately familiar with the assembly-line operation of a fillet processing plant. Nearly all had participated in the traditional salt-fish industry and were used to dealing directly with fish merchants, often bartering for supplies or credit. Toiling side by

LABOUR
AGREEMENT

BETWEEN

FISHERY PRODUCTS, LIMITED

AND

FISHERMEN'S FEDERAL

LABOUR UNION

No. 24560

August 1, 1951

WAGE SCALE BASED UPON CONDITIONS OUTLINED IN AGREEMENT SIGNED 1 AUGUST, 1949, BETWEEN FISHERMEN'S FEDERAL LABOUR UNION, NO. 24560, A. F. OF L. AND FISHERY PRODUCTS, LIMITED

Classifications listed in Agreement signed 29 November, 1949.	Wage Rate 1949 Agreement.	Estimated Wage Scale for Agreement signed 1 August, 1951
Class A:		
Production Line Foremen, Weighmasters	75c. per hr.	86¼c. per hr.
Class B Male:		
Equipment Super-Brine Mixer	70c. per hr.	80½c. per hr.
Class C Male:		
Cullers, Shed Men, Cutters, Trimmers, Skinning Machine Tenders, Candlers and Trimmers, Candlers, Wormers, Selectors (size for 10's, 5's and 1's),		

Classifications listed in Agreement signed 29 November, 1949.	Wage Rate 1949 Agreement.	Estimated Wage Scale for Agreement signed 1 August, 1951
Slicers, Scalers (hand or mechanical), Skinners, Storage Room Workers, Checkweighers (if any)	70c. per hr.	80½c. per hr.
Class D Male:		
Birds Eye Tenders	70c. per hr.	80½c. per hr.
Class E Male:		
Machine Operators, Lumpers, Salt Bulk Workers, Stevedoring, Liver Factory Workers, Smokehouse Workers	70c. per hr.	80½c. per hr.
Carpenters, Machinist Helpers	70c. per hr. or $150.00 per mo.	80½c. per hr. or $172.50 per mo.
Class F:		
Meal Plant Workers, Ice Man, Master		

Wage scale from the official labour agreement between Fishery Products, Ltd. and Fishermen's Federal Labour Union, August 1, 1951 (continued over the next 2 pages).

side with hundreds of others as a filleter, packer, machine operator, or maintenance worker was an entirely different way of working. Employees were paid by cash or cheque; wages depended on the job.

We needed some structure to better manage employees because it was not possible to deal with several hundred employees individually. A more effective system of communication was needed to ensure that production goals, quality standards, and regulations were met. Standard wages had to be established not only in Burin but also across FPL's operations. Monroe understood the need for an

Classifications listed in Agreement signed 29 November, 1949.	Wage Rate 1949 Agreement.	Estimated Wage Scale for Agreement signed 1 August, 1951
Filler, Master Sticker, Master Placer, Handling Smelts and Blueberries, Labour not otherwise provided for	65c. per hr.	74¼c. per hr.
Class H:		
Watchman	$110.00 per mo.	$126.50 per mo.
Boiler House Workers	$140.00 per mo.	$161.00 per mo.
Machinists	$160.00 per mo.	$184.00 per mo.
Machinists Foreman	$170.00 per mo.	$197.50 per mo.
Truck Drivers	$140.00 per mo.	$161.00 per mo.
Electrical Helpers A	$130.00 per mo.	$149.50 per mo.
Electrical Helpers B	$115.00 per mo.	$132.50 per mo.
Machinists Apprentice	$120.00 per mo. or .50 per hr.	$138.00 per mo. or .57½ per hr.

Classifications listed in Agreement signed 29 November, 1949.	Wage Rate 1949 Agreement.	Estimated Wage Scale for Agreement signed 1 August, 1951
Pipefitters	$150.00 per mo. or .70 per hr.	$172.50 per mo. or .80½ per hr.
Welders	$150.00 per mo. or .70 per hr.	$172.50 per mo. or .80½ per hr.
Warehouse Men	$160.00 per mo.	$184.00 per mo.
Cookhouse Attendant	$125.00 per mo. or .50 per hr.	$142.50 per mo. or .57½ per hr.
Janitor	$125.00 per mo.	$143.50 per mo.
Class I:		
The Assistants in the engine room —		

employee organization or representative guild of some sort that the company's management could deal with. So it was that he warmly welcomed union negotiations with the fish-plant workers in Burin. I participated in those negotiations, which led to an agreement being signed in Burin in 1951—the first union contract for a fish plant in the province.

The American Federation of Labor, represented by a well-known and respected Newfoundlander, Cyril Strong of St. John's, negotiated on behalf of the workers. Strong was assisted by local union president Lester Farewell and secretary Tom Gosling. We were negotiating hourly wages in the vicinity of 87.5 cents an hour for nine hours a day, six days a week. We had heated discussions over a quarter of a cent per hour—that gives an idea of the tight

Classifications listed in Agreement signed 29 November, 1949.	Wage Rate 1949 Agreement.	Estimated Wage Scale for Agreement signed 1 August, 1951	Page 30
First Assistant	$155.00 per mo.	$190.00 per mo.	
Second Assistant	$150.00 per mo.	$180.00 per mo.	
Third Assistant	$145.00 per mo.	$180.00 per mo.	
Fourth Assistant		$170.00 per mo.	
Class J Male:			
Inspectors (excepting 3 inspectors excluded from agreement under Clause 2)	.75 per hr.	.86¼ per hr.	
Class K Female:			
Inspectors	.48 per hr.	.55 per hr.	

margins involved.

Cod fillets were selling for 19 cents a pound in the US. We paid inshore fishermen 2.5 cents a pound for head-on gutted cod and 1.5 to 2 cents for round (whole) cod trucked from Lawn to Burin. The finished yield was about 32-33 per cent of the round fish, by weight (equivalent to about 40 per cent in 2013). Given that, we actually paid about 7-8 cents a pound for actual cod fillets, then had to pay labour costs, overhead, packaging, insurance, transportation, and marketing/selling. The profit margin was narrow, and there was little we could do to change it.

Our relationship with the unions in those early days was positive. Differences within our workforce were quickly resolved through negotiations and discussions. Monroe's attitude, which he instilled in all of us, was that remuneration must never be withheld from harvesters or anyone else if we could pay it. FPL always paid a fair price related to the market for raw material, and we were always at the forefront of the industry. This healthy relationship was maintained until the late 1960s and early 1970s, when a decline in the fish stocks began to affect the cost of harvesting fish with trawlers. As the earnings of inshore and offshore fishermen fell, and plant workers had less stable employment, discontent and labour problems arose.

•••

Joey Smallwood, starting what would become two decades as premier of the province, searched enthusiastically for the fastest route to industrialization. Monroe, who had been a vocal supporter of Smallwood throughout the Confederation campaign, saw himself as a pioneer in the Newfoundland fishing industry and was not reticent about conveying that to Smallwood.

In 1950, Monroe sent a letter to Smallwood requesting a government-guaranteed loan to assist in a trawler-building program. He felt that FPL, a vertically integrated, profitable company, had a strong chance of competing internationally. Monroe boasted about his record of achievement and progress in marketing primary and secondary seafood products in the US and Europe. Smallwood was well aware of the size and success of FPL. With some coaxing from Monroe, he identified Monroe as an instrument that would help in his mission to "develop or perish." Smallwood made it known that money was available for expansion in the form of loans at a low interest rate of 3 per cent. A condition of receiving a low-interest loan, however, was building processing plants in certain areas of Newfoundland that did not yet have any, including the northeast coast.

All of FPL's plants were along the south coast of Newfoundland because that coastline was generally ice-free, and plants and fish supplies were accessible year-round. Between the year-round landings by offshore trawlers, the bustling summer inshore fishery, and the strong winter fishery, there was a constant supply of fresh fish for processing. These plants were designed to be operational 50 weeks a year and they had to be so to remain viable. Guaranteeing a year-round supply of groundfish to market was crucial to negotiating sales and prices with the owners of major food service operators that FPL did business with over the years, including Red Lobster, Long John Silver, Shoney's, Krogers, and Denny's. The plants, funded by personal investment, remained open because they were profitable.

Prior to Smallwood's offer of 3 per cent loans, there was little incentive to expand to the northeast coast of Newfoundland, because ice conditions kept communities there inaccessible by water for four to five months of the year. A seasonal fishery was not ideal—not when customers were looking for a consistent supply of product.

However, in 1954 Monroe was granted a $1.5 million loan (at 3 per cent interest) from the Smallwood government. His agreement was to construct fish plants at Twillingate, Joe Batts Arm, Change Islands, Greenspond, and Catalina. The seasonal nature of these plants, a major departure from the more comfortable and proven business model of year-round production on the south coast, may have given Monroe pause. Any hesitation, however, didn't last long. Smallwood and his government made a commitment to the northeast coast of the island, and someone—FPL or another operator—was going to build these plants. Monroe made sure it was FPL.

With the benefit of hindsight, Monroe might have said, "To hell with it. Let them have it—we don't want to build on that coast!" But it was new territory. The government's policy was to expand processing facilities. We had no idea what was coming next, and we did not want to miss an opportunity or be left behind.

As these plants were constructed, and started production, Monroe tried to find ways to deal with the shorter season. It wasn't an easy task. Cod was sourced from fishing communities in the general area and either transported by trucks or collector vessels to the processing plant. When fish was collected from more distant communities, this added to the cost of the raw material. The frequent shortages and inconsistent supply of fish from the inshore sector made a viable operation difficult.

Monroe asked me to go to Peterhead and Lossiemouth, fishing ports in Scotland, to negotiate bringing six 70-foot seiners with crews to Newfoundland's northeast coast to provide additional fish to the plants. We were ready to sign the deal when Scottish fish companies heard about it. They offered seiner owners a substantial increase in the price of haddock to discourage them from leaving Scotland. It worked.

We never found a satisfactory solution to the intermittent supply of fish to those plants. As time went by, declining inshore catches and an increasing number of plants exacerbated the situation. Employees knew that the amount of fish being landed at a plant affected the number of hours they would be required to work. It was only natural for workers to find ways to maximize their incomes, and productivity suffered as employees sometimes worked more slowly and less efficiently to fill the workday. Many potential employees did not want to work for FPL if we could only offer short-term employment. Initially, fishermen and plant workers worked hard to make the plants profitable, but this became more difficult as the 1960s continued.

Most of the fish plants on the northeast coast faced the same difficulties as those on the south coast, almost from the start. Generally the government was ready to help with financial support, refinancing plants and temporarily extending operations that should have faded away. Our expansion to the northeast coast was the start of significant government intervention in the Newfoundland and Labrador fishery. Before then, we were on our own—entrepreneurs left to succeed or fail. In a relatively short time, we were pressured, and given incentives, by the government to keep all our plants working.

The decades of expansion had begun. When Newfoundland joined Confederation in 1949, there were eight fish-processing plants in operation in the province, all on the ice-free south coast, with a continuous year-round supply of raw material. Then the politicians and bureaucrats discovered the fishery's potential to achieve objectives, including re-election. By 1970, there were 89 fish plants in operation, all licensed by the Newfoundland government. Fish-processing capacity in the province was expanding far too fast—and it would only accelerate.

How the government expected the resource to remain viable was a mystery.

•••

The FPL plant in Catalina opened in 1957 as an inshore seasonal plant, operating generally in April, May, October, and November. That year, Monroe appointed me regional manager for the plants in Burin, Trepassey, and Catalina. Home base remained Burin, but for several years I divided my time as best I could between the three communities. Monroe worked hard and demanded the same commitment from those he chose to have work beside him. Although it meant being away from my family, I was up for the challenge. Driving over those rough, unpaved roads week after week, I went through two cars a year. On many occasions Monroe joined me, and we spent hours strategizing how to compete successfully in the international seafood market.

My time in Burin ended in 1958 when Monroe asked me to move to St. John's to become operations manager and director of FPL. Although I was sorry to leave, I accepted the offer and moved to the city with my wife and two sons. My decade in Burin working with first-class staff was the experience of a lifetime. Those who worked in the plant were dedicated to making it an industry model. In years to come, many of them were promoted to demanding positions in management, engineering, production, and quality control.

Even though I had always lived in small Newfoundland communities—mostly on the Burin Peninsula—our transition to St. John's went smoothly. Since the age of 15 or 16 I had been in and around St. John's often, and I always enjoyed meeting new people. Opportunities for our children would be better there.

It was an exhilarating time to step into FPL upper management. FPL was a leading fish producer, and we were expanding operations on the northeast coast and Labrador and increasing FPL's trawler fleet. Cod, redfish, haddock, flounder, and other species were being heavily fished offshore by foreigners but trawler landings were maintained at a reasonably high level. FPL was making a profit and progressing according to plan.

The FPL headquarters were adjacent to Water Street in Monroe's Cove, the same offices I had visited a dozen years before in my first meeting with Monroe.

For 12 years—really, since the beginnings of the frozen-fish industry—I had been immersed in the nitty-gritty operations of fish plants, from their construction and electrification to overseeing production and managing hundreds of employees. We all learned as we went. As the fresh-frozen industry was still relatively new, we studied fishing operations in Europe, Scandinavia, Asia, and North and South America for best practices. Arthur Monroe, who had many contacts in the international fishing industry, made sure that we were exposed to operations similar to ours in the UK, Germany, Norway, Iceland, Canada, and the US. We innovated and improvised as required, striving to meet the demands of our new customers.

Since that Sunday afternoon in the fish plant in Isle aux Morts, when I had seen Monroe and his chief engineer on a scaffold, I had focused on creating the most efficient operations and workforce possible. I had been involved in implementing programs to improve productivity and quality, developing new products, and meeting the demands of an expanding seafood market. Monroe was more than a mentor; I took my cue from him, and my drive and enthusiasm for pushing FPL forward never wavered.

I was asked to come to St. John's because of my day-to-day experience with the operations and production of seafood products in one of Newfoundland's biggest fish plants. I had considerable knowledge of the changes in the industry, in terms of the amount of available product, its size, and its condition. I had spent time on FPL's trawlers on the Grand Banks, off Labrador, and in the Gulf with experienced captains and crews. I knew that the volume of fish harvested had to almost match a plant's processing capacity for it to be considered viable. The size and quality of the fish we received determined the level of productivity in the plant—good-quality mature fish allowed fish-plant workers to be more efficient—and the acceptance of our finished product in the marketplace.

When I moved to St. John's, FPL had fish plants in Isle aux Morts, Burgeo, Burin, Trepassey, Twillingate, Catalina, and Port au Choix. We also had operations in Labrador and a wholly owned subsidiary company called Bay Roberts Fisheries that produced salt fish. We did some secondary processing for the Canadian market at our Burin plant, but the bulk of secondary production was done in the US at our plant in Cleveland (later relocated to Danvers, Massachusetts).

Moving out of the fish plant and into the boardroom led me to a deeper involvement with the overall direction of the company, as well as with fisheries organizations, including the Fishery Council of Canada, and the Fisheries Association of Newfoundland, and eventually as a Commissioner to ICNAF and NAFO.

As I prepared to come to St. John's as part of the management team, Monroe said to me: "Whatever else you do, I want you to keep in the back of your mind the necessity of having a top-class resource to provide raw material for our plants." The availability and quality of fish was central to everything we did. I often returned to these words throughout my career, as I do today.

PART 3: INTO THE BOARDROOM

We are entering an era of great exploitation of fisheries, one in which our competitors have long-range plans, better ships, and usually an assured market at their own price in their own countries.

—Dr. Wilfred Templeman,
Marine Resources of Newfoundland

Chapter 10
State of the resource 3:
Wilfred Templeman, 1966

My introduction to Dr. Wilfred Templeman came just days after I relocated to St. John's. I had hardly unpacked my bags when Monroe arranged a meeting. "Gus is new in St. John's," Monroe told him. "How about if he spends one day a month with you, learning about fisheries science?"

It was one of the most important connections I would make in my career.

On the day of our meeting at the Fisheries Research Board Biological Station[23] on Water Street, though, I had no idea that would be the case. Templeman welcomed me into his office, which was an even bigger mess than mine, with a warning: "Don't expect me to run your fleet for you or tell you where to go fishing."

Templeman, a pioneer in fisheries science in Canada, had spent much of his time on DFO research vessels with other scientists offshore Labrador, on the Grand Banks, on the St. Pierre Bank, and in the Gulf of St. Lawrence, sampling, analyzing, and assessing the state of the fish stocks. In addition to his own considerable research and writing, Templeman taught seminars at Memorial University and supervised graduate students. He travelled to Washington in 1949 as an advisor to Dr. Ray Gushue, who signed the ICNAF convention on behalf of Newfoundland, one of the 11 fishing nations to do so. His tremendous knowledge of the Newfoundland and Labrador fishery and his enthusiasm and determination to better understand the resource wasn't lost on me. Monroe constantly reminded

---

23 This facility was known as the Newfoundland Government Laboratory until Confederation, and the Fisheries Research Board Biological Station afterward. Templeman was appointed director of fisheries investigation in 1944.

me of the business necessity of having a top-quality resource and Templeman gave me a new perspective on the complexity of fisheries research and the pressing need for successful management.

I leaned on Templeman's scientific insight as I became more involved in discussions with the Department of Fisheries over various issues, always holding tight to the goal of protecting Newfoundland's resource. Templeman gave me the background information I required in numerous meetings of ICNAF, the Law of the Sea, and other international gatherings.

In 1965, Templeman wrote *Marine Resources of Newfoundland*, a 170-page bulletin published by the Fisheries Research Board of Canada, offering "information and opinions on all the important marine fishery resources of Newfoundland" (9); he examined the status of a long list of groundfish, shellfish, pelagic fish, and marine mammal species. Haddock, for example, were in "critical condition" ("There has been no very successful year-class since 1955 and survival has been low since 1956. Also, with greatly increased effort when haddock are abundant, the period of good fishing provided by a year-class may be reduced from 3 to 2 years or less"); plaice were vulnerable and could "be readily overfished" (69, 83); and salmon stocks were not predicted to increase, due to the building of hydroelectric dams and roads, pollution, land drainage, and other human-created factors, which were "all either decreasing the summer flow and increasing the temperatures of rivers or creating barriers to salmon movements" (101).[24]

But the bulk of this publication focused on the cod fishery.

Marine Resources of Newfoundland contains a prescient analysis of the unfolding events in the fisheries of the 1950s and 1960s, particularly the impact of foreign fishing on the traditional inshore fisheries of Newfoundland and Labrador. Templeman described the situation in the province, and his predictions were deadly accurate. Since about 1948, he wrote, "a great and rapid change [had occurred] in the fisheries of the Northwest Atlantic, especially of

---

24   Wilfred Templeman, *Marine Resources of Newfoundland* (Ottawa: Fisheries Research Board of Canada, 1966) (cited in text as *WT*).

the Labrador-Newfoundland area." He called it "the final period of discovery of great new resources of groundfish—cod, redfish, and American plaice" (146). Fishing nations around the world, which had invested heavily in new fishing technology, now focused on oceanographic research to help them find better, more productive places to deploy their modern vessels.

As concentrations of fish were located, they were just as quickly subjected to intense exploitation, leading to the other major change Templeman observed between 1948 and 1965:

> The period has witnessed great increases in the European fleets, the introduction of European pair-trawling and longlining to the area, and most recently the great development of factory trawlers and mother ships in which fresh fish can be filleted and processed on the fishing grounds. These new, large factory trawlers are stern trawlers which can fish in much rougher weather than the conventional side trawler. (146)

Fish were being caught in greater numbers year-round. Although Newfoundland (and other Canadian) boats participated in these fisheries, their total catch was well below that of many other countries.

European and other nations had fished off the coast of Newfoundland and Labrador for some 400 years. From about 1935 until after World War II, however, the majority of cod landings were made by Newfoundland and Canada. All that changed in 1947 as the foreign fishing fleets arrived *en masse*.

By 1958, Canadians caught just under half of the total reported landings from the waters off Newfoundland and Labrador. By 1961-64, this had fallen to just 35 per cent—the bulk of the Canadian catch attributed to the Newfoundland inshore fishery. According to ICNAF, the reported groundfish landings off Newfoundland were 611,000 tonnes in 1957; this had increased to 711,000 tonnes by 1964 (*WT,* 150).

This was also happening offshore Labrador. In 1950, Canadians were just about the only ones fishing in the area, accounting for nearly 100 per cent of all landings—but then the European offshore deep-water fishery began: "Since 1960, European trawlers have carried out a great winter and spring fishery on the prespawning, spawning, and post-spawning concentrations of cod on the Southern Labrador Shelf" (*WT,* 29). Total landings of groundfish off Labrador increased from 32,000 tonnes in 1957 to a peak of 296,000 tonnes in 1961, decreasing to 227,000 tonnes by 1964. By that year, Canadians were responsible for only 9 per cent of the total cod landings from that area of Labrador. The rest were captured by the USSR, Portugal, Spain, France, Germany, and other European nations.

The Labrador offshore fishery had only started to ramp up when *Marine Resources of Newfoundland* was published; even so, the effects of the intensive fishing were being acutely felt by those fishing closer to shore: "The new offshore fishery affects the inshore fisheries of Labrador by reducing both quantities and sizes of cod," stated Templeman (29). Indeed, the inshore Labrador fishery already showed "much reduced landings in 1964" (151). The downward trend had started.

> The inshore fishermen of Newfoundland, who relied upon the summer migration of cod for their income, faced the same struggle: In the inshore area, which is under direct Canadian control, the total landings in the cod fishery, far more important than all the other fisheries, have not increased in recent years in spite of considerable increases in men and gear. The landings recently are considerably below those of earlier years, but the inshore stocks are also being caught offshore at other periods by other countries ... (*WT*, 151)

Correctly assuming that offshore fishing efforts would only continue to increase after 1965, Templeman suggested that the "catch per unit of real effort (per hook or per net) in the inshore fishery will continue to decrease" (151).

This was especially grave, given that the majority of Newfoundlanders and Labradorians who were employed in the fishing industry were involved in the increasingly inefficient inshore sector. According to Templeman, only 3 to 4 per cent of Newfoundland fishermen fished offshore—yet they brought in 25 per cent of the province's total landed catch. In 1965, offshore fishermen (accounting for only 700 out of 21,000 men partly or fully employed by fishing) brought in over one-third of landed catches. Put another way:

> The landings of groundfish per man from the offshore fishery are about 10 times as great as those per man in the inshore fishery; and for each person employed at sea in the offshore fishery the number of others employed onshore in the fish plants and services which the trawler landings and earnings make possible is much greater than that for the overcrowded inshore fishery. (*WT*, 153)

The effects of targeted offshore fishing were felt quickly. Templeman and his colleagues conducted an experiment off Bonavista. In the early 1950s, they reported, longlining in the deep waters 30 kilometres offshore was excellent. In 1956, European trawlers and a fleet of Norwegian and Faroese longliners also began fishing in the area, and heavily. By the early 1960s, the average catch by longliner was 40 per cent of what it had been a few years before. Not only was the total catch reduced but the average size of the cod captured was also 2 inches shorter and 1 pound less (gutted weight) (*WT*, 44). As well, by 1964, the inshore cod-trap fishery near Bonavista brought in one-third of the fish it had in 1954.

The catch per unit of effort had decreased sharply. This was happening in all inshore fishing areas of Newfoundland and Labrador. Between 1956 and 1964—the time I refer to as FPL's decades of expansion—the number of fishermen in the province increased by 53 per cent and inshore fishing boats by 57 per cent. More fishing gear was purchased: there were 69 per cent more traps, 68 per cent more trawl lines, and 1,819 per cent more gillnets. This extra investment did not result in more fish being caught:

> Although there were natural variations in the landings, there has been on the average no definite increase or decrease. In spite of more fishing gear per man, annual landings per fisherman declined from an average of 32 thousand lb in 1956-60 to 25 thousand in 1961-64. As a result of normal price increases and of the increases in fishermen, boats, and gear without corresponding increases in catch, the costs of obtaining the same amount of cod increased considerably. (*WT*, 37)

There were 21,000 fishermen in Newfoundland and Labrador in 1964, another 3,000 workers in fish plants, and many thousands more working in spin-off service industries. Fishing employed 18 per cent of the province's labour force in 1963—compared to 82 per cent in 1900 (according to Moses Harvey), and 31 per cent in 1945 (*WT*, 9).

"Although the incomes of inshore fishermen are low," Templeman acknowledged, "the total value of the fisheries, including export values, is of great importance to the economy." He encouraged further development of the offshore fishery as the only way of maintaining a viable, competitive fishing industry (153). The inshore fishery, after all, was already failing. Templeman came from a completely different sphere than I did, but we were both seeing the same thing—the decline of the cod stocks and an increasing effort required to capture the amount of fish we needed to meet our business goals.

Seeing that the fisheries were in a precarious position in 1965, Templeman's advice for the future was much the same as that given in the Walsh Report and he called for all interested parties to work together, immediately and productively:

> To meet the ever-increasing fishing pressure and the
> long-term activities of our competitors in the fisheries
> of the Northwest Atlantic, the federal and provincial
> governments, the fishing industry, fishermen, and sci-
> entists will need to cooperate effectively. (1)

Templeman's timely and well-reasoned advice went unheeded.
In light of its responsibility to manage the fish stocks, the Canadian
government should have provided the leadership to inspire an at-
mosphere of cooperation. With the right direction from Ottawa,
FPL and others in the industry would have gladly worked with
them. That leadership has never been there.

Chapter 11
We had to find more fish

As Templeman so expertly described, Newfoundland's fish-harvesting and -processing capacity steadily increased through the late 1950s and early 1960s. FPL was a major part of that growth. The plants in Trepassey and Catalina, which originally processed fish from inshore fishermen, were converted into "offshore plants," operating with fish supplied from additional FPL trawlers. The Catalina plant was expanded in 1971, with financing from commercial banks, to take and process landings from Trepassey- and Burin-based trawlers. The old, inshore-based Catalina plant employed about 250; the expanded offshore plant employed up to 1,000.

By 1963, it was clear that the fleet of foreign fishing vessels affected our business. FPL had relied heavily on the inshore sector for fish to supply our fish plants and this sector was hardest hit. How could it not be, with 1,400 fishing vessels fishing in the adjacent offshore waters? Inshore fishermen and the Newfoundland offshore trawler fleet tried to compensate for the declining landings at processing plants with increased fishing effort. FPL's offshore plants—those that processed fish caught farther offshore—diversified by processing increased quantities of other species. Markets were developed for redfish, haddock, turbot, flounder, capelin, and, to a lesser extent, pollock, herring, and mackerel products. From the late 1960s until about 1978, cod represented less than 15 per cent of the total production in offshore plants.

As FPL's Chief Operating Officer, I was in a position to see just how the situation was evolving. The slow but steady decline in the quality and volume of practically all fish species confronted me every day, starting about 1960. At each of our plants each morning a document was produced which reflected the previous day's production. It showed the pounds of fish that went through the production lines and weight recovery in terms of fillets. Depending on the species being processed, between 32 to 40 per cent of a whole fish, in terms of weight, ended up in fillet form. This daily production report also showed the cost of the production operation from the ship's side to the storage room—the exact cost, to the penny—and the variety of fish packs produced.

We kept statistics for all of our fishing vessels, including the amount of fish and the species landed. Sample 100-pound batches were counted and examined for quality and size at dockside (federal fisheries officers also monitored the number, gender, and volume of fish caught—information for scientific use). This information helped us establish the average size and quality of fish landed from any given vessel, which in turn helped us predict the cost of producing a pound of fish for the market and the percentage of higher-value product, which came from larger fish, that we could produce.

In St. John's we closely monitored changes in catch rates and fish size. The cost of harvesting and production, as well as expected market returns, were sensitive to changes in the number, size, and quality of fish caught. We had frequent discussions with our trawler captains and crews, federal fisheries scientists, and the senior fisheries personnel who were directly involved with ICNAF negotiations. The viability of a fish-processing company depends on the cost, quality, and size of its raw material. Top quality, firm, mature fish enables the processor to compete in an international seafood market. A continued supply of poor-quality raw material, combined with smaller fish, usually spells bankruptcy.

Every morning I looked at spreadsheets showing our trawler catch rates sliding downhill, production volumes decreasing, and processing costs increasing. The catch per unit of effort—a statistic we kept the closest eye on—was decreasing. It was becoming more expensive to catch less fish. We were entering a situation where our catch per unit of effort was insufficient to allow our fishermen to earn a living.

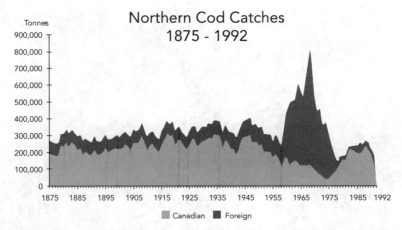

Figure 1: Catch rates were relatively stable from 1875 until 1955, then rose sharply until they peaked in 1969, with a small improvement occurring after Canada's 200-mile limit was imposed in 1977. *Department of Fisheries and Aquaculture, Newfoundland and Labrador, 1995*

All of FPL's production managers were well aware of the numbers and were concerned but helpless to find solutions. It was obvious that our trawlers were not effectively catching cod. Even though, overall, the total landings of cod by all countries continued to increase until 1968 (Figure 1), catching the fish required more and more effort and resources. Competition was high in all known fishing areas.

We had to find other sources of cod.

•••

By 1960, FPL had a fleet of 28 aging 90- to 120-foot side trawlers that we had built or bought second-hand beginning in the mid-1940s. They were all due to be replaced by 140- to 155-foot stern trawlers. Starting in 1962, we began that process with the *Zeeland*, the first stern trawler in Canada. Over the next 20 years, FPL would go on to purchase a total of 20 stern trawlers, from Holland, Norway, Quebec, and Newfoundland.

The *Zeeland* was our first conscious effort to deal with a declining catch per unit of effort.

A stern trawler with a load of redfish on the Grand Banks, c. 1975.

In general, fish could be stored on ice in a trawler's cargo space for a maximum of eight to nine days—enough time for fishermen to fill its hold and return to port. Because our vessels began to require more time at sea, we requested that the *Zeeland* incorporate a refrigeration plant with vertical freezers and a divided hold, allowing fish caught during the first few days at sea to be frozen and stored.

I went on the first of the *Zeeland*'s fishing trips to see if the new setup would meet our needs. Freezing fish at sea did extend the trip but it also permitted a greater volume of fish to be taken, and the extra work involved in freezing in the relatively small space of a 140-foot trawler and the daily variations in catch volumes—which made planning freezing activities impossible—presented difficulties that we could not easily solve.

We decided not to put freezer plants in the other three Dutch-built stern trawlers; we had to find other solutions to source top-quality cod to meet our market demands.

•••

We knew there were areas of good fishing, generally in remote coastal areas of Newfoundland and Labrador, away from processing plants. To access these, we decided to acquire and convert three vessels into floating fish plants to tow to the targeted areas. The refitting process was expensive, but we did it out of sheer necessity. We needed cod badly.

We bought the 256-foot lake freighter *Redfern* from a Great Lakes shipping company and brought it to Marine Industries Ltd. of

The *Zeeland* stern trawler, c. 1962.

The *Zenava* floating fish plant in Packs Harbour, 1965.

Sorel, Quebec, for conversion into a floating fish plant. When completed, the vessel, now capable of processing 150,000 pounds of cod daily, had a holding capacity of 1 million pounds of frozen product. We renamed it *Zenava*. A second vessel was purchased from ferry operators on the Bras d'Or Lakes system in Cape Breton and converted to a floating fish plant by Sydney Engineering Co. in Sydney, Nova Scotia. Rechristened *Zimdowney*, it was first operated in Port Elizabeth, Placentia Bay. FPL also commissioned a third floating plant refit after an unexpected trip to Newfoundland's west coast.

We had decided to deploy one of our floating plants somewhere near Cartwright, Labrador. Monroe and I hired pilot Jim Collins and his Air Transit Cessna 180 to fly us to the area so we could select the specific site. After three or four days going from place to place by plane, we finally decided on Packs Harbour, about 15 kilometres north of Cartwright. During meetings with fishermen in the region, we agreed on tentative arrangements to purchase their cod and other fish and process it in the floating plant. Within weeks, the *Zenava* moved to Packs Harbour, where it operated for four years, employing over 100 people during the spring, summer, and fall until cod became too scarce for a viable operation.

Satisfied with our plans for Packs Harbour, we headed back to St. John's. As we flew over the Strait of Belle Isle, Collins told us that fog covered the east coast and we wouldn't be able to get to St. John's. Monroe suggested flying down the west coast of Newfoundland to attempt to get around the bank of fog. We flew down the west side of the Great Northern Peninsula. It was so foggy Collins had to use telephone lines as his guide from Cooke Harbour to Port au Choix. The fog was relentless, and it was getting dark. Collins advised it would be best if we landed in the small community and stayed the night. As we taxied across the water toward a broken-down wharf, we noticed half a dozen or so punts in the harbour.

That night, after settling into a B&B by the waterfront, Monroe and I spoke with fishermen. They told us about the bountiful cod being landed around Port au Choix and Port Saunders; they even provided statistics. They were catching plenty of large cod, and their only buyer was a man named Swim from Yarmouth, Nova Scotia, who bought their salted fish. There was no fish plant along that stretch of coast. We were encouraged by these fishermen, and anxious to buy their cod. We decided within the hour to put a fish plant in Port au Choix. We also arranged to purchase a strip of land along the foreshore from the families that lived in the area. We promised to bring a floating plant to Port au Choix as soon as possible and to begin constructing a permanent processing plant.

Monroe and I landed in St. John's the next day. I went straight to the Confederation Building with our lawyer, Doug Hunt, registered the new property, and arranged to pay the owners. We had the land, we had the plan—we just needed a floating fish plant so we could start Port au Choix operations. We sent the *Zimdowney* to the community until we could get another floating plant ready.

The *Elmer Jones*, a passenger ferry which had just retired from the commuter route to and from Bell Island, was tied up on the south side of St. John's harbour. It wasn't a perfect boat, but it was available. Monroe contacted Premier Smallwood and Justice Minister Les Curtis and arranged the purchase. The boat was towed to Burin, where our engineering staff converted it into a fully contained processing plant, complete with an electric generator, compressor room, and freezer storage for 500,000 pounds of processed fish. When it was ready to begin its second life as a fish plant, it was towed to Port au Choix, where it operated until the onshore plant was completed. In 1964, the *Zimdowney* was relocated to Gready on the Labrador coast, where it purchased and processed cod from the fishermen in that area; the *Elmer Jones*, however, never did leave Port au Choix. When the shore-based plant was completed the following year, we could not identify another satisfactory relocation site for the *Elmer Jones*, and it stayed where it was.

Port au Choix became one of the most productive fish plants in Newfoundland and Labrador, operating continually as weather and ice conditions permitted. Showing the same initiative they had on the day we landed in the community, the fishermen constructed, through the assistance of federally guaranteed loans, one of the most advanced inshore fleets in Newfoundland and Labrador. They not only fished for groundfish but through hard work and persistence they also developed the first shrimp fishery in Newfoundland and Labrador. The Port au Choix fishermen and plant workers produced top-quality shrimp products, which were a hit in the international marketplace.

One of FPL's most valued customers, starting in the 1960s, was Marks & Spencer, a major British retailer with 1,000 stores in the UK and 40 other countries. The company's demands for quality were recognized throughout the seafood world. Their representatives regularly visited our plants for a full inspection of the premises, performance, and finished product.

In the late 1980s, after I retired, my wife and I stopped at a Marks & Spencer store in Switzerland. I noticed that their frozen-food section contained three products that had been developed and produced by FPL, including attractive packages of Port au Choix shrimp. As of 2013, the fish plant in Port au Choix remains a modern and productive operation. Operated by Ocean Choice International, it focuses almost solely on shrimp processing.

•••

The inshore cod fishery in the Gulf of St. Lawrence remained healthy longer than any other around Newfoundland and Labrador. Although Port au Choix continued to process considerable quantities of cod, production on board the *Zenava* and the *Zimdowney* off Labrador dropped so severely that both operations became unviable.

In the fall of 1964, the *Zimdowney* ran out of fish to process in Labrador. One of FPL's stern trawlers was towing it back to Newfoundland when heavy weather hit. The *Zimdowney* capsized and went down in the Strait of Belle Isle, near Flowers Cove on the Great Northern Peninsula.

The *Zenava* was towed to Rose Blanche in 1963, where it was engaged in buying and freezing herring for several months. Later that year, on New Year's Eve, a fire destroyed the fish plant in Trepassey. We had six trawlers based in Trepassey, and a workforce of over 400 men and women, so we relocated the *Zenava* to the community.

For a year and half the *Zenava* employed the full Trepassey workforce and processed the catch of six trawlers. When the new permanent plant was completed, we had a trawler tow the *Zenava* back to Rose Blanche to resume operations there. En route, however, the *Zenava*'s engine room caught fire. There was a violent explosion and the boat went to the bottom near Lawn Islands. Two people steering the ship escaped without harm.

That was the end of the FPL's floating fish plants, but they had served their purpose.

•••

Two other, vastly different, FPL ventures from this era are wor-

The Trepassey fish plant, c. 1975.

thy of mention: our one out-of-province fish-processing plant and our entry into the whaling business.

In the spring of 1965, Quebec premier Jean Lesage invited Monroe to oversee the construction and operation of a new fish plant in Paspebiac, a small town on the Gaspé Peninsula. Fish for the plant would be harvested in the Gulf of St. Lawrence by local fishermen using two existing side trawlers and two new stern trawlers to be built at Sorel, Quebec. Lesage sent a Quebec government plane to St. John's to pick up Monroe and me and take us to Quebec City for dinner at the Chateau Frontenac with him and his officials. Lesage, a real aristocrat—tall, stately, grey-haired, and elegant—sat at the head of the table, flanked by six or seven of his cabinet ministers.

The offer from Lesage was an attractive one. The Quebec government would build a plant and assist in the building of trawlers to service it, if Monroe and FPL would enter into a 10-year agreement to manage it. FPL already had a contract with Marine Industries to construct five stern trawlers; an additional two of identical design were added to the contract. After dinner and some discussions, we signed on and were flown back.

Paspebiac was added to my responsibilities and I flew there once a month to check on the operation. It was a big plant, employing about 400 and processing mainly cod and redfish. Obtaining sufficient experienced trawler crewmembers for Paspebiac, however, was a problem—but not one I couldn't solve. I travelled to Portugal and hired an experienced crew to work on the first stern trawler for Paspebiac. The Portuguese captain was retired Captain Chinita of the famous White Fleet hospital ship *Gil Eannes*, his mate was Joao Pinto, and they led 12 experienced Portuguese who had fished the Grand Banks for years. After fishing out of Paspebiac the Portuguese crew transferred to trawler operations in Trepassey and eventually most of the crew and their families immigrated to Newfoundland.

Operating the Paspebiac plant was a good experience. Managed by senior personnel who had worked in Burin, it was profitable for the 10 years we operated it. When the time we had committed to was over, we left. It continued to operate successfully under local management until the Gulf fishery collapsed.

Our whaling operation in Williamsport, White Bay, Newfoundland, lasted from about 1966 to 1972. We had a joint agreement with Taiyo, a Japanese fishing company, to operate the plant under the name Atlantic Whaling Co. Taiyo's whalers landed two whales a day for six months of the year and towed them to the Williamsport whaling plant, where FPL staff would process the meat and oil. During its six years of operation, this plant employed over 80 people and processed 1,248 fin, humpback, and sei whales for frozen meat and 33,063 barrels of oil.[25] It was a boost to the economy of that area until Canada, under pressure from Greenpeace and other groups, imposed a moratorium on commercial whaling in 1972. The Williamsport plant was closed.

•••

Even as it was costing us more to catch groundfish, the prices being paid for it were low and suppliers from practically every fish-

---

25   C.W. Sanger, A.B. Dickinson, and W.G. Handcock, "Commercial Whaling in Newfoundland and Labrador in the 20th Century," http://www.heritage.nf.ca/environment/whaling2.html, accessed July 15, 2013.

ing nation were vying for a piece of the American market and would go to extremes to achieve success.

Fishery Products Inc. was the only Canadian fish-marketing organization based in the US. Fishery Products Inc. and its secondary processing unit both grew significantly through the 1960s; as we fought to keep a steady flow of fish going to market, new regional Fishery Products offices were set up in the US. Our product-development group created products that reached new customers in the food-service industry, including restaurant chains, hotels, universities, the armed forces, prisons, and other commercial clients. Only a small portion of our production went into retail stores. This marketing organization was crucial to FPL's success and the reason we survived the challenges of those years.

In the mid-1960s, the American seafood market paid about 19 cents per pound for frozen cod fillets. Even at that price, which did not include a huge profit margin, our American customers were anxious to find cheaper fish, and suppliers in many fish-producing countries were willing and anxious to answer the call.

Fishery Products Inc. was told that high-quality Chilean hake was available to the market for 15 cents a pound and that many of our major American customers were interested. If this was true, it would have a disastrous effect on our operations. Pressure was being applied on us by some of our customers to reduce our prices.

I was sent to Chile, along with a food-service representative from one of our biggest customers, Gorton's of Gloucester, and an independent representative of the Food and Agriculture Organization of the United Nations to evaluate the situation. My goal was to protect our interests and keep our customers—this development was a threat that had to be confronted. Our margins were tight enough; we could not cut further.

We spent six weeks in Chile, fishing out of the ports of Valparaiso and Concepción five days a week. We'd leave every morning at 6, fish until the boat was full, and return to the processing plant. The Chilean continental shelf was only 40 kilometres wide but 4,600 kilometres long and it was teeming with Chilean hake. In only six to eight hours of fishing we could fill a 65-foot vessel and return to port. Chilean hake, unlike the South Atlantic variety, were not only plentiful but also appeared to be of good quality. The catch was brought to a huge plant built by Germans who had immigrated to South America immediately after World War II. In fact, immigrants from coastal Germany in that era built some of the finest fish plants in the world: modern, efficient, able to produce top-quality fish, and in direct competition with us in the US and European markets.

To my great relief, although Chilean hake could indeed be delivered to Los Angeles for 15 cents a pound, the flavour, taste, and especially the texture did not measure up to our cod. It was an excellent fish, but the quality could not be retained through harvesting, processing, and storage to the same degree as cod.

The trip to Chile consumed a considerable amount of time but the effort was worthwhile, considering the trend that might have developed if Chilean hake had replaced Newfoundland cod. FPL was not the only Canadian fish processor who took comfort in our findings. That trip crystallized two issues: the pressure FPL and Fishery Products Inc. were under to keep costs down and the pressure to produce a consistent, continuous supply of top-quality fish in packages the customer wanted.

As unpalatable as it is for me to say, our quality was not always what it should have been. Although our receiving and holding facilities met high standards, the care and handling procedures from the time the fish were taken out of the water and transported to the processing plant left, in many cases, much to be desired. This was a problem faced not only by FPL but also by the industry in general, just as it had affected the traditional Newfoundland salt-fish industry.

We continued to battle the same challenges we had in the early days. In general terms, fish caught by trawlers and immediately gutted, washed, and iced in fish holds produced a consistently good-quality product. Inshore, however, the situation was different. Inconsistent handling procedures by fishermen, lack of proper storage facilities, prolonged exposure to sunlight and heat during the trap season, truck transportation over long distances, and the additional handling of the product before processing all affected its quality. There could be vast differences in quality between these practices at different plants, in spite of the best efforts of some concerned fishermen and processors.

As Templeman had indicated, overfishing on the Grand Banks and elsewhere offshore impacted the size and weight of the fish our inshore fishermen could catch. By 1970, for example, the average fish brought to the Port Union and Burin plants had fallen in weight to 2.2 pounds from 4 pounds. The catch per unit of effort by our 140-foot stern trawlers was reduced from 2,000 pounds to 850 pounds per fishing hour.

We became aware that our main competitors, Iceland and Norway, often received 10 to 20 per cent more for the same products, due to their reputation for providing a reliable supply.

In spite of all the challenges we faced, FPL was a profitable company for its first 20 years in business. We built new trawlers and operated plants in Isle aux Morts, Burgeo, Burin, Trepassy, Port Union, Port au Choix, and Twillingate. We made money and there was little input from government. Our workers were happy, and business was progressing.

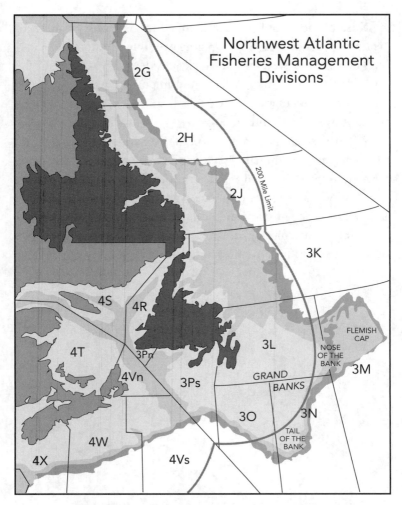

Figure 2: Northwest Atlantic Fisheries Management Divisions. The 200-mile-limit line is an approximation. *Department of Fisheries and Aquaculture, Newfoundland and Labrador*

Figure 2 shows those areas and sub-areas of fishing grounds in the northwest Atlantic established by ICNAF in 1949 to identify and manage various fish stocks. The areas, or "divisions," 2J, 3K, and 3L (more commonly referred to as 2J3KL), extending from the main spawning grounds on Hamilton Inlet Bank off Labrador to the Nose of the Grand Banks, identified the migratory pattern of the northern cod stock. Some spilling over into divisions 2GH and 3NO occurred. A separate cod stock was identified as 3NO on the Tail of the Grand Banks. A large and important American plaice stock was located in area 3LNO; at its height it provided 2,000 jobs in Marytown, Burin, and Trepassey.

ICNAF's scientific committee used these areas to develop its assessments and recommend TACs. Commissioners from the member nations then discussed and determined TACs by species in each area. National allocations or quotas were assigned to each member nation and the regulatory and enforcement regimes implemented accordingly. The commissioners were not bound to follow the advice of the scientific committee; often they did not.

Chapter 12
The ins and outs of ICNAF and NAFO

Watching our catch per unit of effort decline despite everything we were doing was frustrating. Knowing that the international commission charged with managing fish stocks was doing nothing to stop the unrestricted overfishing was infuriating. It was in the 1960s, and it is today.

Monroe insisted that I spend as much time as possible on matters provincially, nationally, and internationally relevant concerning fisheries management. I readily agreed to his request that I be involved with ICNAF and NAFO and participate where possible in activities concerning the conservation of our resource.

I started as an advisor for the Canadian delegation in the early 1960s, a role I filled for about eight years. I was appointed by the federal government as one of Canada's three ICNAF commissioners in 1971 and served in that capacity for eight years. When ICNAF evolved into NAFO in 1979, I served as Canadian commissioner for two years. In all, I participated in 20 years of ICNAF and NAFO meetings world-wide: Tokyo, Washington, Havana, Toronto, London, Bergen, Brussels, Madrid, Rome, Halifax, and many other cities.

It always bothered me that, despite every effort to solicit support from the Canadian government to hold an ICNAF/NAFO annual meeting in St. John's, we never succeeded, even though the Newfoundland and Labrador fisheries and its participants were impacted the most by the fishing practices of member nations. An annual meeting in St. John's would have enlightened the foreign representatives considerably about the enormous damage they were doing to our province's economy.

The mandate of ICNAF, an organization "aimed to protect and conserve the fish resources of the Northwest Atlantic area on the basis of modern fishery science," was a good and necessary one. NAFO's goal is in keeping with the same spirit: "NAFO's overall objective is to contribute through consultation and cooperation to the optimum utilization, rational management and conservation of the fishery resources of the NAFO Convention Area."[26] It is tragic that these organizations did not fulfill these mandates.

Member nations had competing and overlapping interests in the fisheries of the northwest Atlantic; there had to be one organization to oversee the assessment and allocation of resources. For better or worse, ICNAF/NAFO was it. ICNAF *was* effective in bringing scientific knowledge that would not otherwise have been available. There is no doubt that the organization itself was required, and the ICNAF secretariat did its best to focus members' attention on its primary purpose. At ICNAF annual meetings, member nations reviewed the previous year's activities and decided on plans and programs for the following 12 months. Each nation was entitled to three commissioners, and the meetings generally lasted between three and four weeks.

An important component of each meeting was to hear the report from the scientific council. The council, which was comprised of scientists from every member nation, met for weeks prior to the annual meeting. Each country provided the council with information about its fishing operations and annual catches. The scientific council would analyze the reports and assess the status and future prospects of each fish stock. They would then come to a consensus on recommendations, including the total allowable catch (TAC) for each species, which the chair would present at the start of the annual meeting. The commissioners would decide the national TAC allocations for each stock during the meeting.

I have always had great respect for the scientists who, with very few exceptions, were not influenced by governments or fleet owners. They worked long and hard with the information submitted to

---

26   North Atlantic Fisheries Organization (NAFO), www.nafo.int, accessed July 15, 2013.

them, and their recommendations were as solid and reliable as the information about catches and discards they were given.

During the first week of the official meetings, ICNAF commissioners reviewed the scientific documents, discussing and arguing about their contents. Participants were allowed time to ask questions and request clarification from the chair of the scientific council. At the end of that week, most of the scientists returned to their home countries. Only the chair of the scientific council and his advisors stayed to be questioned when necessary. During the second week (and lasting as long as necessary), the commissioners from each nation started to formally establish total allowable catches (TACs) for the year ahead. They either accepted the scientific council's recommendations or established higher TACs than those recommended. They never went lower.

Then came the extraordinarily difficult task of allocating national quotas. That's when the fights began: "We can't take that!" "You took that much from us last year!" "Jesus, we can't live with that!" "We can't go back home with that; we're finished if we accept that!" The debates and arguments went on, sometimes well past midnight. I didn't get back to the hotel until 5 a.m. one morning during the 1972 meeting in Denmark. On that occasion, the American delegation had announced at 2 a.m. that they would resign from ICNAF if the present situation prevailed—the "situation": an attempt by European members to establish a TAC for a species that was, in the opinion of the Canadian and American delegations, too high. It took Dr. Alfred Needler, Canada's lead commissioner, hours to dissuade the head of the American delegation from leaving the organization. He did not, however, succeed in substantially lowering the TAC.

In the midst of all the fighting, there was some give-and-take between member nations. Each country would get its allocation, for example, of cod from area 2J3KL near Newfoundland. Then came further negotiations: so much cod would be traded for a break on flounder, redfish, or haddock. Getting agreement on national allocations was a huge undertaking and led to bitter exchanges during, before, and after the meetings.

The final numbers required majority approval of ICNAF commissioners. Before the annual meeting concluded, there would be lengthy discussions regarding fisheries regulations, infractions, and punitive measures. This was a useless exercise for Canada. The many hundreds of infractions by foreign vessels were never dealt with because, according to ICNAF and NAFO regulations, punitive action could only be taken by the flag state (the country in which the ship was registered). Even if the captain of a Canadian ship reported seeing a foreign fishing vessel overfishing or otherwise ignoring regulations, Canada could do nothing. Foreign fishermen were free to fish as they pleased.

Member countries could propose TACs or national allocations of a species, but the will of the majority always prevailed. Canada and the US, although they were the countries adjacent to the fisheries under discussion, with their fishermen fully dependent on responsible management of the fisheries, had one vote each in an organization of 20 members. The mandate of ICNAF and NAFO did not mesh with the interests of foreign fishing nations that deployed fleets of the latest freezer trawlers and factory-freezer trawlers thousands of miles from their own fishing grounds.

Ensuring the sustainability of fisheries on the continental shelf offshore Newfoundland and Labrador and complying with regulatory and enforcement measures to achieve that sustainability were of little interest to Spain, Portugal, the USSR, or any of the other ICNAF nations from Europe and Scandinavia. Anyone who has been exposed to the fisheries management of ICNAF and NAFO will understand this statement.

One example of an attempt by Canada to reduce a TAC in order to protect Newfoundland's inshore fishery and "provide substantial increases in the economic yield per recruit, to the benefit of all" is given below. Portugal and Spain refused, Spain blaming the Canadians' "inefficient fishing" (and not offshore overfishing) for the plight of Newfoundland fishermen. The other member nations agreed with Spain. The discussion was recorded in the official proceedings of the 1974 ICNAF annual meeting in Halifax:

> Div. 2J-3KL cod stock. The Canadian delegate pro-
> posed that the TAC for 1975 for this stock be estab-
> lished at a level below the biological maximum sus-
> tainable yield and accordingly suggested that the TAC
> for 1975 be 470,000 metric tons, instead of the 550,000
> metric tons ... In support of this proposal, he pointed
> out that establishing the TAC at this lower level would
> in the long term permit all participating countries to
> bring about changes in their fishing patterns which
> would provide substantial increases in the economic
> yield per recruit, to the benefit of all.... The sustained
> development of an extensive offshore fishery in this
> area had created an especially difficult situation for
> the many inshore fishermen along the northeast coast
> of Newfoundland and Labrador who depend almost
> entirely on the inshore migrations of cod for their live-
> lihood and whose catches have declined markedly as
> a result of removals from the same stocks in offshore
> waters during the winter months ...
>
> The Portuguese delegate could only very re-
> luctantly accept a reduction from the 1974 TAC of
> 650,000 metric tons to 550,000 metric tons for 1975, as
> recommended by the scientists, since unusually severe
> ice conditions had limited fishing in recent years and
> accordingly protected the stock. The Spanish delegate
> agreed that this cod stock had not been fully exploited
> in recent years and suggested that the plight of the Ca-
> nadian inshore fishermen was due to inefficient fishing
> which could be best improved by changing the tech-
> nology of fishing. Several delegates, although sympa-
> thetic to the plight of the Canadian inshore fishermen,
> expressed agreement with the arguments advanced by
> Portugal and Spain.

> The Canadian delegate ... reiterated that a reduc-
> tion of the TAC to 470,000 tons for 1975 would be a
> progressive and advanced step in the best interests of
> everyone fishing this stock complex....[27]

The Canadian delegate was unsuccessful in convincing other delegates to lower the TAC and, eventually, the Canadian proposal was withdrawn and the original TAC of 550,000 supported by a majority of ICNAF members and established by 1975. It was impossible to win even a slight reduction in TACs in this format.

Another example of Canada's request for more conservative measures being turned down by member nations comes from the official proceedings of ICNAF's annual meeting at the State Department in Washington in 1975:

> Division 3NO cod. The <u>delegate of Canada</u> pointed out
> that the 1975 TAC for this stock was above the level
> of 85,000 tons recommended by [the scientists] ... He
> also pointed out that this was a depressed stock very
> dependent on recruiting year-classes and well below
> its long-term MSY [maximum sustainable yield], as
> indicated by the failure of recent catches to achieve
> TAC levels. In addition, the substantial by-catch of
> flounders in this fishery has caused the decline in the
> abundance of flounders to the detriment of Canadian
> fishermen who are heavily dependant on such species.
> Furthermore, the delegate of Canada noted that, be-
> cause of the lack of data difficulties, no new assessment
> of this stock has been provided ... and their recom-
> mended TAC level of 85,000 tons for 1976 would con-
> tinue over-exploitation and allow large by-catches of
> the depressed flounder stocks. The delegate of Canada

27   ICNAF: Proceedings of the Third Special Meeting October 1973, [and] Fourth Special Meeting, January 1974, [and] 24th Annual Meeting June 1974 (Dartmouth, NS: 1974), 205.

could not accept such advice and proposed a TAC of 60,000 tons, accompanied by action of full utilization of by-catch of valued flounders.

The delegate of the USSR, supported by the delegates of Portugal, Spain, and the UK, felt that since no new assessment was available for this stock the Commission should accept the recommendation of the Scientific Advisers that the 1976 TAC be maintained at the 1975 level of 85,000 tons. The delegate of Canada reiterated the opinion of the delegate of the USA that the lack of support by Panel members for the Canadian proposal suggested a real failure in the mechanisms of ICNAF to effect recuperative action on depressed stocks and stated that this was due to the failure of the Commission to provide the scientists with appropriate terms of reference to which scientific advice on TAC levels should be associated.[28]

A "real failure" is an understatement. No country was interested in helping to conserve a species, not if it meant a reduction in the overall TACs and specific national quota allocations.

The 3NO cod fishery was the most prolific fishery in the northwest Atlantic. It was practically destroyed by foreign fishermen, who continue to fish in 2013 on what is left. That stock has been under a moratorium for 21 years, with no sign of recovery.

•••

ICNAF meetings usually meant a busy time for commissioners and scientists, but not for all. Often these annual meetings, held in major cities of member nations, were used by politicians and others to provide a holiday for friends or supporters.

---

28   ICNAF Proceedings: Proceedings of the Fifth Special Meeting November 1974, [and] Sixth Special Meeting January 1975, [and] Joint ICNAF/NEAFC Meeting on Joint International Enforcement March 1975, [and] 25th Annual Meeting, June 1975 (Dartmouth, NS: 1975), 192.

One ICNAF meeting, in Rome in 1976, stands out in my memory. Usually, each of the 20 or so member nations was represented by five to 10 people, including one to three commissioners and technical staff. A check of the annual proceedings of ICNAF meetings over the years shows, however, shows Canada's delegation to be regularly the largest of any country's, by far. In 1976 were 60 in the Canadian delegation—far too many to be of any use—all living in a five-star hotel in Rome for 23 days. That hotel hosted clientele like Richard Burton and Elizabeth Taylor, who were in a room on the same floor as many in the delegation. Hotel and all other expenses associated with the ICNAF meetings were paid by the Government of Canada.

Of the bloated delegation, eight or 10 individuals were fully occupied for the entire slate of meetings. The rest enjoyed the sights and social events. These social affairs had their own purposes—commissioners would have discussions with one another and those conversations would likely be reflected in the final national allocations. Despite the frustrating discussions, arguments, and expense to Canadian taxpayers, these meetings were not entirely a waste of time. Its participation in the organization indicated how important, socially and economically, the fisheries were to Canada. It was the only forum in which Newfoundland's fisheries were discussed, face-to-face, with representatives of the 20 plus countries fishing in the waters adjacent to Newfoundland.

But that doesn't change the fact that I look back at ICNAF as a complete failure in terms of meeting its mandate. It failed because European and other members, foreign fleet owners, captains, and crews weren't interested in listening to the advice and recommendations of the scientists, most of whom were men and women of integrity and had the professional skills to provide commissioners with the necessary information to sustainably manage the fish stocks of the northwest Atlantic.

Records prove that the majority of commissioners did not accept the advice or warning of the scientific council. Certainly the fishermen of their countries did not—and greed was evident in all directions. Large quantities of fish were discarded and not reported, and catches were underreported by the nations to ICNAF or NAFO headquarters. It was extremely difficult for scientists to accurately assess the state of the various fisheries—not that it would have mattered. ICNAF member nations were not willing or capable of managing the great fisheries of the northwest Atlantic.

•••

ICNAF and NAFO (and, to a certain extent, domestic fisheries management) had another major shortcoming. Years passed between data collection from offshore and inshore research surveys and the decisions that flowed out of that data. Reliable or not to begin with, the information became less reliable as time went on.

By the time information was compiled and reviewed by scientists and moved through all levels of bureaucracy and into print, at least one or two years had elapsed. Then the data from each member nation would be received and assessed by the ICNAF scientific council and their recommendations presented to ICNAF commissioners.

Meanwhile, fishing levels established a year or more previously were maintained and having a negative impact on the stocks:

> The results of a recent Canadian assessment of the groundfish resources incorporating increases in fishing efficiency from 1955 to 1975, reinforce the conclusion of the Assessments Subcommittee that fishing effort has approximately doubled, and stock size is decreased by half in the sub area in the period 1961-1973.[29]

This 50 per cent decrease in stock size was caused by actions taken in 1969, 1970, and 1971. The stock had been reduced by half by 1973. But it took another two years for the data to be collected,

---

29   Ibid., 197.

analyzed, and confirmed. As a result, these numbers weren't mentioned in an ICNAF meeting until 1975, for possible implications on the 1976 fisheries. Three years of relentless fishing in the interim would only have done more damage.

The scientific committee did the best it could with the numbers it had; there was no guarantee, of course, that its recommendations would be accepted by the member nations. ICNAF commissioners fought for every fish they could for their nation's fishermen. The overall sustainability of the resource did not enter the equation. Canada had the opportunity to position itself as a responsible fishing nation within ICNAF. As early as 1965, Canada shared all the evidence needed to show that the Canadian fishing industry was headed for disaster. But the commissioners didn't have the conviction to back up the information.

Having been an ICNAF and NAFO commissioner for many years I can vouch that Canada rarely, if ever, took an uncompromising position in either organization regarding repeated infringements by member nations on matters of management and resource conservation. In that way the failure of ICNAF was Canada's failure to take a stand and be heard.

Chapter 13
Pushing for fish-plant productivity

Other matters, arguably more pressing ones, were tended to onshore. Our plants were not operating as efficiently as those of our international competitors and, adding further complications, our employees were showing signs of unrest.

The relationship between FPL management and the fish-plant unions had been generally positive for years. We were proud that the contract we had signed with the Burin plant workers in 1951 was the first of its kind in the province and a model for subsequent contracts. Signing it had been an important step for FPL, and one that Monroe supported as an important step forward in labour relations. For the decade or so after the first union contract was signed, everything ran smoothly. There were no strikes. Wages and working conditions were negotiated openly and professionally about every two years. In terms of our relationship with workers, we felt we were at the forefront of the Newfoundland fishing industry.

As fish plants were constructed around Newfoundland through the 1960s, the province reached an over-concentration of processing facilities. The supply of fish was not increasing—it remained the same or less, even with increased fishing effort—and had to be split among three times as many fish plants as in the 1950s. We were becoming accustomed to regular announcements of new fish plants and we dealt with each situation accordingly. One new plant, however, took us unawares.

•••

In the mid-1960s the worldwide price of sugar increased steeply—which in itself was of little concern to the fish-processing companies of Newfoundland.

The Toronto-based Atlantic Sugar Refineries Ltd., finding itself with a surplus of cash, decided to diversify its business. Atlantic Sugar's top brass searched Canada and abroad for business investments, and the fishing industry was on their list. They approached the Newfoundland and New Brunswick governments, cash in hand, looking for opportunities. Atlantic Sugar's first move was in New Brunswick. In October 1965, it purchased a 75 per cent interest in Canadian Tuna Corp., a new company that would build and operate a $2 million tuna processing and canning plant in that province.[30] The tuna was brought in from the west coast of South America and through the Panama Canal, a lengthy voyage that was not only costly but also had a negative effect on fish quality. Nonetheless, the tuna plant operated for decades, packaging low-quality tuna, most destined for export.

This tuna operation, which employed about 400 people, ended abruptly in 1985 when it was discovered the plant had packed and shipped a million tins of spoiled tuna (StarKist brand). The tuna made it to store shelves and the resulting political scandal—"Tunagate"—resulted in repercussions in DFO circles, including the firing of federal fisheries minister John Fraser.

In Newfoundland, Atlantic Sugar planned a total investment of $13 million in Marystown, a growing town on the Burin Peninsula: $3 million to build a huge fish plant and $10 million to purchase 10 new steel trawlers to service the plant.[31] FPL didn't know anything about these plans until the official announcement was made in January 1966. We were horrified. A processing plant requiring a workforce of more than 1,000 less than 20 kilometres from our own plant in Burin would have a major negative impact on us. It threw a wrench into our own plans for the area.

Our Burin plant, which had been operating since 1942, need-

---

30 Nicholas L. Thomas, "Atlantic Sugar Broadens Entry into Fishing," *Montreal Gazette*, January 19, 1966.

31 Dave Butler, "Newfoundland Town Gets Economic Boost," *Ottawa Citizen*, January 26, 1966.

ed upgrading. FPL's board of directors had decided in the spring of 1965 that, in light of an excellent workforce, the plant's level of productivity, and the long-term development plans for Burin, we should build a modern replacement plant there. Engineering and construction plans were being developed and money allocated for the construction. We were about to break ground when we heard about Atlantic Sugar's plan.

I telephoned Arthur Monroe immediately and we arranged a meeting with Premier Smallwood. At 8 a.m. the next Saturday, Monroe and I travelled to Smallwood's house on Roaches Line, and presented our case. We explained that there was already a good plant in Burin—our most productive—employing 450 plant workers and 110 trawlermen. There wasn't enough manpower in the area, we argued, to support two plants. The raw material we depended on, after 15 years of foreign fishing, was showing signs of decline. The shortage of fish wasn't an immediate problem, we said, but it was an impending one. On and on we talked. I can sum up our three-hour presentation to Smallwood in one question: "For God's sake, Mr. Smallwood, do you know what you're doing?"

Smallwood listened to us. But at the end of the meeting, he said, "Sorry gentlemen, I understand your concerns and I see why you feel the way you do. But it's *fait accompli*. The deal is done."

Our next plan of attack was to meet with a representative from Atlantic Sugar to determine, at the least, who we would be dealing with in the future. We also wanted to learn details about the Marystown plant, including where and when it would be built and the scope of its operations.

A man named Emerson Gennis, hired as plant manager, had announced on CBC that his company was "going to revolutionize the trawling industry." The plant would replace the established share arrangement—trawler crews were generally paid a set amount plus a share of the catch—with salaries, unrelated to how much was harvested. This method of remuneration removed incentive for the crew to be exceptionally productive.

The day after that announcement Monroe and I had a breakfast meeting with Gennis at the Newfoundland Hotel in St. John's.

Atlantic Sugar was flush with cash, but the company was entering the fishing industry with no previous experience. Monroe and I felt it would be of mutual benefit to help the company fully understand the state of the resource, processing capacity saturation in the province, and the limited availability of production and harvesting personnel.

Just as we were getting into the conversation, a man came by and asked Gennis to step away for a moment. Monroe and I waited 15 minutes or more for Gennis to return, then we looked for him to see what was going on. Gennis had gone outside for a CBC interview he had arranged the previous night. He was deep in a discussion with a reporter on the "revolutionary trawler crew settlement schedule" that Atlantic Sugar would implement.

That was the end of the discussions with Emerson Gennis of Atlantic Sugar.

The Atlantic Sugar plant was built as planned, and it opened in 1967. It was the largest fish plant in Newfoundland, requiring some 75 million pounds of fish a year to make a reasonable profit.

Sure enough, 12 months later 50 per cent of our Burin production workers and 50 per cent of our experienced trawlermen—including captains and mates—had gone to Marystown. The wages weren't necessarily better but it was a more modern plant and, for some of our employees, it was closer to home. It was an enormous blow, which we took personally. We had pioneered the fresh-frozen-fish industry on the south coast, particularly on the Burin Peninsula. The loss of so many productive plant employees and experienced deep-sea fishermen, many of whom had worked for FPL for decades, put FPL in a precarious situation.

But we survived. Due to the Smallwood government's resettlement program, residents of some of the more isolated communities in Placentia Bay and elsewhere moved to the Burin Peninsula. Marystown became a growing community, and we struggled along. Atlantic Sugar operated the new Marystown plant for about 10 years, until they decided to sell. Their new trawler plan didn't work out as planned and, with dwindling resources and other problems looming, they decided to get out of the fishery almost as quickly as they had arrived.

As soon as word came down that Atlantic Sugar was leaving Marystown, many of the players in the province's fish industry perked up. We learned that the Lake Group in Newfoundland and National Sea Products and Nickerson of Nova Scotia planned to jointly purchase the plant and pressure us out of the Burin area.

We had no choice but to step in and purchase the plant. We borrowed the $12 million we needed and bought the Marystown plant from Atlantic Sugar in 1975 for one reason: to salvage our flagship Burin operation. For six years we managed to run both plants, sharing resources where required.

•••

With the increased costs of finding and catching fish, it became more crucial than ever to find ways to improve efficiency at our fish plants.

In 1965—just as Atlantic Sugar was devising its plans for Marystown—FPL hired Inbucon, an international firm specializing in productivity studies for resource-based industries, to conduct a six-month study of fish-processing plants in Denmark, Grimsby (England), Lunenburg (Nova Scotia), and Burin. We wanted to find out how we measured up on an international scale.

The plant in Denmark, which Inbucon determined the most productive of the four, was assigned a productivity level of 100; the Ross plant in Grimsby, 70; the plant in Lunenburg, 55; and the plant in Burin, 45. The Burin plant was considered to be one of the more productive plants in Newfoundland and Labrador at that time—our other plants would have scored even lower. We knew we had to elevate productivity. Concrete numbers from that study pushed us into action.

The assembly-line fish-plant process required hundreds of workers, which made it difficult to control and measure individual productivity. It was in the early days of the mechanization of processing plants and filleting, skinning, and weighing machines were just being introduced. Most of our employees had been involved in the salt-fish industry, which basically worked at a rate determined by the head of the family or the senior person of each small operation. As expected, the level of productivity, therefore, could vary greatly between inshore producers or families.

In a fish plant with 400 or 500 people working in a restricted area, a controlled flow of production through the stages of filleting, selecting fillets, packing, weighing, and overwrapping the final product was essential to prevent product buildup and to maintain quality. The Inbucon report indicated that we had to change our management and control of the processing lines if we hoped to compete in the same markets as our Danish, English, or even Nova Scotian counterparts. Our immediate actions fell into two categories: we developed new training programs, but, more importantly, we launched an incentive scheme to reward employees for performance improvements.

The incentive program was simple: fish would be delivered to the filleters in 100-pound boxes. Similarly measured quantities of fish were moved to the fish packers. Each box had a tag; as the worker finished with a box, he or she would collect the tag. At the end of the shift, a tally of tags would be submitted. This idea came from a plant in Grimsby, England. When the production manager there, David Hill, had given me a tour and I had seen the boxes and the tags, I asked him about this. He refused to elaborate at the time, saying it was a company secret. I knew then it must be something good.

A year or so later we hired Hill. He came to Burin and stayed with us for 25 years. Together with people like production manager Lew Fizzard and quality-control supervisor John Crewe, Hill implemented the Grimsby incentive program, along with other initiatives that improved the performance of FPL operations. When we were ready to begin this program, we brought the Burin production workers to the local parish hall for a daylong presentation. We explained that we would continue paying union-negotiated hourly rates but that we would pay extra for anything above "standard" production levels. We had the numbers: the basic standards and the potential level of earnings as productivity increased.

The workers embraced the plan—otherwise it would never have worked as well as it did. We gradually introduced the program in our other fish plants. Most, if not all, production workers exceeded the standard levels, with many earning 125 per cent of their usual wages. Eventually the Burin plant reached an overall level of 110 compared with the Danish output of 100. The Inbucon program not only enabled us to achieve a higher productivity level in the short term but it also inspired us to maintain that competitive level during subsequent years.

•••

Processing fish by hand is labour-intensive. Every step—receiving the round fish with the head on, removing the fillet, skinning and deboning, and packaging it for retail or secondary processing at our plant in Danvers—required that people knew their jobs and did them well. Fish-plant jobs were repetitive, even monotonous, but essential, and we did our best to ensure year-round jobs.

The introduction of filleting, skinning, and weighing machines reduced the number of production workers in mechanized plants but provided new operational and maintenance jobs. The first cod filleting and skinning machines came to Burin from Baader Fish Machinery Co. in Lubeck, Germany, in 1955. These machines were being used to a limited degree by our competitors in Europe. We needed to keep up, but we had to tread carefully; we were well aware that our employees were protective of their jobs. We considered our first foray into mechanization an experiment.

The chief engineer from Baader stayed in Burin for three months to adjust the machinery and streamline the process. The filleting machine was marvellous—it may not have been as efficient as the fastest, most skilled filleters, but all it required was to feed the fish in, and it automatically did the job.

Filleting machines, skinning machines, and machines to sort fillets of different weights eventually came to most of our plants, including the one in Paspebiac, Quebec. We maintained hand-fillet lines in seasonal plants and a limited number of trawler-supplied plants to enable the processing of species other than those usually provided to that plant. A good filleter is more flexible and responsive than a machine, after all.

Baader Fish Machinery Co. was the largest manufacturer of its kind and FPL became its largest customer in North America. We cooperated with them in developing filleting machines for species other than cod, including flounder and redfish. We sent employees from Newfoundland to Germany for training and hired one of their top-level engineers permanently to service the machinery and train FPL personnel in proper maintenance procedures.

•••

Despite operational improvements, the decline in the fish stocks affected our business. There were fewer fish and higher costs and longer hours were required for the trawlers to catch what we needed. The fish were smaller and thus more expensive to process. Whether filleted by hand or machine, by the late 1960s we needed, on average, two fish to get the finished product one fish would have previously given us. We commissioned a study that compared the size of fish being landed in Newfoundland with that in Norway and Iceland. Our fears and observations were confirmed: a 100,000-pound catch in Norway and Iceland was composed of about 25,000 cod (an average fish was 4 pounds); a 100,000-pound catch in Newfoundland, by contrast, comprised 50,000 cod (of about 2 pounds each). It's not difficult to see how we were quickly losing ground to these countries in the marketplace.

We noticed the difference in the fish coming in on our trawlers and in the inshore fishery, despite the best efforts of the fishermen. We were confident we knew the reason for the change, given our informal monitoring of foreign fishing activity on the Grand Banks and elsewhere offshore.

We were gradually producing a higher percentage of lower-value packages. Our overhead costs were fixed—the cost of running the plant, the management, the number of employees involved in plant and trawler maintenance, insurance, and transportation—but we were handling less and less product. Our business model was changing, and we were not in control of it. We were losing ground in the marketplace. We had never experienced anything like this: the plants were there, the management was in place, the workers were in place, and the inshore and offshore fishermen were working hard. What was missing was the large, plentiful fish we had depended on for 25 years.

We had no choice but to look to the federal government to protect the common property resource in the name of all citizens; we expected Canada to take the lead and save our fisheries. We lobbied Ottawa to deal with the biggest problem of all—foreign overfishing. We urged the provincial government to stop licensing more processing plants, which were placing more and more demands on a diminishing resource. We offered our observations to both levels of government, but no action was taken.

By the 1970s, maybe even before that, we should have been closing plants. But that wasn't even a consideration.

Closing a fish plant would have meant chaos in the affected community. It would be impossible to select which plants to close— and if FPL closed a facility, another company would likely set up shop in our wake. There would be no conservation of fish stocks, just negative attention for FPL. Besides, even as FPL and others in the fish business struggled, Smallwood and other politicians encouraged the building of more plants. There was no way we would shut down one of our operations, only to see new ones opening in the next bay or harbour.

Instead of closing plants due to fewer fish, we opened more. In 1970 there were 89 licensed plants in Newfoundland—too many. Smallwood's reign soon ended and Frank Moores and Brian Peckford had their turns—still, more plants were built, for a total of 246 by 1982. With these developments came an era of seasonal workers, greater dependence on employment insurance, requests for greater government assistance, and increased labour strife.

The 1970s began in a state of crisis for FPL and for the future of the fish stocks.

Chapter 14

SOFA: major success and heartbreaking failure

Under present conditions, there is little hope of reversing the long-term decline in Newfoundland's cod landings, says Dr. Wilfred Templeman, director of the St. John's Biological Station of the Fisheries Research Board of Canada.

—Evening Telegram, *1971*

S o began an article entitled "Biologist Sees Little Hope of Saving Province's Cod,"[32] which reported on a speech Templeman had made the previous day to the St. John's Rotary Club.

I had spent considerable time with Templeman and his scientists and had heard his warnings about our cod stocks for years. Given my respect for Templeman and my day-to-day experience overseeing FPL's struggling operations, I was convinced that he knew what he was talking about. And he believed that the resource was finished unless serious changes were effected.

In his Rotary Club speech, Templeman laid out the situation, with scientific data to support his assessments. In the Labrador inshore area, for example, cod landings had fallen from 170 million pounds in 1933 to 10 million pounds in 1969 and to 4 million in 1970. Salmon, too, had fallen dramatically, from 7 million pounds in 1963 to 2.5 million pounds in 1971. Templeman pointed out that "cod have been reduced in both numbers and size, especially the mature fish, and this, together with an increase in participation in the offshore fishery, has had a disastrous effect on the inshore fish-

---

32   "Biologist Sees Little Hope of Saving Province's Cod," *Evening Telegram*, September 10, 1971.

ery of Labrador and northern Newfoundland."

Templeman also highlighted the damage done by fishing during the winter, when "great migrations" of cod occur for spawning. While spawning, cod gathered in large concentrations and were easily available and vulnerable to trawlers. Given the expected increase in the number of trawlers, especially those targeting cod, and the overall offshore activity, "the cod stocks must be expected to decline further." He did not tell his Rotary Club listeners anything different from what he had already laid out in 1966 in *The Marine Resources of Newfoundland*, but he did have five more years of data to show that his predictions about the depletion of the northern fisheries were correct.

Had the politicians and bureaucrats in Atlantic Canada, and especially those in Ottawa, paid attention to what their top scientist was telling them, hundreds of millions of dollars in taxpayer money spent on Commission reports, restructuring, assistance programs, and Lord-knows-what-else would have been unnecessary. As Templeman noted in his address, the problems in the Newfoundland fisheries were not difficult to see, but solutions were "not that easy to find." It was time to find the answers, though.

The *Evening Telegram* editors recognized that Templeman's speech required further commentary, and wrote an editorial entitled "A Word of Warning":

> When someone with the authority and the scientific background of Dr. Wilfred Templeman, Director of the St. John's Biological Station of the Fisheries Research Board of Canada, is pessimistic over the future of the fishing industry it is time for the provincial and federal governments to sit up and take notice. He sees the cod, salmon and herring fisheries as declining in productivity, with a decrease in fish size.
>
> The statistics he used to illustrate the decline in fish stocks were depressing indeed. In almost every area the story is the same. Heavy catches by off-shore

draggers and trawlers are cleaning out great concentrations of fish on the spawning grounds. This means that fewer and smaller fish are able to move into inshore waters ...

The only way our fishermen can increase their catch is to go farther out in search of fish, for the days of great schools of fish crowding our shores are over. Moving farther out means bigger boats, mainly in the dragger and trawler class. This would, of course, add to overfishing but it is either that or get out of the fish business entirely and leave it to the foreign fleets. Fishery Products Limited is forced to buy three new trawlers to keep its Catalina plant in full-time operation. This is good news for Catalina but it shows how local companies have to invest more and more money to compete with foreign ships on the most productive fishing grounds.

There are solutions to the problems resulting from overfishing and Dr. Templeman mentioned some of them but he was not optimistic about other countries accepting them.

If Canada is prepared to allow her Continental Shelf to be ruined by foreign fishing fleets there seems to be little future for our fishing industry. And waiting around for a Law of the Sea conference in 1973 is not going to do much good.[33]

•••

It was time to stop the ongoing uncontrolled and unrestricted overfishing that threatened FPL's viability and, frankly, Newfoundland's economic and social well-being.

According to FPL's records, the trawler fleet servicing the Burin plant had its catch per hour reduced from 2,000 pounds in 1965-

---

33   "A Word of Warning," *Evening Telegram*, September 13, 1971.

66 to 880 pounds in 1970-71. The inshore fishery was also in steep decline: the total catch of 108 quintals in 1971 was only 40 per cent of the 270 quintals caught in 1967. Only 440 million pounds of cod were caught off Labrador in 1971 compared to about a billion pounds in 1968.[34]

Offshore the total catch from the northern cod stock (ICNAF area 2J3KL, which ranged from the Labrador coast to the Grand Banks) was higher than the official figures reported to ICNAF. In 1968, the total catch was reported to be 810,000 metric tons (1.78 billion pounds). In 1972 an ICNAF Special Assessment Committee of scientists determined that the actual catch had been 1,200,000 metric tons (2.64 billion pounds) because it had been misreported by ICNAF nations.

The salt-fish industry was experiencing the same pressures, as it relied entirely on inshore fishermen to provide raw material. Salt fish was still important to the province, but producers were finding it more difficult to compete. Customers—certainly those countries which would pay top dollar—demanded high-value products from large, mature fish and guaranteed continuity of supply. Unfortunately, Newfoundland and Labrador's marketable salt fish was comprised of increasing amounts of smaller fish which could only be sold in the Caribbean and other lower-end markets.

The situation had become so serious that concerns, once aired only behind closed company doors, were becoming more widespread. Voices from the Newfoundland and Labrador fishing industry were joined by those from other fishing provinces in Canada.

Canada had to stand up and take control of her waters. As Ottawa didn't seem prepared to take the lead, Newfoundland needed to be heard. With the full support of Monroe, I convened a meeting of colleagues and industry players at the Newfoundland Hotel in September 1971. Its goal: to discuss the state of the fisheries and together determine the best course of action.

---

34 "Province's Fishery in Danger … Facing Possible Collapse," *Evening Telegram*, September 7, 1971.

There was no shortage of interest and experience. A steering committee included Captain Max Burry from Glovertown, a veteran vessel owner and representative of the Gander Chamber of Commerce; Richard Cashin, head of the Newfoundland Fishermen, Food, and Allied Workers Union; Roy Myers of the Newfoundland and Labrador Chamber of Commerce; Don Hollett of the Newfoundland and Labrador Federation of Municipalities; P.J. Antle, general secretary of the Federation of Fishermen; C.R. Barrett, president of the College of Fisheries, Navigation, Marine Engineering and Electronics; Rupert Prince, provincial department of fisheries; and me.

Over 50 interested supporters also attended; these included Aidan Maloney of the Canadian Saltfish Corporation, and representatives from the College of Fisheries, Memorial University's Division of Extension Services, Marystown Board of Trade, Newfoundland and Labrador Fish Trades Association, Newfoundland Ship Owners Association, Newfoundland and Labrador Chamber of Commerce, Newfoundland and Labrador Federation of Labour, Northern Development Association, St. John's Board of Trade, and the Labrador Rural Development Council. Politicians from the governing and opposition parties were also present.

We decided to start a formal organization and call it the Save Our Fisheries Association (SOFA). I was named president.

"The main object of the association is to take whatever steps the association deems reasonable to influence the Government of Canada or the governments of the province of Newfoundland, Nova Scotia, New Brunswick, Prince Edward Island, and Quebec, to take whatever legislative or other action is necessary to protect and conserve the fisheries off the east coast of Canada," stated our press release.

We had 11 specific goals, including immediate extension of the territorial 12-mile limit to all areas off the coast of Newfoundland and Labrador, the end of gillnet fishing on offshore banks, the closure of all fishing on the Hamilton Inlet Banks during spawning and pre-spawning seasons, increased air and sea surveillance of foreign fishing boats on the continental shelf, and increased scientific capability.

But our largest and broadest aim was to see Canada take control over its entire continental shelf, which would include jurisdiction over the prolific fishing areas of the continental shelf that fell just outside 200 miles. These zones, the Nose and Tail of the Grand Banks, as well as the Flemish Cap, were part of Canada's continental shelf and slope and, therefore, we believed, should be managed by Canada. For 20 years, ICNAF had proven its incapability of controlling the irresponsible fishing habits of more than 20 nations. Canada had to step up.

Precedents for the 200-mile jurisdictional limit had already been set. Chile and Peru had both claimed similar maritime zones in 1947. For those two countries, the 200-mile zone extended far beyond the limits of their continental shelves and therefore gave them full protection for their fisheries. Extending Canadian jurisdiction to the edge of the continental shelf was the only way to stop foreign overfishing, regain Canadian control of the fish stocks, and allow them to rebuild.

Our going public prompted enthusiastic support from all sectors of Newfoundland and Labrador. SOFA took out a full-page ad in the St. John's *Evening Telegram* to recognize, by name, the hundreds of organizations and individuals who vocally supported us. Financial contributions came in from across the province, even from schoolchildren.

Don Hollett, Roy Myers, and I travelled through the Maritime provinces and Quebec and met with regional fishing association and industry representatives. All supported SOFA's objectives.

Smallwood, nearing the end of his tenure—and fighting to hold on to the premiership—was vocal in his support of SOFA. He assigned his deputy minister of fisheries, Rupert Prince, to represent his government on the organization's board. Smallwood also requested the support of the premiers of Nova Scotia, New Brunswick, and Prince Edward Island. They declined to support our group, presumably for political reasons, in spite of the fact that industry players in each province did. I kept copies of the telex messages between Smallwood and the Maritime premiers' negative responses.

Industry representatives from Nova Scotia, New Brunswick, Prince Edward Island, and Quebec agreed to join us for a meeting with the federal government on October 7, 1971. At the meeting, we planned to show the Canadian government—the government that was supposedly responsible for managing the country's fishing resources—that heavy foreign overfishing was causing a monumental change in Newfoundland's offshore.

In total, 25 SOFA members met with federal Fisheries Minister Jack Davis, External Affairs Minister Mitchell Sharp, Transport Minister Don Jamieson, and their senior staff. The meeting was to be held behind closed doors, but that changed after Newfoundland Progressive Conservative MP Jim McGrath demanded, in the House of Commons, invitations to the meeting for him and the other Newfoundland MPs. The invitations were extended.

We presented the latest scientific data on the state of fishing resources, pointing to the greatly reduced fish catches by inshore and offshore fishermen and a reduction in the average size of cod between 1965 and 1971. Our evidence: DFO surveillance data, observations by those of us directly involved in harvesting offshore, stock assessments made by DFO research ships, and the scientific council of ICNAF. Supporting documentation from Templeman was also included.

After presenting the hard science, we described the negative impact of declining stocks on the economic and social lives of east-coast residents. Reduced catches and a reduction in the size of fish, we continued, already affected the cost of production and quality of the finished product and brought a lower market return. Jobs were in peril. The only solution was to take control of the waters over the entire continental shelf, including every piece of the Grand Banks and the Flemish Cap.

Our presentation had the desired impact. The three federal ministers present requested that we make a similar, abbreviated, presentation to Prime Minister Pierre Trudeau and his senior cabinet the next day. They said that the prime minister should know the seriousness of the situation.

We spent the evening working on our shortened presentation. At 9 a.m. we met with Trudeau, the deputy prime minister, and several other cabinet ministers. The discussion lasted three hours. We pointed out the urgency of extending fisheries jurisdiction to the slopes of the continental shelf. The 200-mile limit, which had already been discussed by the federal government, was a good start—but it *had* to be extended to all of the Grand Banks. Otherwise, the migratory stocks would continue to be devastated. Liberal MP Jeanne Sauvé from Quebec remarked, "I don't know anything about the fishery, but anyone knows that if you're catching smaller fish, and less fish, then something has to be done." We were heartened by such comments; we had no doubt we had succeeded in getting the message to the prime minister and his cabinet.

The SOFA delegation left Ottawa believing there was an appreciation of the importance of the fisheries to the east coast and that some action would be taken. I was proud to bring home a positive report to Monroe.

On October 13, 1971, one week after SOFA's meeting in Ottawa, Smallwood received a message from Davis:

Hon. Joseph R. Smallwood, Premier
St. John's, Nfld

[Referring to your telegram:] appreciate concern and support of your Government for future of Atlantic Fishery Resource. My position and the policy of the Federal Government is that Canada must assume responsibility for fisheries resource management and conservation over the entire continental shelf and slope. We will vigorously pursue this policy in all international forums and particularly at the 1973 Law of the Sea conference.

In addition we will endeavour through existing international organizations or by means of bilateral and multilateral discussions to reach agreement as early as possible on any measure which we believe to be beneficial to the Canadian fishing industry.

Jack Davis[35]

We were elated. This was first time the Government of Canada had made a commitment, in writing, to implement Canadian jurisdiction over the entire continental shelf. We had the promise; we had seemingly achieved our goal.

A month later, we were informed that the federal government had created a special committee to respond to SOFA's demands. The St. John's *Daily News* published a notice of the group's inaugural meeting on November 2, 1971, under the headline "First Fisheries Study Committee meet slated":

> The two-day meeting will be held on November 30 and December 1. The Fishery Study Committee is a group that was set up following a meeting in Ottawa on October 8 between a delegation from the Save Our Fishery Association and federal authorities. Three federal cabinet members and their officials sat in on the meetings.
>
> The SOFA organization was initially started in Newfoundland earlier this year by various groups concerned with the depletion of fish stocks in the North Atlantic. The movement quickly spread to other Atlantic Provinces and Quebec following which it made representation to the federal government....

The meeting brought together representatives from the federal government, including officials from the departments of Fisheries and Environment and External Affairs, the Federal Fisheries Service, Dr. Templeman from the Fisheries Research Board Biological

---

35   Copy of telex in author's personal files.

Station in St. John's, and SOFA members from the Atlantic provinces and Quebec.

We were pleased that the committee would begin its investigative work so quickly. The federal government had established a committee with a senior DFO official as chair. We had raised awareness, gotten the federal government onside, and had a telex from the fisheries minister promising the extension of jurisdiction to the edge of the continental shelf. We kept SOFA going for a few months, and then disbanded it to concentrate on the fishery study.

But then I received a note in November 1972, written by a fisherman in Burin, in barely legible longhand:

> Dear Sir, I saw you on television today. You say SOFA is finished. Sir, I am shocked at such a statement. I thought you would not be bought off with words or $ but sir as a fisherman I think so. Jack Davis, yes, and Rick Cashin are mug fish. I think they want to keep the cod for the Russians, the seals for the Norwegians, the salmon for the Danes ... I think they want to get us off this Nfld island like they got them off the islands down the bay. I think it is over. Keep fighting for us.
>
> A not so happy fisherman because of your statement.[36]

That letter really got to me: that that's what people thought—that they still wanted and believed in SOFA, that we needed it more than ever. That they thought I had been bought out. The fact of the matter was that SOFA was taking up a lot of my time, and I believed there was no longer a need for it.

It remains one of my greatest regrets that we did not keep SOFA going, because we had the whole province, including Smallwood, the schools, industry, and the service clubs, behind us. SOFA could have been a major watchdog group. There was so much involvement

---

36   Lightly edited for clarity.

from the Newfoundland population that, had we kept it going, it would have been impossible for anyone to ignore us. I've never seen the people of Newfoundland come together like they did for SOFA. Many citizens in hundreds of communities around Newfoundland and on the coast of Labrador had observed the lights of hundreds of foreign vessels fishing close to our coastline for years. They felt the effects of the uncontrolled foreign fishing. They understood what was happening, and SOFA was clear about what needed to be done.

We felt we had made a difference. And we would have, if only the action that was promised had materialized, and if the Fishery Study Committee had followed through on SOFA proposals and communicated regularly with the prime minister and his politicians as was solemnly promised, month after month and year after year. But as happens so often, federal politicians and bureaucrats failed miserably to meet their commitment.

•••

The Canadian government reneged on its pledge to protect the Grand Banks fisheries.

In 1977, six years after SOFA's meeting in Ottawa, Canada finally implemented the 200-mile exclusive economic zone. The precious Grand Banks Nose and Tail fisheries and the Flemish Cap were left exposed to the continued unrestricted practices of foreign fishing fleets.

When the announcement came, I was furious. I wasn't the only one. Given that cod and other groundfish are migratory species, leaving parts of the Grand Banks open to foreign fishing ensured continued destruction of the resource.

So what had happened? In 1971, the prime minister and his senior cabinet members had expressed their concerns about the diminishing resource, foreign overfishing, and the impact on the social and economic lives of fisheries participants. They had assured us, in writing, that Canada would extend jurisdiction to include all of the continental shelf.

I received my answer about two years after the 200-mile limit had been put in place. A federal politician, after retiring, told me that a senior fisheries bureaucrat had convinced Trudeau and his cabinet that there was not sufficient "geography" outside 200 miles to provide an economic fishery for the European community fishing nations, that no country would bother mounting a fishery there, and that those areas weren't worth fighting for.

Between 1971 and 1977, the 200-mile limit was discussed and negotiated in several forums, primarily the Law of the Sea Conference and annual ICNAF meetings. These meetings presented ideal opportunities for Canada to claim jurisdiction over the entire continental shelf. Canadian delegates would have had a strong negotiating position. They could have acknowledged that other countries that had a history of fishing on the continental shelf, and pledged to discuss reasonable TACs in the area, if and when the resource strengthened. Canada could have said and done much.

It seemed that the federal government expected that the 200-mile limit would result in a rebound of fish stocks—after all, most of the huge armada fishing inside the 200-mile limit were now pushed farther out to sea. Everyone from the prime minister down was sure we were in for a period of rebuilding. It didn't happen that way.

•••

The negotiations leading to the formation of NAFO in 1979 as a successor to ICNAF were disastrous to the future of Newfoundland and Labrador's fisheries. NAFO would be no more effective than its predecessor at blocking foreign fishing.

Canada had an opportunity at those transitional meetings to negotiate stricter arrangements with those fishing nations that had caused the most damage to the resource. For example, Spain, Portugal, the USSR, and other countries known for heavy overfishing could have been given small quotas only in exchange for iron-clad agreements that they would fish responsibly outside the 200-mile limit. Instead, NAFO nations overfished, just outside 200 miles, a reported 1.5 million tons of cod over the next six years. The combined catch of NAFO fishing nations outside 200 miles and on the migrating stocks in that time period was over four times the allocated quotas of cod and other species. Canada failed miserably by not presenting this recorded data and pressing for jurisdiction over the total continental shelf. Even as NAFO set TACs for its members, there was little surveillance and little anyone could do to punish those who fished more than their quotas. As before, only the home country, or flag state, of a vessel could take any punitive measures. The coastal state—in this case, Canada—could do nothing.

Blatant overfishing went on for decades. In 1991, Victor Rabinovitch, then assistant deputy minister of DFO, made headlines when he stated that NAFO needed more teeth. "Certainly, what we have seen in the last year is that catches by vessels from the European Community are five or six times greater than their legitimate quota," he told the Canadian Press. "They are contributing to a major conservation problem."[37] In 1990, the article stated, the quota set for the European Community in the area outside the 200-mile limit was 15,377 tonnes. It was estimated that an additional 80,000 tonnes of fish, including cod, were captured that year. That was a "straddling stock"—the fish were known to travel on both sides of the 200-mile limit—and severe damage was being done to the total stock.

What would happen to the Canadian fishing fleet if *they* overfished for 30 years in European waters? If Canadians conducted their fishing operations in a similar manner in the Bay of Biscay off Spain or Portugal, they would be escorted back to Canada within a week.

Fifteen years after the 200-mile limit was put in place, Newfoundland's stocks were in worse shape than ever, teetering on the verge of a moratorium on northern cod. I believe that an extension of the jurisdiction to the slopes of the continental shelf would have prevented the fishery collapse in 1992. Of many errors in fisheries management that the Canadian government made, this

---

37   Erin Dwyer, "NAFO Needs More Teeth, Canadian Fisheries Official Says," *Evening Telegram*, September 7, 1991.

was the most grievous.

Canada's fisheries on the east, west, and north coasts are vastly different, in terms of species, migratory patterns, international implications, harvesting, processing, marketing, and seasonality of operations. I have never been confident that our federal government has displayed adequate understanding of our country's complex fisheries resources. The debacle of the 200-mile limit is just one example.

Chapter 15

Finally, a victory:
The Spanish pair trawler experiment

With or without a 200-mile limit, FPL needed enough fish to stay in business. We invested heavily in additional boats and equipment and increased our fishing effort to keep the plants supplied. We were basically throwing money at the problem—an interim measure, we believed, while waiting for Canada to take control over the continental shelf.

The demand for FPL products continued to grow, thanks to the hard work of our American marketing arm. About 80 per cent of our products were sold in the US; the rest went to Asia and Europe.

Cod had become uneconomic for us to catch offshore as a directed fishery; the only cod we caught offshore were generally bycatch. FPL trawlers instead focused on other groundfish, including flounder species (American plaice, yellowtail, and grey sole). Our marketing arm found buyers for flounder products in the US and Europe, and those species represented 75 per cent of the fish processed in our Burin, Trepassey, and Marystown plants. Those three employed over 2,000 plant workers and fishermen.[38] In other words, Grand Banks flounder had become crucial to FPL and to the economies of many coastal communities.

Our trawler captains and crews always kept an eye on foreign fishing activity on the offshore fishing grounds and reported back to management. Blatant infringement after blatant infringement of the ICNAF guidelines threatened our business and the employment of thousands of Newfoundlanders. We were powerless to act.

---

38   Between 1975 and the 1992 cod moratorium, FPL's offshore plants operated mainly on flounder species. Some redfish, turbot, and cod (in that order) were also captured.

But there was one practice we could stop by making a staged intervention to stave off the complete destruction of the flounder stocks.

•••

In 1974 FPL management received a report from an experienced skipper of one of our Burin-based trawlers. "The Spaniards are out there making a mockery of the flounder fishery," he said angrily. According to his best estimates, backed by several other trawler captains and crewmen, there were 50 pairs of Spanish trawlers out on the Grand Banks, fishing for seven, eight, nine, or more hours at a time.

Pair-trawling, a technology embraced by Spanish fishermen, had been used for decades offshore Newfoundland. These trawlers were smaller than most of FPL's and many of the other trawlers working in the area. They worked in pairs, towing a huge trawl net between two vessels. Pair trawlers did not have freezing equipment on board and depended entirely on salt to preserve their catch. They targeted fish that could be salted for market, primarily large cod, but also hake and pollock. The flounder species were not suitable for salting and were of no use to these fishermen.

According to our skipper, about 50 per cent of the fish the pair trawlers pulled in were flounder and other "unwanted" species. The Spanish crew separated the fish, kept the cod, and threw the rest overboard. The FPL skipper also believed that small cod, less suitable for salting, were included in the discards.

With our growing reliance on flounder, we were especially concerned.

We informed the federal government about yet another massacre going on in Newfoundland's offshore waters. Their first response: they didn't want to get involved in any international issues—and certainly weren't interested in anything that might lead to a confrontation with Spain, especially given the ongoing tense negotiations around the 200-mile limit. However, we arranged a meeting with government officials and outlined what we'd heard about the Spanish pair trawlers. Government was still reluctant to get involved.

Arthur Monroe, Denis Monroe, and I devised a plan, which we presented to the government. Our idea was to outfit three stern trawlers for pair-trawling and try this method ourselves. The purpose would be two-fold: to test the technology to see if we should adopt it and to determine the composition of the catch. We knew the Spanish did not have any use for flounder; this operation would help us prove how much and what they were discarding. We proposed that the federal government support us by sharing the cost of the initiative.

Called the Spanish Pair Trawler Experiment, the joint venture between industry (FPL) and the federal and provincial governments (Environment Canada and the Industrial Development Branch of the Department of Fisheries) started in the spring of 1975. We modified and outfitted three 155-foot stern trawlers, *Zenica*, *Zeila*, and *Zidani*, as required. No one in our company had any experience in pair-trawling, so we hired 12 Spanish fishermen, four for each vessel, to aid with the transfer of fishing technology. The rest of the crew was Canadian. The Department of Fisheries agreed to place an observer on each vessel.

The final government report of the Spanish Pair Trawler Experiment included this explanation of the equipment and method:

> The most striking feature about pair trawling is the huge size of the light-weight net. The headline of 300 feet and the footrope of 360 feet are over three times as long as traditional Canadian groundfish trawls. Pieces of chain are used to hold down the groundline, and a continuous string of about 180 floats raises the headline to give the net a tremendous mouth …
>
> Each trawler fishes its net in turn. After the net is thrown over, one wing is transferred to the twin trawler and attached to the end of the towing warp … The trawlers drag the net at a speed of approximately three

miles per hour for periods of four hours and over. Tows of up to eleven hours duration were sometimes required. It takes about three-quarters of an hour to haul back and shoot away the net. (1)[39]

We fished this way for six months, between May and November 1975. We learned how to pair-fish. We carefully recorded the details of our catches and collected important data related to pair-fishing. We subdivided the catch into two categories: Cod, etc. (this included perch, turbot, catfish, and halibut); and Flatfish, etc. (flounder, grey sole, and yellowtail). There was no doubt that we caught just as many flatfish as we did cod. Some trawler trips yielded 99 per cent cod—but others, just 2 per cent. As the report stated: "Exceptionally high catches of flounder demonstrated the effectiveness of the technique for harvesting species other than cod" (4).

Unlike the Spanish fishermen, we were relatively close to our processing plants and we could take our catch—no matter the species—to shore. One of the three vessels, when full, would return to shore while the other two continued. This enabled us to have a continuous operation with two vessels fishing.

The method presented problems, however. Although the gear itself performed well, the fish were generally of poor quality: "The quality problem was caused as a result of the long tows ... and also the heavy sets of fish being taken, which caused excessive bruising" (*SP*, 4). Some fish were hauled along in a net for hours, being bumped and bruised along the way. Given the scarcity of medium and large cod, the expense of the operation, and the damage to the fish, Canadian pair-trawling was discontinued after six months, along with the experiment. The federal government established an industry committee, of which I was chair, to present the results of our experiment to the Spanish government.

Knowing that for decades the Spanish pair trawler fleet had

---

39   *1975 Spanish Pair Trawl Experiment* (St. John's: Fisheries and Marine Service, Newfoundand Region, Industrial Development Branch, 1975) (cited in text as SP).

directed its effort to catching cod, particularly large cod for salting, and knowing its catch had included a high percentage of other species, it is not difficult to imagine that millions of tons of unwanted fish were discarded at sea. Spanish officials denied our charges at first. But they could not disagree with our catch numbers. They finally admitted that they did throw away a substantial amount of fish. They agreed to find a way to use the fish they would previously have sent overboard or stop pair-fishing entirely.

Their solution had some merit. After they separated the catch in the pair trawl, their fishermen would put the flounder in a bag, attach it to a buoy, and advise FPL so that we could retrieve the fish for processing. We agreed to their plan—how could we not? The fish wouldn't be wasted and we would get usable raw material out of the deal. The arrangement went ahead as planned for six months. This worked for us but eventually proved too labour-intensive for the Spanish. They soon agreed to stop pair-trawling all together.

After 25 years of catching and throwing away perfectly good flounder, the practice finally ended—at least the use of pair trawlers did. It was an expensive effort on FPL's part, but the result was worth it. It was a rare success for us in our fight against overfishing.

•••

The Spanish Pair Trawl Experiment highlighted one of the biggest problems in the fisheries of those days.

All fish caught by pair trawlers except large cod was discarded at sea and never reported. That fish could not have been contained in any scientific assessment of the state of various stocks. No doubt this meant that the advice of the scientific councils to ICNAF, and their recommendations for TAC limits, were considerably off the mark.

Fish above and beyond the allocated quotas was caught year after year. No one knows for sure, but it's a safe bet that millions of tons of various species were taken by foreigners, as in the case of the Spaniards, and never reported. The experiment also confirmed that scientists rarely received accurate catch levels for use in their stock assessments. It's certain that fishing boats other than Spanish pair trawlers threw vast quantities of fish overboard, but we just didn't have proof.

This example of blatant destruction of a fishery by one of the world's major fishing nations was never discussed in an ICNAF meeting. Corrective measures would never have been taken if our trawler captain had not reported the activity to FPL management. It was not industry's job to intervene—after all, the mandate of ICNAF was to protect offshore resources—but we had to do what we could. Foreign fishing boats ignored ICNAF and NAFO regulations as though they were non-existent. This continues, long after the 1992 moratorium, and it will never change until Canada takes the action that will lead to restoration of the fisheries—or until there are no fish left in the water.

No one can know how many thousands of tons of fish were discarded by the Spanish fleet over the years. The catch chart from our experiment only scratched the surface of this deliberate massacre.

Chapter 16
Struggles of the Canadian Saltfish Corporation

As FPL management was dealing with smaller and fewer cod, the Canadian Saltfish Corporation experienced similar challenges. Given a broad and unrealistic mandate to "buy all salt fish," the Corporation struggled to find markets as the quality of the salt fish deteriorated. Aiden Maloney was president of the Canadian Saltfish Corporation from its beginnings in 1970 until 1979. Here, in his words, is how he got into the industry, and how he watched it fall apart.[40]

•••

My first job, after graduating from Grade 11 in 1938 in my hometown of King's Cove, Bonavista Bay, was as a bank teller in the Royal Bank of Canada in Trinity. It was a two-man operation, that branch, and between us we did everything. I was a manager and I also held all the positions beneath manager: assistant manager, teller, and bookkeeper. I lit the fire in the morning and swept the floor in the evening.

The bank moved us around constantly, considering it part of our training. Over the course of six years I worked in bank branches in Trinity, Placentia, Gander, and St. John's (in the west end and in the main office downtown). Back then, the fish merchants kept their eyes on the banks, using them as a place to headhunt accountants and bookkeepers and reliable, educated workers.

Sure enough, in 1944, after half a dozen years in the banking business, the Penny family offered me a job at a very attractive salary to work out of their fish operations in Ramea: $1,400 a year, twice what I was getting at the bank. My first thought was, "How am I going

---

40   Aiden Maloney was interviewed by Ryan Cleary, September 2010.

to cope with all of that money?" I didn't hesitate. I was 24, single, and ready for anything. The Pennys wanted me to go in and take over the accounting end of the business, which was a bit of a stretch. I had six years at a bank but absolutely no experience in accounting for a company that was in the business of selling, buying, retailing, and exporting. It was on-the-job training, to be sure.

I arrived in Port aux Basques—after my first train trip across Newfoundland—on the night of October 22, 1944. I got off the train and the captain of a banking vessel in the harbour came out and said, "We're looking for a Mr. Maloney." I responded, "Yes sir, you're looking at him."

We left straight away, at about 8 p.m. By 8 a.m., we were in Ramea.

In 1871, brothers George and John Penny started John Penny and Sons, a fish business. Penny's was a prosperous enterprise and George had set up sawmills and a small shipyard within a few years, enabling him to construct his own fishing fleet. When George Penny died in 1929, his nephew, George Penny Jr., took over, steadying the business through the Depression and gradually converting the operation from salt fish to frozen fish.

This was the George Penny I met on my first day in town. The boss was 44 and a formidable businessman—but quite ill. A veteran of World War I, Penny had been in contact with toxic gas and had severe lung trouble. I spent a few hours with him, and he was frank with me from the start: "You're taking care of the accounts for our business," he said, "but I'd like to see you down in the plant and you should get down there and watch the filleting and the processing operation."

On the second day I was in town, Penny made me a director of the company. I was given a qualifying share in the company.

I remember it was a dull October day, grim and raining and cool, and as I walked around the community I wondered what exactly I had gotten myself into. The shock of the job and the big money was wearing off as I realized where I was. In a matter of days I had gone from a bank teller in the capital city to a director of one of the island's big fishing firms, located in an isolated island community off

Newfoundland's south coast.

I planned to give myself six months to see how it would all go. I grew into the job and I guess the thing that kept me there was the work. It was non-stop and I didn't have time to question what I was doing. We'd get up at 7 a.m. and go to work. Then we'd come back for breakfast, head back to work, return for lunch, and work again until 6 p.m. And I'd generally go back again at night. That was six, sometimes seven, days a week.

Ramea was a fishing community with a good source of cod nearby on the Burgeo Bank and I was completely caught up in the job. I was working hard, constantly, and we had a good product. The American market was opening up and Penny opened a sales office in Boston—Caribou Fisheries—in 1945 that was doing well for us. I was a director of that, too, which again enlarged my job. I travelled to Boston regularly to see how the sales office was doing.

I had arrived in Ramea and the Penny's operation in the middle of the transition from the salt-fish business to the frozen-fish business. George Penny was a pioneer, much like Arthur Monroe. He could see the end of the salt-fish business and, even though he was not well, he saw the future was frozen fish and was determined to get into the new industry. By 1946, we were completely into frozen fish.

In 1946 we decided to fish for species other than cod, which meant getting away from the fleet of small fishing trawlers we had. We placed an order for our first dragger that year from a shipyard in Maine. I went down to Maine with Penny; and again he said, "You've got to get into every aspect of this business."

Penny died in 1949 at age 49. About the same time, Jim Rogers, Penny's managing director, took a job in Corner Brook. I had been in Ramea for five years and was working well with all the other directors, enough that they promoted me to managing director. Now I was the boss man—but I reported to Marie Penny, George Penny's wife and chair of the board. John Penny and Sons would continue to operate until 1982, when it became part of Fisheries Products International.

I spent a total of 14 years in Ramea, learning the fishery from top to bottom. Perhaps if I'd had spare time on my hands I would have been moved on—but work was fast-paced. I married a girl from Placentia who came to Ramea and ran a small nursing station in the community. There was great salmon fishing in the area too. We had a good life there.

In 1957, we decided to leave, partly so that our daughter could go to school in St. John's, and partly because I was 37 and ready for a change. We moved to St. John's and, for the first time since 1938, I was out of a job. Eventually I got a call from the province's minister of fisheries, saying there was a problem at the fish plant and whale meat plant in Dildo—and so began three years of cleaning up those operations, which were making food for Smallwood's mink-ranching business.

After that I moved into government, back into the fisheries, where I was most comfortable. They appointed me assistant deputy minister, where I served from 1960 until 1966. In 1966 I made another big leap, and successfully ran for Smallwood's Liberals in the district of Ferryland. In 1967 I was named minister of fisheries, a portfolio I held until 1970.

As minister, I worked with the province to try and bring about some federal programs—I thought some agricultural programs could also apply to the fishery. There was a program to help farmers with crop failure, so why not one for catch failure? I was also working to organize the marketing of salt fish in the wake of the dissolution of the Newfoundland Associated Fish Exporters Limited (NAFEL), a once-powerful salt-fish marketing organization that had tumbled from "exclusive" salt-fish marketing to "voluntary" through the 1960s. As we told the federal government, there was a wheat board on the Prairies, so perhaps there should be a salt-fish board. They bought into the idea. I applied for the job as head of the Canadian Saltfish Corporation, and I got it.

I'd had enough of politics. I enjoyed the public part of being a politician. But the bureaucracy of it? I didn't enjoy that at all. I thought I was better off involved in production and marketing, like I had been with the Pennys, and the Saltfish Corporation got me right back into that again.

At a time when frozen fish was taking over the marketplace and prices were unstable, the Canadian Saltfish Corporation was the federal government's attempt to ensure a stable salt-fish industry and reliable incomes for fishermen. The Canadian Saltfish Corporation regulated and marketed salt fish from Newfoundland, Nova Scotia, New Brunswick, and part of Quebec. Fishermen from the Gaspé Peninsula, where they had a cure of salt fish prized in Italy, asked to be excluded so they could manage their own marketing.

It was a brand new entity, a new way of doing things on the east coast, and setting it up was a challenge. The Corporation's mandate was, quite simply, to buy all salt fish on offer and find a market for it. Our other main requirement was to set a price for salt cod in the spring of the year, which we would then pay the fishermen in the fall. The goal was to end speculation and uncertainty, but it wasn't easy. We'd go to the market and get an idea of what we could hope to get for good-quality salt fish, or medium-quality salt fish, and then we'd name a price. The fishermen were guaranteed that price come the fall. And at the end of the year, after all the bills were paid, including my salary and rent, if there was any money left over, it went to the fishermen.

We marketed mainly in Europe—Portugal, Spain, Italy, and Greece—and in the Caribbean and Brazil. Although frozen fish was heavily in demand, there was always a market for the salted product. And for many years there was always salt fish to be sold. The fresh- and frozen-fish business was big in Burin, Trepassey, and the south coast of Newfoundland, but there were still plenty of fishermen in the north and in Labrador still producing salt fish, and they did it the traditional way.

Here's how the Saltfish Corporation worked: we would draw on the federal government for capital each year, $10 million being the limit. That's what we would use to cover our operations and buy the salt fish. As we sold the fish, we had to pay back the government what we had borrowed.

In setting up the Canadian Saltfish Corporation, we'd had to dislocate the merchants who had been in the business of selling salt fish for decades. But we relied on those firms—companies like the Fishermen's Union Trading Company in Port Union, Steer's Ltd. in St. John's, Bay Roberts Fisheries, and a number of others—to buy salt fish from the fishermen, at the negotiated price that we had set in the spring. We paid the firms out of the money from the government. We therefore removed the risk from the fish business for them and shouldered it ourselves.

In the years I was involved, from 1970 until 1979, we averaged about 500,000 quintals of salt fish a year. In our best years, we would buy and sell a couple million quintals. But there were problems. The dark clouds in the salt-fish business started to gather around 1973.

Fish size is an important factor when it comes to selling salt fish, even more than with frozen fish. I was looking at the supply coming to me by the tens of thousands of quintals, and I was seeing the average size going down and down and down. I'd go to the market, and I'd hear, "Mr. Maloney, the Norwegians can give us big salt fish, or the Faroese can give it to us or the Icelanders. The size of what you're offering is going down." When I went to Brazil, which was and still is one of the top markets in the world for salt fish, I didn't have the right product to sell them.

I got really concerned about it: the percentage of small fish was a burden I could not get off my back. I was looking at the rich markets of Italy, Greece, and Brazil, the ones who could afford to pay high prices for good fish, and then I'm looking at the markets that would buy the small stuff at a lower price, these being the West Indies, Puerto Rico, Jamaica, and Barbados. I alerted the federal government to what was going on but their response was to simply reiterate my mandate: to buy and market all salt fish.

With fresh fish at least the processors could take the small fish and turn it into blocks. We couldn't do that with salt fish. I had these tiny little salt fish, some that weren't as long as your hand. It cost us the same to package and ship the product and to employ staff and salespeople, no matter what the size of fish. But we couldn't sell the fish for a good price. The markets wanted big, top-quality salt fish.

Worse still, most of these small fish were under the age of reproduction—so we were not only losing the return from the market but we were also destroying the resource. There wasn't anything I could do. The government insisted we buy all salt fish that was produced, regardless of size, at the agreed-upon price.

I made one valiant attempt to deal directly with the problem, by getting the board of the Saltfish Corporation to bankroll two vessels to fish off Labrador, north of Black Tickle, in the mid-1970s. We fitted those vessels out with salt and put some real money into the venture. The voyages went for two years, but they got nothing in either year, no big fish at all.

I became a member of SOFA to bring attention to the government about what I saw happening to the industry. Trying to advocate from my position of head of the Canadian Saltfish Corporation didn't seem to make a difference.

Eventually, the Saltfish Corporation hired boats to go to the southern Grand Banks to try to get some big fish to salt, because we couldn't get them off Labrador. They even bought some cod from the Portuguese. I left the Saltfish Corporation in 1979. The organization held on until 1991, but it was not viable. There simply wasn't enough of the codfishery left to market.

There are still a few small-scale producers of salt fish in Newfoundland and Labrador but, by and large, I would say Canada is no longer a factor in the international salt-fish industry. We just couldn't meet the standards that the market demanded.

Chapter 17
1970s: False optimism
and asinine political decisions

By mid-1974 the groundfish industry's appearance
of health had vanished abruptly as the cost of gear,
fuel and labour shot skyward. In that year it cost
the large-vessel fleet ten to twelve cents per pound
to catch fish, compared with five to six cents in the
late 1960s.
—Policy for Canada's Commercial Fisheries

In the early 1970s, the Newfoundland fishing industry players were confident that SOFA's efforts to convince the Trudeau government that our fisheries were in desperate shape had been successful. We anxiously anticipated the extension of Canada's jurisdiction over the entire continental shelf. It was like we were waiting for an epiphany, blindly optimistic about the future. Certainly the provincial and federal governments felt that the fishing industry was one to invest in, as they encouraged more plants to be built and more people to enter the fisheries.

In May 1976, the federal government published *Policy for Canada's Commercial Fisheries*, a 100-page document outlining their strategy for creating a healthy, stable fishing sector from a struggling industry. It demonstrated a shift in government philosophy, but unfortunately it was a shift in the wrong direction. Another opportunity to take the action required to revitalize the failing fisheries, particularly in Newfoundland and Labrador, was missed.

Presented by the Minister of State for Fisheries, Roméo LeBlanc, the policy document was driven (in government words) by the need to rebuild an industry in the midst of an "acute economic crisis" and to be ready for the impending extension of Canadian jurisdiction over "what could, with wise management, become one of the richest fishing areas in the world" (Foreword).[41]

The policy document was flawed in many ways. The fundamental problem, though, was encapsulated in one paragraph in the foreword:

> Although commercial fishing has long been a highly regulated activity in Canada, the object of regulation has, with rare exception, been protection of the renewable resource. *In other words, fishing has been regulated in the interest of the fish. In the future it is to be regulated in the interest of the people who depend on the fishing industry.* (5, emphasis added)

This is completely backwards. Had LeBlanc forgotten that healthy, sustained fisheries allow people to make a good living? Caring for and protecting the resource should always have priority. Fish cannot be processed if they aren't caught; companies cannot compete in the international marketplace without consistently producing high-quality seafood products that meet consumer demand. If the fish aren't in the water, no one has a job.

One of the stated goals of this new policy, in fact, was to "[base] total allowable catches (TACs) and annual catch quotas on economic and social requirements (including the requirement for stability), rather than on the biological-yield capability of a fish stock or stocks" (*PC*, Appendix I). Again, it was completely backwards. If fish are not there, how can fishermen operate? How can they make a living?

Perversely, the policy document also demonstrates that the government was not completely ignorant of the issues faced by the industry, including the problem of decreasing quality and related wastage:

---

41   *Policy for Canada's Commercial Fisheries* (Ottawa: Fisheries and Marine Service, Department of the Environment, May 1976) (cited in text as *PC*).

Competition for an increasingly scarce supply of fish has been followed by deterioration of product quality, and consequent market losses. In the large-vessel groundfish fleet, for example, trips grew longer and fish size smaller.... The end result is a situation in which groundfish landings with an estimated potential value of $25 million are rejected outright as unfit for human consumption each year, and a further substantial loss sustained in the production of a lower quality product than could be obtained with proper methods. An additional loss, occasionally on a serious scale, is sustained from discards of undersized fish and of unwanted species taken while fishing for the sought-after groundfish species.

Variation in the quality of Canadian fish products has reduced their acceptability on the market. In some cases, foreign competitors get a higher price for the same basic product, because of a perceived difference in quality. (43)

Federal government officials obviously had the information before them. They knew that, as of 1975, Canada's share of the catch of all species in the northwest Atlantic was about 20 per cent, ranking well behind Spain and the USSR. They had evidence of the travesty of foreign overfishing, the reduction in fish stocks and the increasing expense of harvesting them, and the crisis of quality the industry was facing. This made it all the more frustrating that, throughout the 1970s, countless short-sighted political decisions were made by both the federal and provincial governments, with devastating effects on the east-coast fisheries.

•••

With the "new direction" in federal fisheries management came the dissolution of the Federal Fisheries Research Board. First established in 1898, this Board was long the principal organization in Canada for fisheries and aquatic research. It established and controlled budgets for scientific programs which assessed the state of fish stocks before and after the formation of ICNAF in 1949. The Board counted among its employees and members some of Canada's most important and knowledgeable scientists from DFO and Canadian universities. Industry was also well represented by people such as Paul Russell of Bonavista Cold Storage and Arthur Monroe of FPL.

The Board was in charge of several biological research stations across the country and its contributions were crucial to the ongoing understanding of the fisheries. Financed by the Canadian government, the Board's direction came primarily from academics and scientists, but with some industry input:

> In 1968 the Board had considerable support and good relations with its major clients: the universities, the fisheries industry and the Ministry of Fisheries, and could securely function, as it was mandated, providing research support for the fisheries and contributing generally to the advancement of knowledge. At this time the Board had eighteen members, ten from the 153 universities, seven from the fishing industry and one from government. This intersectoral body set objectives and policies for ten research establishments which together employed a staff of 959.[42]

In 1973, the Fisheries Research Board was rolled into the Department of Fisheries and the Environment as part of government restructuring (other natural resources departments were also combined), as well as an overall movement to so-called government efficiency. The Board's interests became more closely aligned with government policy than the pursuit of good science and fisheries management:

42   Frances Anderson, "The Demise of the Fisheries Research Board of Canada: A Case Study of Canadian Research Policy," *HSTC Bulletin: Journal of the History of Canadian Science, Technology and Medicine* 4.2 (1984), 151-156. doi: 10.7202/800193ar.

In the eyes of the [Treasury] Board, science is not regarded as a thing in itself, but rather as a means to an end. In general, particular scientific projects are not examined on their own merits but rather as components of programs which have defined objectives.[43]

After 75 years of operation, the Fisheries Research Board became an advisory body; it was no longer responsible for research facilities and unable to set its own research goals. Ottawa's disdain for science- and research-based fisheries management was showing.

Whatever the true political reasons were for the change, the power of the Fisheries Research Board had been revoked. The group continued to meet, as a relatively successful advisory board, until 1978, when it met its official demise.

With the dissolution of the Fisheries Board, everything passed over to the minister of fisheries, just as LeBlanc was stepping into the role. The fish, our future, everything was now in one man's hands.

•••

One of the most painful examples of the 1976 fisheries management "policy" directly targeted cod on their spawning grounds. It was yet another asinine political decision made under LeBlanc's leadership with apparently no understanding of its implications for the Newfoundland and Labrador fisheries.

In 1977, at the annual ICNAF meeting—just before declaring the 200-mile limit—Canada came out strongly against any foreign fishing on Hamilton Inlet Bank, off the coast of Labrador, during the winter cod-spawning season. Between January and early April, the northern cod stock concentrated on Hamilton Inlet Bank to spawn. For 30 years, beginning in the early 1950s, large ice-strengthened foreign factory-freezer vessels fished those concentrations, which contained a high percentage of small fish as well as the spawning

---

43   Senate Special Committee, *Proceedings* 26, 3695-3696, quoted in Anderson, 154.

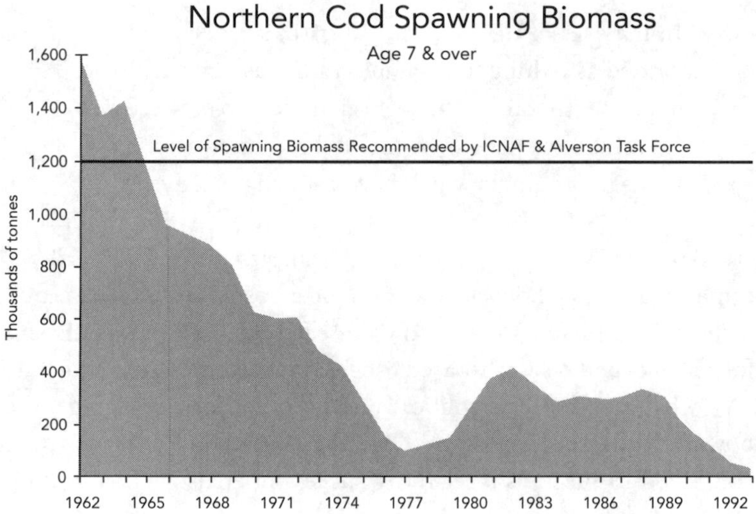

Northern Cod Spawning Biomass

Age 7 & over

Figure 3: The spawning biomass, cod seven years and older and considered capable of reproduction, was at 1.6 million tonnes in 2J3KL in 1962, and has fallen steeply since. Limited scientific analysis available from DFO or others indicates in 2013 it is approximately 130,000 tonnes. The recommended biomass level by the Alverson Task Force and ICNAF is 1.2 million tonnes. *DFO*

population. Enormous amounts of fish—over 1 million metric tons in 1968—were caught there, year after year. Despite warnings from ICNAF scientists that the resource was in trouble, ICNAF's 20 member nations did not agree to reduce TACs or take any measures to reduce fishing during the spawning period. They were not interested in reducing their fishing effort on northern cod anywhere, particularly on the Hamilton Inlet Bank.

Canada's implementation of the 200-mile limit in 1978 brought that fishery to a close. (Since the northern cod stock actually migrates from Hamilton Inlet Bank off Labrador to the Nose of the Grand Banks, outside 200 miles, foreign fleets could continue to overfish the stock—just not in spawning season.)

I thought that the protection of the Hamilton Inlet Bank spawning grounds was one issue that would go away after the 200-mile limit was effected. After all, the northern cod-spawning biomass (considered to be cod seven years and older) was at its lowest level ever—it had been reduced to 70,000 tonnes in 1977 from 1,600,000 tonnes in 1962 (see Figure 3). And sure enough, after the foreign fishing boats had been gone a year or so, there was evidence that the fishery was starting to rebound.

But then a group of trawler owners from Nova Scotia lobbied the federal government for permission to fish northern cod on the Hamilton Inlet Bank, just as the foreign nations had. It was assumed that indications of a rebound pointed to an early recovery of the resource. The trawler crews needed new places to fish as only very small cod were being caught on the traditional fishing banks adjacent to Nova Scotia. Since the foreigners had been ousted from the popular winter fishery off Labrador, the Nova Scotians now wanted in.

It is difficult to imagine any response to this request other than an immediate "No." But the federal government was ready to give the thumbs-up.

When the FPL board heard about the Nova Scotia request, I was directed to go to Ottawa and confront Fisheries Minister LeBlanc. My job was to convince him that agreeing to the Nova Scotians' request would further delay, if not forever destroy, any possible recovery of the all-important northern cod stock.

I spent four hours in LeBlanc's Ottawa office, pleading our case. I pointed out that only a short while ago Canada had made a big show at the ICNAF meetings, trying to get foreign fishing ships off these same spawning grounds. I pointed out that, unlike European fishermen, east-coast fishermen didn't have ice-strengthened vessels fit for a Labrador fishery at that time of the year. The potential for losing a trawler crew and a multi-million-dollar vessel was high, and the results could be tragic. "Good judgment will be used," I remember LeBlanc telling me. I begged him not to allow the fishery.

LeBlanc said he understood my arguments, but they were of no use. After a continued heated exchange, he advised me it was too late: the Hamilton Inlet Bank winter fishery had already been agreed to and terms and conditions had been mailed to regional headquarters in the Maritimes and Newfoundland and Labrador.

Sure enough, a letter from the federal fisheries department was waiting in my office when I returned. It laid out all the terms and conditions for participation in the fishery. Not only did the letter permit the fishery but it also offered a healthy incentive by way of a "special assistance program to encourage fishing in INCAF Divisions 2GHJ and 3K during January, 1978."[44]

The subsidy to *encourage* participation in this reckless and dangerous fishery was based on a per-sea-day payment of $500 "to offset increased insurance and gear costs" and an equivalent catch guarantee. This was based on the calculated value of catching 16,667 pounds of cod each day at 11 cents a pound for a maximum of 13 sea days (or a maximum makeup payment of $23,833.81). With that incentive removing the risk, few fishing companies would refuse to take part.

As upset as we were, as insulted as we were that our Nova Scotia counterparts had put forward this proposal, we had to make a difficult decision: should FPL trawlers participate? If we joined, we would be taking all the risks of winter fishing in harsh conditions, and we would contribute to the decline in our own fisheries. We would be attacking spawning grounds and doing exactly what we had fought to outlaw. If we didn't participate, however, we would allow other fishing companies, many from another province, to catch cod. Our plants would lose out on that business and we would potentially lose customers to our Nova Scotia competitors. We would be considered fools in the minds of people who didn't understand the situation.

The captains and crew of our trawlers let us know that they wanted to fish the northern fishery and earn more money; trawler deckhands calculated that their earnings would increase from $25,000 to $40,000 annually with the addition of the winter fishery.

---

44   RE: Assistance for fishing ICNAF sub-area 2GHJ & 3K. D.A. Tilley, Department of Fisheries and Environment to Fishery Products Ltd., January 9, 1978.

We were left with no choice. If our crews didn't fish for us, they would leave and fish for others.

I'm not proud to say that we joined in. Not surprisingly, the fish we caught were small, fetching a minimal return from the cod-block market and costing us twice as much to process as larger fish.

It's unbelievable. We went in and fished on the same spawning population that the foreign fishermen did. It was massacre after massacre and certainly contributed—along with the ongoing foreign overfishing outside 200 miles—to the continuing demise of the fisheries. The cod stocks had no chance to recover.

Chapter 18

A personal price

Through the 1970s I put in long hours in Newfoundland and elsewhere on behalf of FPL. I led the same lifestyle as any executive of a major fish company, especially one facing the problems created with a declining resource and increasing costs. I wasn't just president and COO of the company; I was deeply involved in management issues and in our lobbying efforts. I worked day and night to raise awareness of those issues facing our industry and to effect change in the face of government's procrastination in dealing with the destruction of the fisheries.

This meant long hours in the office and a lot of time on the road, out of town, and overseas. I was thoroughly committed and devoted to work, as were the Monroes. Everyone involved in the management of FPL and, I would say, a majority of plant workers and trawler personnel, were still enthusiastic about the business. We were focused and determined, trying to find ways to improve the fisheries and ensure a future for all concerned. It didn't come without a price.

I missed holidays and family events. I vividly remember spending a lonely Christmas Day in London, waiting for an Air Canada flight home. There were many occasions I prefer to forget. My family were understanding and I always took comfort in knowing they were well looked after, even when I wasn't around to participate directly in their day-to-day lives.

On March 16, 1975, I went shopping with my wife, Nora, in Churchill Park while the boys were in school. We came home from our outing and settled in for the evening as usual, and I got ready to leave for a business trip with Arthur Monroe to Spain. I cherish the memory of that normal, comfortable day. The next morning,

Monroe and I caught the plane, landed in Madrid, and then transferred to a smaller plane for San Sebastián, on the northern coast of Spain—the heart of Basque country and the home of my ancestors. We were about 20 kilometres from our destination when fog forced the plane to turn around. We landed about 40 kilometres from San Sebastián in a small airport near Pamplona. From there we got a bus and arrived at our destination about midnight.

The bus left us at the San Sebastián terminal. There were no taxis to be seen. I waited with our luggage while Monroe went around the corner to find us a lift to the hotel. I stayed there for half an hour, then an hour, and I wondered what was going on. I was getting worried. About 90 minutes later Monroe came back, driving a car owned by the company we were going to meet the next morning.

Monroe got out of the car and came straight to me. "Gus, was your wife not feeling well when you left?"

"What are you talking about?" I replied.

"Gus, I've got bad news for you," Monroe said. "Your wife is dead."

There I was on a street in San Sebastián, in the middle of the night, completely stunned. There had been absolutely no indication that Nora was ill when I left. I couldn't move. Monroe led me to the car and took me to the hotel. The first family member I managed to contact was my sister; the family had been trying to reach me for 24 hours but I had been completely out of touch and unreachable by telephone.

The morning I left home, I crept quietly out of the house to catch the early flight. A little later, our two boys—they were just 15 and 11—got up to go to school. Their mother wasn't up, so they went into the bedroom, and found her dead in the bed. She had died of a heart attack in her sleep. It was horrible. And here I was in San Sebastián in the middle of the night and many miles from Madrid, where I needed to be to get a flight across the Atlantic. I had to get home as soon as possible to my two boys—I needed to be with them to try to make sense of these tragic and shocking circumstances.

It was difficult but I met with Monroe and briefly discussed the project that had brought us to the Basque country. Within an hour I was in a limousine, provided by the company we were visiting, en route to Madrid. It was a long, numb, lonely eight-hour drive though the Pyrenees to get a plane to Toronto and finally home to St. John's.

My two boys were broken. They immediately told me they didn't want to live in the same house anymore. After Nora was laid to rest, the three of us went to Florida and spent three weeks there, together, trying to come to terms with what had happened. We spent a lot more time together after that; every weekend we took the car and went one place or another. They didn't want to stay at home, and I didn't much want to either. As quickly as I could arrange it, we sold the house in Churchill Park and moved to St. Philip's, a 15-minute drive from St. John's.

I suppose my sons realized that I was busy—or at least they were used to it. I did get back to work, but I needed help to manage everything else. I had a dozen housekeepers over the next seven or eight years, just trying to keep up with the house and life for the boys and me without Nora. The housekeepers didn't measure up, to be honest, but we managed to get through it somehow.

Glenn and Grant grew up into responsible young men, and I am intensely proud of them in every respect. Glenn, who graduated from Memorial University with a degree in economics, has done well in the business world and spent a year with a German fishing company, Nordzee, in Bremerhavn, and several years as trawler manager with FPL and Fishery Products International. As of 2013, he is vice-president of Oceanex, a successful marine transportation enterprise. Grant, on the other hand, demonstrated his mother's love and talent for music from an early age; he studied music at Memorial University, as well as the universities of Western Ontario and Regina, and received a Masters degree. He is completely involved in the world of music and became director of music at Holy Heart of Mary High School in St. John's.

Chapter 19
Trade meetings and trade-offs

There are many accounts of the Government of Canada's trading fishing rights, including quotas, to other countries for benefits—market access, reduced tariffs, air space rights, or the construction of manufacturing plants. But don't expect to read details of such transactions. The prime minister's office, the minister of fisheries, and senior fisheries bureaucrats would never permit such information to reach the public press.

Most of these agreements, at least those occurring before 1977, have been muted, denied by politicians and bureaucrats, with no publicly available record.

There were participants in the Canadian fishing industry, however, who knew of agreements that were made with foreign fishing nations and that they had negative impacts on the Canadian fisheries. These international agreements were almost always to the detriment of the Newfoundland and Labrador fishery, while the benefits, should there be any, flowed to other regions of Canada. One example: the UK, a major customer for British Columbia halibut, agreed to remove the tariff on that fish in exchange for Canadian support for a larger UK northern cod quota at ICNAF. I learned about that deal through the Fisheries Council of Canada and contacts in the British Columbia fishing industry. And another: Canada reportedly offered its support in a NAFO voting procedure for a Korean request for a quota outside 200 miles, in exchange for a car-manufacturing plant to be built in Quebec. Spain and Portugal, in exchange for Canada's support for more cod quotas, agreed to grant landing rights for Canadian Pacific Airlines at airports in Madrid and Lisbon.

There is no paper trail, no accessible record of these agreements and others like them.

Commissioners like me, while not directly party to such discussions (and certainly not signatories to the agreements), were nonetheless in a position to have some knowledge of what was being negotiated at that level.

For all of my frustrations, Canada—as the coastal state adjacent to the fisheries of the northwest Atlantic—did have considerable influence on decisions made in both ICNAF and NAFO on the allocation of resources. For that reason, Canadian representatives were often approached by commissioners from other countries seeking to make deals exchanging support at ICNAF/NAFO meetings for something valuable to Canada.

Those of us who weren't at the table will never know for sure, but there is little doubt in my mind that ICNAF members influenced the United Nations Law of the Sea and the Canadian government on their final decision to extend jurisdiction to 200 miles and not the entire continental shelf. During that crucial period when discussions were being held about the extension of jurisdiction, I did not know a single Canadian politician or bureaucrat who understood the need to protect all fish stocks on the continental shelf from foreign overfishing.

•••

After the 200-mile limit was established, bilateral agreements, commensurate benefits, and over-the-side sales were three ways in which foreign countries could still directly participate in Canada's fisheries. These initiatives were fully welcomed by the federal government and designed to smooth international acceptance of Canada's 200-mile limit. The agreements were also an opportunity to share fish that were surplus to Canada's homegrown industry. After the establishment of the 200-mile limit, after all, there was hope that the stocks would improve. Newfoundland's minister of fisheries went so far as to say:

> Canada's extension of fisheries jurisdiction to 200 miles will have a profound impact on the volume

of fish available to our domestic fishery in the years ahead. This also means that we will have greatly increased volumes ... available for world fish markets. It is no secret that the Canadian fishing industry is looking towards the European market as a major outlet for our greatly expanded production.[45]

It was thought that, after extending the jurisdiction, Canada would suddenly have access to more fish, which many Canadian politicians worried they would not be able to sell. After all, Canada had only been taking about 20 per cent of the total catch off Newfoundland and Labrador—foreign fishing nations were harvesting the vast majority. Surely, some believed, Canada would have plenty of fish for its own markets, and enough to share.

In 1978, the federal fisheries department officially announced a policy of commensurate benefits—agreements "under which the various countries wishing to fish in Canada's territorial waters had to offer commercial compensations in exchange for the quotas granted in their licenses." For example, "Canada estimated that, by the end of 1978, Spain would have been obliged to buy Canadian fishing products to the value of $1.5 million in exchange for the quotas offered to the Spanish fleet." The quota was a reported 19,600 tons of cod.[46]

The official commensurate benefit program, also introduced at the time of extended jurisdiction, involved an exchange of "surplus" fish for market advantages:

In 1978, 25,000 tons of northern cod were declared surplus to Canadian requirements. Seventy-five hundred (7,500) tons of this were allocated to foreign countries which had signed bilateral agreements with Canada.

---

45   Quoted in Michael Leigh, *European Integration and the Common Fisheries Policy* (Croom Helm, 1983), 128.

46   Rosa Garcia-Orellan, *Terranova: The Spanish Cod Fishery on the Grand Banks of Newfoundland in the Twentieth Century* (Boca Raton: BrownWalker Press, 2010), 216.

The remaining 17,500 tons were considered available for commensurate benefits. Of this total, 8,000 tons were allocated to Portugal in view of its traditional cod fishery and its expressed willingness to expand markets for salt cod from Canada.[47]

The idea of commensurate benefits was unpopular among the fishing industry. Not only that, but by 1981 even the federal government had to admit those 25,000 tons of cod were not surplus—Canadian boats could take their share of the quota and more.[48]

Nevertheless, over-the-side and over-the-wharf sales were still allowed, inflicting more damage to the struggling industry players. These direct sales permitted foreign fishing boats, including massive factory-freezer vessels, to enter and tie up at wharves in Newfoundland fishing ports and purchase various species of fish from fishermen. At certain times of the year, fishermen might have a glut of cod, for example, and be eager to sell it to a waiting vessel.

Year	Over-the-side Sales (tonnes)	Over-the-wharf Sales (tonnes)
1979	565	
1980	5,504	0
1981	4,429	8,525
1982	7,018	10,230
1983	6,248	4,222
1984	7,203	3,587
Total	**30,967**	**26,564**

Department of Fisheries and Aquaculture, Newfoundland and Labrador

47   "History and Management of the Fishery for Northern Cod in NAFO Divisions 2J, 3K, and 3L," in *Perspectives on Canadian Marine Fisheries Management*, edited by L.S. Parsons and W.H. Lear. *Canadian Bulletin of Fisheries and Aquatic Sciences* 226 (1993), 55-90, quote at 72.

48   Ibid., 72.

The foreigners would then process this fish into products that were in direct competition to those made in Newfoundland and Labrador. Between 1979 and 1984, Newfoundland fishermen sold over 57,500 tonnes of fish over-the-side and over-the-wharf. The Department of Fisheries had, once again, initiated a program that replaced the Newfoundland and Labrador exporter in traditional markets.

•••

A report written by Joseph Gough, who worked for DFO in 2005, explained the bilateral and other agreements this way:

> In return for surplus fish, Canada requested economic benefits from its bilateral partners, through new markets for fish products or through other arrangements. This had some good results with certain nations, notably Portugal for a time, and some members of the East Bloc. Besides fish purchases, economic arrangements included co-operation in over-the-side and over-the-wharf sales, developmental fishing arrangements using foreign vessels, and use of Canadian ports and ship-repair facilities.[49]

These were, in effect, deals between Canada and other countries whereby foreign vessels could fish inside the 200-mile limit for certain trade considerations. Ottawa used cod or turbot or squid—anything they considered surplus—as bargaining tools.

The government definition of "surplus" fish was obviously much different than that of the Newfoundland and Labrador fishermen. Those of us in the industry were optimistic but none of us would have agreed with the federal government when it decided (arbitrarily, it seemed) in the mid-1970s that the turbot fishery on the

---

49   Joseph Gough, "Review of Canada's Bilateral Agreements and Foreign Allocations in Relation to Atlantic Straddling Stocks, 1977-2004," Advisory Panel on the Sustainable Management of Straddling Fish Stocks in the Northwest Atlantic, Fisheries and Oceans Canada (Ottawa, 2005),1.

Signing the bilateral agreement in Moscow. Gus Etchegary (first on left) and Roméo LeBlanc (fifth on left) are seated at the table.

northeast coast of Newfoundland was "surplus." At the time, local fishermen depended almost exclusively on that species to stay in the fishery, because it was about the only groundfish species available to gillnet fishing—northern cod catches were at their lowest levels in history. That didn't seem to matter; in this instance the USSR was the beneficiaries of the federal largesse.

I was present during the signing of several bilateral agreements, and I can speak about the one signed with the USSR in 1977. I was not a signatory to the document, but I participated in the related junket with Romeo LeBlanc and other officials and I was present during the signing of the agreement. Canada awarded a quota of so-called "surplus turbot" in exchange for access to the market—$12 million worth of sales in the Soviet seafood market, to be exact. The meeting with that country's minister of fisheries, Alexander Ishkov, and his staff took place in Moscow. LeBlanc was there, as were some his deputies, and three or four representatives from the fishing industry, including me.

After signing the bilateral agreement we were royally fêted and treated to an extensive tour of the country's culture and fishing operations. We were transported in style to watch the opera *Carmen* from the czar's box overlooking the stage at the famous Bolshoi Theatre and served vodka and caviar during the intermission. We also visited the State Hermitage Museum in St. Petersburg. From Leningrad, home to the country's southern distant-water fishing fleet, we were flown to Murmansk on the Barents Sea, home to the huge northern distant-water fishing fleet. Probably the largest fishing port in the world, Murmansk also contained numerous fish-processing plants. For the next three or four days, we were invited to tour factory-freezer trawlers and processing plants.

At one particularly large modern assembly-line plant, LeBlanc and I were given details of the operation by the plant manager, through an interpreter. As we observed the operation, I noticed a line of 1-kilogram packages being conveyed from the automatic packaging machines. Clearly marked on each cover was "40 kopeks"—in other words, about 40 American cents. Through the interpreter I asked the plant manager the significance of the price on the package; his response was, "Don't pay any attention to that price; it's been on that package for three or four years." I asked LeBlanc if the bilateral agreement he had just signed included a set unit price for Canadian fish. As we found out in reviewing the agreement details that evening, I was right to be concerned. There was no reference to a per-unit price that the Canadian producer would receive for a pound of exported fish.

The net result of that bilateral agreement: not a pound of Canadian-processed fish was sold to the USSR for the simple reason that the price offered represented about 20 per cent of the cost of creating the finished product in Canada. The Soviet vessels, however, took full advantage of the turbot quota available to them. So much for that bilateral agreement.

How many other agreements were signed between Canada and foreign fishing nations? Don't ever expect to locate public documents as evidence. They never were, or ever will be, available to the public. But I do know from detailed conversations and discussions with former ambassadors, advisors, and bureaucrats that trades and other programs involving fish and fish products were negotiated with foreign fishing nations—many of them prior to the 1977 200-mile extension.

Chapter 20

The situation deteriorates:
Ottawa barges in

In 1975 FPL management learned that the Lake Group, National Sea Products, and Nickerson were working together on a deal to purchase the Marystown fish plant. Atlantic Sugar was getting out of the fishing industry, and our three main competitors wanted to take over the operation and push FPL out of the area.

We had no choice but to borrow $12 million and purchase the plant and trawlers ourselves, even though our Burin plant, less than 20 kilometres away, was struggling to find enough fish to operate at capacity. We still believed that the diminishing fish supply was a short-term issue that would be resolved when the Canadian government extended jurisdiction over the entire continental shelf. We told ourselves we could make both plants work until the fish stocks rebounded. And we did, for a few years. We had 20 trawlers supplying the two plants, and we transferred fish between them, as required, to balance the operations as best we could.

To compensate for the lower catch rates, we invested in additional large, more efficient trawlers. We financed new ships and improvements to our operations by borrowing money. Because the catch per unit of effort was much higher in the offshore fishery, we focused our efforts there. The inshore fishery catch was at its lowest level in history.

We weren't the only ones to invest in FPL through the late-1970s. Processing capacity in Newfoundland and Labrador continued to expand dramatically; there was nothing but enthusiasm for the imminent recovery of and a bright future for the fisheries. The federal government encouraged our investing in more vessels and offered subsidies as high as 50 per cent of the total cost of building new trawlers in Canada. (This was not the great incentive for fishing companies that it appeared: as we sought construction quotes from shipyards across Canada and Europe, we discovered we could have trawlers built in Europe for less than we could in Canada, even *after* the generous federal subsidy. The files on this are long gone, but I remember that the quotes we gathered ranged from $2.5 to $5 million [USD] per trawler built in Spanish and Portuguese shipyards and $7.5 to $9 million [CAD] in Canadian yards.)

Companies from Nova Scotia and elsewhere on the mainland built or bought processing plants in Newfoundland. Nickerson constructed plants in Charleston and Triton and acquired another in Jackson's Arm. They invested on the premise that their new trawlers could supply those plants from the huge rebounding northern cod stock.

Many fish-processing companies threw caution to the wind, pushing for even greater fleet expansion than that first proposed by the federal government. In 1978, Nickerson, with some help from wealthy Nova Scotians and their provincial government, took over National Sea Products. Together they were a formidable company and angled heavily for a part in the Newfoundland fisheries. Nickerson-National Sea published a booklet that year ("Where Now? A Discussion of Canada's Fishery Opportunity and the Considerations Involved in Realizing It") pushing for aggressive expansion, beyond even what the government had prescribed:

> Canada cannot reap the potential benefits of the 200-mile management zone if its fleet does not have the capacity to harvest the fish stocks available during the next decade. If it is to take the initiative in fleet replacement and development, the industry requires comprehensive policies that will allow the industry to proceed with confidence in:
>
> • The replacement of the inshore fleet;

- The replacement of the offshore fleet;

- The expansion of the inshore fleet and the off-shore fleet as fish stocks permit; and

- The development of a new generation fleet of Canadian trawlers, with freezer capability and possibly some on-board processing.[50]

As a result of the increase in Canadian fishing, landings, particularly of northern cod, increased after 1977. Newfoundlanders entered or re-entered the fisheries at an impressive rate. There were fewer than 13,000 fishermen in the Newfoundland and Labrador fisheries in 1976; that number doubled or more than doubled in the next four years. By 1980, there were an estimated 35,000 fishermen in the province.

FPL did not let all the construction happen without some protest. In 1980, Nickerson-National Sea cleared a space on the waterfront in St. Barbe and erected a steel frame that was supposed to become the newest fish plant in the area at an estimated cost of $1 million. St. Barbe is midway between Port au Choix and St. Anthony—two towns with FPL fish plants, both of which were operating at between 30 and 40 per cent capacity.

As soon as we found out about the St. Barbe construction, I confronted the minister of fisheries, Liberal Pierre de Bané: "What is the fisheries department doing giving a licence to build a plant so close to two plants that were not even operating at half capacity?" He agreed that I had a point.

If I hadn't spoken up, Nickerson would have received a processing licence from the province government and a substantial subsidy from the federal government to build the plant. In the end, although Nickerson had reportedly already been given federal money for

---

50   Booklet quoted in L.S. Parsons, *Management of Marine Fisheries in Canada*, *Canadian Bulletin of Fisheries and Aquatic Sciences* 225 (1993), 359.

construction, the steel frame had to be taken down. The people of St. Barbe were not happy with FPL *or* Nickerson.

FPL did everything possible to improve the quality and value of our primary and secondary products to get maximum return from the market. Every conceivable move was made to reduce costs and improve our finances. We introduced incentive programs to increase productivity. We stopped processing fresh fish at the plant in St. Anthony because of a shortage of raw material and turned it over to the Canadian Saltfish Corporation to operate.

But FPL faced a serious dilemma. On the one hand, we were struggling to process enough fish to supply our large customer base in the US, Europe, and Asia, and our business was vulnerable. On the other hand, Canada had implemented a 200-mile limit and experts predicted that the resource would recover. We believed we had to maintain our plants, hold on to our experienced workforce, and encourage the inshore and offshore fishermen to remain with the industry until the fish came back.

Closing more fish plants was almost impossible. Doing so would have been suicidal for the company; it would have meant a loss of product for the market and the end of a job for too many fishermen and processors. A sense of uncertainty already prevailed in many of the communities because there was less work available in the plants.

Closure would have been the end of employee loyalty. We made the best of what we had and struggled to maintain operations until the situation improved.

•••

In stark contrast to the modern Marystown plant we had added to our holdings, the Burin plant was showing its age. It had been built in 1942 and, although additions had been made over the years, it was an old plant, long overdue for replacement. On the positive side, Burin had an efficient workforce and a first-class management group led by Joe Moulton, Lew Fizzard, Harvey Shave, Ern Moulton, and others. Even though we had the plant in Marystown, we were deeply committed to Burin and planned to spend $10 million to build a new facility. By 1979, however, our optimism had faded again, and we knew we had to delay the construction.

Catch rates continued to drop, and it became increasingly difficult to maintain continuous employment in both plants. Trawlermen and plant workers were working fewer hours and thus earning less money and union leadership began to pressure FPL management to increase hourly wages to compensate for the loss in hours by fish-plant workers. They also pushed for larger share arrangements on trawlers to compensate for reduced catches. As was the case in other trawler operations, FPL paid its trawler crews based on a standard per diem rate and a share of the catch. This worked well, especially when catch rates maintained an average level. The FFAW, under Richard Cashin and Des McGrath, wanted to throw out all incentives and implement a guaranteed wage; we couldn't do that—there would be no motivation to catch fish. After much argument, we agreed to increase the daily rates but maintain the share agreement. It was an effort on our part to compensate for a reduction in catch volumes over which we had no control.

Labour negotiations, which used to be a mere formality, stretched over longer periods of time as agreements became more difficult to reach. While production levels dropped, costs increased. In addition, our inability to consistently provide products to long-established customers in the food service and retail trade meant that returns from the market were reduced. And then interest rates went up and the market price of fish went down. Borrowing money to construct new trawlers was fine when Smallwood provided fisheries development loans at interest rates of 3 per cent. But when interest went to a crushing 22 per cent in the 1980s, many fishing companies, including the larger ones in the province, faced bankruptcy, having spent too much borrowed money while not having produced the volume or quality of fish required to break even, let alone stay profitable.

Only a small number of family-run operations, with their minimal capital investments and bank loans, managed to stay viable.

These smaller operations purchased their fish supplies directly from inshore fishermen and did not have to own and operate expensive company trawlers. Their flexibility in dealing with the changing situation was a huge benefit.

The viability of FPL was seriously threatened. Thus we were surprised when the Canada Development Corporation (CDC) contacted us in 1980 and indicated their interest in the fishing industry. Specifically, they were interested in taking shares in FPL.

The CDC was an arm's-length organization of the federal government with a mandate to invest in resource-based industries with potential and to work with companies within those industries to foster growth. Although the fishing industry on the east coast was experiencing difficult times, CDC officials decided FPL was a worthy candidate for their support.

Our company boasted features that must have intrigued CDC—I can't see why else they would have wanted to get involved. Our relatively new fleet of offshore stern trawlers, experienced crews, productive plants, dedicated workforce, and long-established marketing organization and secondary processing plant in the US were all valuable assets. Over the years, Monroe had built a solid management organization that CDC personnel found easy to work with, which solidified a strong business relationship.

Then again, with the general conviction that recovery of the resource would be just a matter of time, I suppose the future looked relatively bright in spite of the immediate financial struggles we faced.

In the final deal, CDC agreed to invest $33 million in FPL in exchange for 49 per cent ownership. The FPL management team would stay in place and the Monroes would hold majority ownership, but CDC would have representation on the board of directors and participate fully in the strategic planning and development for the company.

That $33 million made a world of difference for FPL. New trawler construction, the purchase of the Marystown plant, and the modernization of other plants added up to a substantial debt for

FPL by 1980. Soaring interest rates and the depressed American market prevented us from retiring the debt as quickly as the bank would have liked.

The CDC deal buoyed us up, as a business and as individuals. The injection of cash allowed us to pay off some debts, bringing us close to the break-even point in 1981 and enabling us to forecast a modest profit for 1982. We took comfort in the optimism of CDC's representatives. The organization held considerable influence in Ottawa and its members were well positioned to lobby for action against the foreign overfishing that continued outside the 200-mile limit. We hoped that our new partnership would allow us to finally have the ear of federal politicians.

CDC representatives were enthusiastic, brimming with ideas about how to increase our marketing efforts and get our products noticed. We knew there was a more immediate problem: rebuilding the resource to ensure a continuous supply of high-quality seafood products to help put FPL back on a firm financial footing. It wasn't long before CDC fully understood the issues, and supported our position. They also quickly recognized the enormous processing overcapacity in the province. They suggested that production efficiency could only be achieved by reducing the number of plants in operation and increasing production at those remaining—at least until the fisheries were restored to a healthy, sustainable level. We had avoided closing plants for years, even when we should have. We could no longer afford to do so.

A painful decision had to be made: Burin or Marystown? We could only keep operating one plant. Burin's workforce, after 40 years of operational experience and training, was probably the most experienced in the province. Their productivity rivaled the best plants anywhere in Canada or Europe, according to our own records. However, the newer Marystown plant could easily handle the landings of inshore and offshore fish available in the area. We decided to close Burin instead of rebuilding it as we had hoped and to put our efforts into making Marystown a profitable plant.

We devised a way to provide work for nearly all of our employees. Because many of the plant workers had worked in both locations, the seniority clause in the union agreement applied to the total workforce. Accordingly, many displaced Burin workers would be eligible for employment in Marystown. Others could work in Burin, in new positions. We planned to close the Burin primary plant but expand its secondary processing operations. All the maintenance work and annual refitting of our 25 stern trawlers would also be carried out in Burin, allowing us to continue to employ a large portion of the Burin production and maintenance employees.

Despite these plans, I knew the people of Burin would be deeply hurt by the closure of the primary plant. I knew it would bring discontent and resentment. Unfortunately, there was no other defensible option for FPL.

Of FPL's management team, I had the closest relationship with our employees in Burin and with most of the town council—they were all my friends—I was given the job of telling them our plans. I was flown by helicopter to the town, where a meeting was convened with the town councillors. Their first reaction to my announcement was not surprising: "My God, Gus, you can't do that, for the love of God." As I relayed the details of the company's decision, I could feel the resentment build in the room. I assured the council that everyone would still have a job, but it didn't soften the blow. They were angry that their plant was to shut down in favour of Marystown's.

It was a dreadful day. I had lived in the community and been Burin plant manager for 10 years. I knew everyone there. I had a close relationship with the people and they had stuck with FPL, always giving their best. I felt horrible and the town felt let down.

To make matters worse, the earlier understanding we had had with the union that seniority would entitle some Burin workers to employment in Marystown did not materialize. The union executive found it difficult, if not impossible, to implement the process, even if it was in accordance with normal union-sanctioned practice. It was another slap in the face to the devoted Burin workers.

But the people of Burin were ready to fight; the workers were prepared to take every measure to save their source of employment.

Most memorably, they dug a moat across the entrance to their plant so FPL could not move any of its equipment or product off the premises. It was a nasty, sometimes violent, situation.

After 40 years of year-round FPL trawler and plant processing operations, the relationship between the company and the people of Burin ended.

Chapter 21
Fishery Products International is born

Thanks to the $33 million CDC investment and tough decisions such as closing the Burin plant, FPL could stave off the bankruptcy that closed in on many of its competitors. Although FPL's profits had declined through the 1970s and it carried a multi-million-dollar debt, it was probably the best off of any of the large fish-processing companies. In fact, after a tough decade, we thought we had ridden out the storm. We believed that, with careful management, reduced operation cost, and a new investor, we would survive.

Although our cod landings had fallen steeply, we succeeded in developing a large market for flounder products in the US and Europe, and we negotiated access to 92 per cent of the flounder resource quota on the Grand Banks to supply that market.

The ill-advised Labrador winter cod fishery resulted in landings of very small fish, which were processed into low-value cod blocks. While this provided some employment for our plant workers in Marystown, Trepassey, Burin, Harbour Breton, and Catalina, it was a losing venture. There were too many small fish coming in and too many cod blocks on the market.

The demand for cod blocks was flat, and inventories grew. Some processors opted not to buy small cod until the market stabilized. Faced with the possibility that many processors might slow down or cease operations, the federal government purchased the surplus until markets recovered. This intervention didn't help. American buyers were all too aware of growing inventories. Information about the number of cod blocks in storage was easily available and buyers used it to manipulate purchase prices.

The inshore fishermen and processors who were unable to

access Labrador northern cod were without fish to catch or process. To fill this gap, DFO created a "Resource-Short Plant Program." During the program, which ran throughout the 1980s, special quotas of groundfish were established. These had to be landed by 65-foot longliners at designated "resource-short" plants on the northeast coast of Newfoundland. Because the longliners continued to bring in small catches, the program was discontinued.

The inshore plant in Port au Choix became a bright spot for FPL. A strong shrimp fishery had developed, and the plant continued to operate successfully. Unlike so many others, the plant there prospered after the 1992 groundfish moratorium, due to an aggressive and energetic group of fishermen who had developed a first-class fleet of vessels and an equally productive workforce.

FPL management was kept busy trying to keep the company on the road back to profitability. CEO Denis Monroe and financial vice-president Harry Earle concentrated on dealing with financial matters. I publicized, in every possible forum and manner, to governments, the workers, and the public, that the heart of the fishing industry—the once huge and diversified fisheries—was in deep trouble and had to be restored.

Busy as we were, we were not aware of an ongoing behind-the-scenes dialogue between the Bank of Nova Scotia and senior federal government officials about the financial situation of the fish companies in Newfoundland and Nova Scotia. Nickerson-National Sea Products in Nova Scotia was struggling with a debt load of about $250 million; the Lake Group in Newfoundland was nearly bankrupt; the Pennys and others had accumulated various but serious debt loads. FPL carried some debt but, due to the investment of the CDC and its valuable inventory, we were better off, financially, than any other east coast fish company. The Bank of Nova Scotia, which held most of the loans, worried about the money it would lose if the fishing companies declared bankruptcy, pressed the federal and provincial governments to step in.

The situation was about to get much worse for FPL.

•••

In 1982, the federal government under Prime Minister Pierre Trudeau made its move. The public relations spin went something like this: Ottawa would find a solution before fish companies went under and thousands of Newfoundlanders, Labradorians, and other Atlantic Canadians were left unemployed. The social and political problems in eastern Canada had to be dealt with, and Ottawa was going to act.

Ottawa's first move was to pump $13 million into the Lake Group, allowing it to stave off bankruptcy and keep all plants operational for another year. That was only a fraction of what the federal government was about to spend on "saving" the fisheries.

Next, the Trudeau government appointed Nova Scotian Michael Kirby as chair of a task force that would examine the Atlantic Canadian fisheries and make recommendations for a way forward. Kirby was a former university professor and high-profile public servant—he served as assistant principal secretary to Trudeau and secretary to the Canadian cabinet for federal-provincial relations, among other posts—who would go on to be appointed to the Senate in 1984. None of us at FPL were aware of the type of discussions taking place or where the Kirby Commission would take the industry.

Navigating Troubled Waters: A New Policy for the Atlantic Fisheries (commonly known as the Kirby Report)[51] was driven by raw politics. The first priority seemed to be to bail out the banks, primarily the Bank of Nova Scotia, the main bank of the fishing industry. The second was to deal with immediate social concerns, including saving jobs and communities. The underlying cause of the problems in the fisheries—mismanagement of the resource since 1949—was never mentioned.

Kirby was put under severe deadline pressure: the bank was ready to pull the plug on the fish companies and many thousands

---

51   Michael Kirby, *Navigating Troubled Waters: A New Policy for the Atlantic Fisheries: Report of the Task Force on Atlantic Fisheries* (Supply and Services Canada, 1983) (cited in text as *KR*).

of jobs in the fishing industry were at stake. He had nine months to complete the report.

> Why the need for such haste? Because the fishery, viewed from either an economic or a social perspective, is in serious trouble. Change in the way a great many things are now done is essential and must be undertaken as quickly as possible if the fishery is to survive. And survive it must. (KR, vii)

The task force surveyed over 1,000 fishermen and studied about 100 fish plants in Atlantic Canada. I was president of FPL, the largest vertically integrated fish company in Newfoundland, which harvested, processed, and marketed millions of pounds of seafood products a year, yet I was not interviewed once by Kirby or anyone on his commission.

I attribute this to the fact that I, and other FPL managers, had publicly maintained that Canada had failed to protect the fisheries off the coast of Newfoundland and Labrador. It wasn't only cod that had been neglected but also flounder, redfish, haddock, turbot, capelin, and other species. The Spanish pair trawler fleet was evidence of that.

The redfish fishery, important for offshore plants, was dealt a similar blow in 1971 when DFO permitted the introduction of mid-water trawlers by Nickerson's and National Sea. Redfish was a viable fishery when caught by bottom trawls—as a light-seeking species, redfish concentrate in the mid-water column at night, which affords it protection from overfishing by bottom trawls and ensured a healthy stock. When the DFO minister permitted the Nova Scotian companies to use mid-water trawls to catch redfish, trawler catches doubled or more, eventually reducing redfish to very low levels. Redfish are a slowing growing species and have not recovered.

We could have provided Kirby and his team with evidence of the effects of decades of foreign overfishing. We could have shown him that, because of the decision to reopen the winter fishery on

Hamilton Inlet Bank spawning grounds, the northern cod stock would likely never recover. Of course, Kirby and his associates would not have wanted to hear any of that—it didn't fit into their plans.

•••

The Kirby Report was built on the baseless assumption that cod and other fish stocks were improving and that issues within the industry resulted from incompetent management and marketing:

> The fishery confronts us with a disturbing paradox. On one doorstep, we have one of the world's great natural fisheries resource bases, one that has made dramatic improvements since the extension of fisheries jurisdiction to 200 miles on January 1, 1977. The resource is manageable and is being capably managed by Canadians.
>
> On our other doorstep is the United States, a major and accessible market for fish. In between is a Canadian fishing industry mired in financial crisis, plagued by internal bickering, beset with uncertainty about the future, and divided on how to solve its problems. (7)

This point is often repeated in the report: "Although the industry has many problems, a shortage of fish is not one of them. By 1987, the groundfish harvest should reach 1.1 million tonnes, an increase of 370,000 t[onnes] over 1981" (9). Just about all of this increased tonnage was expected to be in cod, the vast majority to be harvested on the northeast coast of Newfoundland and Labrador. This turned out to be utterly false.

The stocks *had* shown a slight improvement since 1977, but they were still vulnerable and the long-term effects of the damage they had suffered during decades of overfishing—which was still continuing—was either disregarded by Ottawa for political reasons or simply not understood.

Kirby attempted to find the best way to work with a resource he believed was on a fast road to recovery, pinning high hopes on the recovery of the northern cod. History has shown this was not a realistic starting point.

In late 1982, Kirby and his task force proposed 57 recommendations in economics, social issues, and marketing. Attention was paid to creating efficiencies within the production line and improving the final fish product delivered to the market. Training and skills development were highlighted, as was a better use of existing infrastructure. Over-the-side and over-the-wharf sales were encouraged as a way to deal with "surplus" fish and to offer fishermen an additional source of income. No attention was paid to a recovery plan for the groundfish, except to report on its projected rapid growth:

> The Total Allowable Catch of northern cod is forecast to increase by at least 170,000 t, or 70 per cent, between 1982 and 1987, with the Canadian quota projected to be at least 380,000 t in 1987 [vs. 215,000 t in 1982]. (91)

Kirby did not find any issue with the supply of fish, but he did criticize the over-investment made by fish processors in the wake of the declaration of the 200-mile limit. Eagerness to compete and secure a piece of the alleged stronger resource brought on "a surge in investment and employment in the fishery." Over-capacity led to a financial crisis and, wrote Kirby, the problem needing immediate attention was "the near collapse of several major processors with extensive operations in Newfoundland" (122).

Under that directive, consultations continued in the wake of the Kirby Report as its recommendations were evaluated and decisions made. It cannot be forgotten that the banks were owed some $54 million by east-coast fishing companies. The banks wanted their money; the governments wanted to keep their constituents employed and happy.

In 1983, the *Atlantic Fisheries Restructuring Act* was passed.

It gave DFO the legislative power it needed to dismantle the fish companies that had been operating in Atlantic Canada, paying off their debts and taking over their operations. When the dust settled, two major organizations remained: National Sea Products in Nova Scotia and Fishery Products International (FPI) in Newfoundland.

•••

Negotiations to create National Sea Products and Fishery Products International did not come easily—or cheaply.

In Nova Scotia, the federal government put more than $50 million into the new company, paying off some of the outstanding loans held by National Sea and Nickerson in return for equity in the new firm. The federal government became the controlling stakeholder of National Sea Products, angering the nearly 200 smaller independent Nova Scotia fish processors, who were worried that the new supercompany would force them out of business.[52] That fear spread across the Maritimes. As Donald Cousins, owner of the family-run, 90-year-old French River Cannery Ltd. in Prince Edward Island told *Maclean's*:

> It's a family business and I work hard to keep it that way. But this new company is getting government funding and the government is going to come out and use it against us, while we have just got our own money to work with. That is what we are very much against.[53]

In Newfoundland, the deal-making was even messier, dragging on for over nine months. The first attempt to bring three major Newfoundland fish companies—FPL, the Lake Group, and Penny and Sons—together was mired in government ineptness and suspicion.

---

52   Parker Barss Donham, "A Deal That Upsets Fish Firms," *Globe and Mail*, October 22, 1983.

53   "The Largest Fish Company," *Maclean's*, October 17, 1983.

Ottawa unilaterally announced the reorganization of New-foundland and Labrador's fishing industry, in accordance with the Kirby plan, on July 4, 1983.

Newfoundland premier Brian Peckford accused the federal government of making a "secret deal" with the Bank of Nova Scotia without including the province in the negotiations: "Peckford ... suggested that it was suspicious that the receiver appointed by the bank for all three companies was Clarkson Co. Ltd. This, he suggest-ed, was possibly part of the federal government plan and the bank's secret plan."[54] The national media also reported that Ottawa began planning the restructuring without the agreement of the province—or the players in the fishing industry, for that matter:

> The Cabinet also approved recommendations from Mr. Kirby on reorganization that found some form of opposition from Newfoundland municipal lead-ers, the fishermen's union, the fishing companies, the provincial Government, provincial opposition par-ties, and most opinion-shapers in Newfoundland. In fact, Cabinet approved his recommendations only a few days after a broadly based Newfoundland People's Conference had recommended the restructuring be done differently.[55]

Fisheries Minister Pierre De Bané took the recommendations of the Newfoundland People's Conference to cabinet, but cabinet didn't bother to reply—Kirby continued to call the shots. Not surprisingly, "the negotiations themselves ... never escaped an at-mosphere of paranoid suspicion."[56] As noted in the national press, the province, represented by Fisheries Minister Jim Morgan, did

---

54   "Province May Bid for Assets of Three Big Fish Companies," *Evening Telegram*, August 27, 1983.

55   Michael Valpy, "A New Agreement," *Globe and Mail*, October 25, 1983.

56   Ibid.

nothing to instill confidence among Newfoundlanders. He "twice initiated agreements in principle in Ottawa that were politically unpalatable to Premier Brian Peckford and were subsequently reneged upon."[57] The press carried stories of an embarrassed Morgan being sent to Ottawa on Peckford's orders to undo a deal he had signed. It was a mess.

Without any support in the province, the plan crumbled. Another attempt, this time engaging the Newfoundland government, and under the control of De Bané, got underway by Labour Day.

The Bank of Nova Scotia, however, was not interested in waiting for governments to do a deal. In August 1983, it boldly attempted to retrieve its millions in outstanding loans by placing FPL, the Lake Group, and Penny and Sons into receivership:

> But Fisheries Products (FP), the largest fish processor in the province with eight fish plants, 40 trawlers and some 5,000 employees, did not go easily into receivership. John Penny and Sons, with one plant and five boats, and Lake Group with seven plants and 23 trawlers, accepted the bank's move. FP, however, sought an injunction preventing the sale of its assets. The firm, which carries an estimated debt of $67 million, alleged that the bank and Ottawa had illegally conspired to push the company into receivership to hasten the federal restructuring plan.[58]

The Supreme Court dismissed FPL's injunction, saying it had not convincingly proved that a conspiracy had existed. I maintain that we did. The management of FPL maintained that it did.

One afternoon in August 1983, when Denis Monroe and Harry Earle were in the US, a representative from the receiver, Clarkson

---

57   Ibid.

58   Bonnie Woodworth, "Salvation for the Fisheries," *Maclean's*, October 10, 1982.

Co. Ltd., came to FPL offices in St. John's. We turned him away. I ordered that the doors to the building be locked to ensure that no one from Clarkson entered. There was no way anyone at FPL was going to give up our company so easily.

August 1983—the same month Clarkson banged on our door—was the first productive month FPL had had in years. Our monthly report, showing we had broken even, maybe even had a tiny profit, was given to government. As far as we were concerned, FPL's future was sturdy.

That's why we fought the government's restructuring plan in any way we could. While I focused on maintaining FPL's daily operations, Monroe and Earle worked on legal action. In addition to filing for the injunction with the Supreme Court, they went to the US and separated the marketing arm of the company from the Newfoundland operations. The hope was that the marketing arm could be kept out of any deal the government was going to impose. The CDC remained committed to FPL and worked with us to stop the takeover:

> Talks between the CDC and federal negotiators aimed at bringing Fishery Products' assets under the umbrella of the new Newfoundland company were more like white collar guerrilla warfare than negotiations. The CDC valued the assets at approximately $32 millions more than Ottawa thought they were worth, and when negotiations to transfer them to the new federally controlled company fell through, the Bank of Nova Scotia called Fishery Products' huge loan.
>
> Complex litigation followed. The CDC and Fishery Products sued the federal Government, the Bank of Nova Scotia, and federal negotiator Michael Kirby, alleging an attempt to defraud the Fishery Products shareholders. The bank, in turn, sued Fishery Products and the CDC, alleging a fraudulent transfer of FPL's

assets to a numbered [company] in Ottawa.[59]

We then made a counter-proposal to the government's restructuring plan, suggesting that a group of Newfoundland companies form one private company and have it refinanced as a new entity. That at least would have protected the investments of our shareholders. Again, we were denied.

FPL had enough value in its inventories and receivables to pay the Bank of Nova Scotia in due time—but we weren't given the courtesy of time. Of course, FPL's repaying its loans was not actually in the best interest of the bank or the federal government, as it would not have solved the financial problems of the Lake Group, Penny and Sons, Nickerson, and the other companies.

Nothing we tried was successful. The bank made impossible demands, including immediate loan repayments.

The shareholders of FPL, the Monroes and CDC, were bought out by the Canadian government. FPL, the largest and most successful of the major fishing businesses in Newfoundland, became the centrepiece for the new FPI. The Lake Group, Penny and Sons, and other smaller operations were also bought out and drawn into the new operation. The federal government became 60 per cent owner of FPI. The Newfoundland government held 25 per cent, and the Bank of Nova Scotia, 15 per cent.[60] The company would operate as a crown corporation until 1987, when it was privatized.

All lawsuits were dropped as part of the final deal. Monroe and Earle were fired. CDC was paid off, and left the scene. The deal was done.

---

59   Michael Harris, "Troubled Fishery Firms All in Federal Hands," *Globe and Mail*, October 25, 1983.

60   Ibid.

Chapter 22
The evolution of FPI

The day that Denis Monroe and Harry Earle got the boot they came home with me. Denis called his father from my kitchen and said, "Dad, I've just been fired." None of us could believe the words. I have no idea what Arthur Monroe's reaction was to his son's call but, knowing his fierce dedication to building the Newfoundland fishing industry, it must have been a heavy blow.

The Monroes, after a century in the Newfoundland fishing industry, were forced out. This began an extremely difficult period and I, and many others, still resent it. The Monroes were great people who had had invested heavily in the industry and the province, taken risks, and, in the process, built an incredible business that had weathered many storms. Their contribution to the economy of Newfoundland and Labrador was enormous and required skill, guts, and perseverance.

In 1983, when it all ended, FPL had over 6,500 employees, a tremendous group of people with whom we had, by and large, a good rapport. The Monroes had never been equalled in the Newfoundland and Labrador fishing industry, and they have never been replaced.

Arthur Monroe helped to develop the fresh-frozen industry under the most difficult circumstances. There were virtually no roads or communication systems outside the Avalon Peninsula when he launched FPL. Transportation between all coastal communities was by sea; the limited freight-train service through the centre of Newfoundland and an unreliable ferry service to Nova Scotia often created more headaches than they solved. Yet FPL competed with fish-producing nations that had superior training, transportation, and communication networks. FPL had established an international reputation as a premium producer of fisheries products. The company prospered until the most important component in the production of fisheries products, the fish, began to decline.

Working with the Monroes through nearly 40 years of expansion and change was highly rewarding for me. Arthur Monroe and I had always been close; Denis and I developed a rapport in the later years of FPL. Denis had spent many years in the US managing Fishery Products Inc. He succeeded his father as president of FPL in 1971 until 1976 when he replaced him as chairman of the board. That was when I became the company's third and final president.

Fishery Products Inc., incorporated in 1941, was the first foreign-owned seafood marketing company and secondary processing operation in the US. Through regional and international sales offices, products were marketed across North America and Europe. In Asia, the company was represented by Nichiro Ltd., an established Japanese seafood company.

Arthur Monroe was probably one of three true frozen-seafood pioneers in Canada. (I would count C.J. Morrow of National Sea and Hazen Russell of Bonavista Cold Storage as the other two.) Through years of hard work, Monroe built one of the first successful vertically integrated fish companies, involved in all parts of the fish and seafood industry. I have never felt that Monroe's business efforts and savvy were properly appreciated; certainly they weren't in 1983, when the government barged in and took over.

Under Monroe's leadership I, along with others in FPL senior management, was able to establish excellent working relationships with leaders in the fields of fish harvesting, processing, and marketing in the UK, US, Norway, Iceland, Alaska, Germany, Spain, Portugal, and elsewhere. I have binders filled with thousands of business cards that I was given over the decades from businessmen, scientists from research institutions, presidents of fishing companies, etc.—contacts we relied on to market our products and stay successful. FPL management always maintained an international presence, thanks to appointments or election to leading fisheries organizations, including the National Fisheries Institute of the United

States, Fisheries Council of Canada, the Federal Fisheries Research Board, and various international fisheries commissions.

Over half a century Monroe and FPL built up a huge network that helped the company attain the success it did. It was an insult to Monroe and all the work he and everyone at FPL had done to think that government appointees with virtually no experience in the fishing industry would be taking over.

I had some say in choosing a name for the new company. The government employees in charge were going to change the name to something ridiculous, so I suggested: "Let's use Fishery Products but add 'International,' because the company conducts considerable international business." This name allowed us to keep a sense of legacy, although there was some spitefulness at play too. If the Nova Scotia operation was *National* Sea, then the Newfoundland group was going to be Fishery Products *International*.

•••

An interim board for FPI was established in 1983, comprised primarily of government and bank representatives. The new board asked me to stay on and manage the company during its transition.

I wanted to leave the whole mess behind me. But I still felt loyal to the company that the Monroes had built, and especially to the people who worked for us. I received a request from some of FPL's former vice-presidents—all experts in their fields and distraught over the turn of events—that I remain with them. Out of respect for them I agreed to stay on, report to the new board, and manage the operations until a new president was appointed.

It was a painful purgatory, but the appearance of "business as usual" had to be maintained. The company needed to maintain operations and connections with our clients, the people the Monroes and I had dealt with for decades. In that interim period, Ramea and other fish plants were closed because of low production and continuing losses. It was a shock to those communities, but there was no great furor—the fight was gone, it seemed. FPI maintained 15 plants and kept the business operating steadily until new management was established.

During the period between FPL and FPI, representatives of the "Big Three" (the federal government, the Newfoundland government, and the bank) were kept fully informed of the activities of the interim management group through weekly or bi-weekly meetings with the transitional board. To their credit, they did not interfere in my day-to-day decisions, and they were interested in our management strategy and its implications.

Those vice-presidents who had worked for years with FPL were kept on to manage the harvesting, processing, and sales and marketing operations of FPI. As for the trawlers, plants (those that remained open), and US marketing operations, business continued as usual and our customers were supplied with product as they had been for years.

Meanwhile, headhunters were busy on behalf of the Big Three to find a new president.

•••

After about a year and a half of uncertainty, the new management team and board of FPI were officially installed. Thanks to millions of dollars of taxpayer money, FPI began its corporate life debt-free and with money in the bank.

Vic Young was appointed head of the company. Young, who had an MBA, had been a manager at Newfoundland Hydro, but he didn't come in knowing much about the fisheries. We travelled together, visiting processing operations and customers in the US, Europe, and Asia. I introduced him to my key contacts as we went.

A crop of public servants was hired to fill new and old jobs at FPI. I remained with the company as executive vice-president of operations and, later, vice-president of marketing and sales.

None of the new board members was immediately familiar with the fishing industry, but most were quick to learn the basics. The board included some of the top businessmen in Canada, including Paul Demarais (president of the Power Company of Canada and one of the richest men in the country), Frank Stronach (founder of Magna International), and other competent and well-travelled individuals.

At the first board meeting, everyone was new, except me. I was asked to give an overview of the industry and offer my opinion on why it was in the shape it was. When I finished my presentation, I don't think there was a 10-second pause before Demarais said, "Dammit, the problem is with the resource!" And I said, "Yes, it is." At least there was one board member and maybe others who understood what FPI was facing and how it had arrived at this juncture. That's a lot more than I can say for most politicians and bureaucrats, provincially and federally.

Neither Demarais nor Stronach stayed on the board for any length of time. It's unfortunate, because perhaps they could have raised some alarm bells that the Government of Canada would have listened to.

Still, FPI stayed in business. The supply of fish to FPI plants was maintained by a large number of trawlers that worked aggressively to catch from a diminishing supply of raw material. The cost of our finished products rose, but our long-established markets were relatively strong. Interest rates finally dropped to normal levels and, most important of all, the newly restructured company carried no debt.

•••

Throughout the mid-1980s, FPI went about the business of harvesting as much fish as quotas permitted. Our processing teams were kept busy; the product-development group responded to demands in the marketplace with new products, and FPI held its own.

In 1987, there was a surge in the popularity of fish, thanks to an aggressive American marketing campaign touting the nutritional value of fish. Jumping on the bandwagon, the University of California, Los Angeles (UCLA) increased the fish served in its campus cafeterias from one to two meals per week.

It wasn't going to be easy: serving one meal of fish a week presented logistical challenges. Getting thousands of meals of fish ready on time required that the staff start preparing lunch at 1 or 2 a.m. About 80,000 students and staff were on campus each day, of which a high percentage preferred to eat fish. The university put out a call for proposals from fish companies. It was a big potential contract. FPI went after it.

The vice-president of purchasing for the university invited three companies—FPI, a company from Iceland, and one from Norway—to meet to discuss supplying fish for the new venture. The requirements were straightforward, but not simple: UCLA wanted first-class-quality fish in a form that would allow it to be prepared efficiently.

FPI had a six-person product-development group, three people from the production side of our company and three from our US marketing team. We gave them UCLA's requirements. We needed to produce enough to feed tens of thousands of students and staff, twice a week. The preparation had to be simple and efficient, and the fish had to be top quality. The university committed to paying 20 per cent over and above the average market price for a suitable product.

It was a big incentive and a prestigious opportunity. We went to work. The product we designed was a prime-quality cod loin, taken from the thick upper portion of a cod fillet of a certain size, packaged and fast frozen for easy preparation. To create the finished product we had in mind, the cod had to be mature, 24 to 30 inches long, with firm, fresh flesh—the absolute best texture. First-class raw product to these specifications would allow us to produce 4-, 6-, and 8-ounce cod loins. Combining these three would satisfy the requirements of a lunch, which might be made up of two pieces, or a dinner, which would consist of three.

We devised the specs for an overwrapping machine and commissioned a machinery company to assist in developing it. The machine used a square piece of heavy plastic, with various size indents to allow for the three sizes of cod loin. After the fish was put in place, another sheet was put on top, then vacuum-sealed and frozen. The kitchen staff would simply have to pull back the top layer of plastic

Launching Imperial Cod at the Boston Seafood Show, 1987.

and immediately 16 pieces of cod of known size would come out. We called it "Imperial Cod."

This was exactly what the university wanted. They saw our product, accepted it, and offered us the contract with the promised 20 per cent premium. We got 80 per cent of their business; the other 20 per cent was split between the Icelandic and Norwegian suppliers. We had come out ahead of two of our fiercest competitors.

For the next six months we went all out and produced the product as best we could. From the beginning, however, we had difficulty getting enough fish of the size and quality required to meet the specifications of the product. To make a long story short—it still is painful to think about this—we had to inform UCLA that we were unable to provide the consistent supply they required. Six months in, we lost the contract.

Despite the fact that FPI had the largest fleet of fishing vessels in Canada and the people and the plants required to produce the product, we just could not meet the demand. Our trawlers could supply some of the cod needed for the Imperial Cod intermittently, but we did not have continuity of supply. It should not have been unexpected—our industry was going downhill, we knew that—but it was a crushing blow that resounded through the company.

I tell this story for two reasons. First, winning the UCLA contract over our competitors in Iceland and Norway was a tribute to the innovative and dedicated work of our product-development group. Second, that we were not able to provide the product as promised clearly demonstrates the state of the resource on which we were dependent. Norway and Iceland, on the other hand, with their better-managed resources, were able to meet the demand in 1987, and are still thriving in 2013.

•••

Notwithstanding the UCLA fiasco, FPI was debt-free, thanks to Canadian taxpayers. The years 1986 and 1987 were profitable, and it was decided that FPI would be privatized. This had been the federal government's plan from the beginning, and five years of careful business management had made the company an attractive investment. I accompanied Young and a group of representatives from financial institutions to sell shares in FPI to interested people in cities across Canada and Europe, including London, Paris, Frankfurt, and Zurich. The public relations campaign surrounding the event created great enthusiasm, and we sold close to $180 million worth of shares.

The Fishery Products International Ltd. Act, passed by the provincial government, prevented any single shareholder owning more than 15 per cent of the company, ensuring it would preserve local interests—the company's mandate was not only to turn a profit but also to be responsive to the needs of the communities in which it operated.

Well financed as a public company, FPI continued to contribute to the economy of the province. Vic Young remained CEO and, though it had its ups and downs, FPI survived everything that came its way, even the 1992 cod moratorium. When its fishermen were unable to catch cod and other groundfish, FPI focused on other species, including the burgeoning shrimp and crab fisheries around Newfoundland, as well as purchasing fish from foreign producers. Young kept the company out of debt, socially conscious, and on relatively stable footing.

Nevertheless, the owner of the Nova Scotia-based Clearwater Fine Foods, John Risley, attempted a takeover of the company in 2000. He failed. But he returned in 2001, this time with new partners, including Newfoundlanders: businessman Derrick Rowe, former fisheries minister John Crosbie, and Newfoundland fishing industry heavyweight Bill Barry. Risley and his cohorts wooed FPI shareholders, promising they would be more aggressive in business than the current team and would bring in more profit for all.

The shareholders were convinced. The provincial government, which could—and I would say *should*—have intervened, did not. Young and his team were ousted.

In allowing FPI to be taken over, the government of Newfoundland and Labrador failed to protect the interests of its fishing population. Nova Scotia-based interests, which had worked for half a century to end the competition presented by Newfoundland's seafood products, were allowed to prevail. The takeover was the end of the days of profitability for FPI. Allowing outsiders to run what was once a family-owned, Newfoundland-first company was its death knell. Shares tumbled, plants were unceremoniously closed, and debt piled up. Actions that were once unthinkable—including shipping fish from Newfoundland all the way to China for processing—were taken, even embraced.

Piece by piece, the building blocks that had created the Newfoundland and Labrador fishing industry were closed down, sold off, or shipped overseas. The Burin plant, once the flagship FPL operation, had been rebuilt as an $8 million secondary processing plant in 1984, right after FPI's restructuring. Between that plant and the trawler refit and repair operation in the community, practically all of those displaced by FPL's plant closure in Burin had steady work.

In 2007, the faltering FPI sold off its assets. The secondary plant in Burin was purchased by High Liner of Nova Scotia (which closed the plant in 2012, putting 120 people out of work). High Liner also purchased FPI's American marketing arm—the company Arthur Monroe had set up in 1941—at the same time. Ocean Choice International bought FPI's remaining fish plants, including Marystown and Port Union (both of which were shuttered by 2012).

Practically nothing is left of the old FPL. The company which had once operated in every corner of the province, from Cartwright to Trepassey, is gone. Rebuilding an industry, even if the resource comes back, would be a steep uphill climb, at best.

•••

Occasionally I refer to the Kirby Report, and I'm still angry about the devious manner in which it was born and implemented. The collaborators on the report had a plan from the beginning, and they were hell-bent on implementing it. Michael Kirby—who became a senator in 1984—was a smart guy, no doubt about that.

Unfortunately for us, influential members of the task force were from Nova Scotia and were biased toward the well-being of the industry in that province.

The groundfisheries adjacent to Nova Scotia were heavily overfished and Nickerson-National Sea actively built and acquired processing plants on Newfoundland's northeast coast to keep their businesses viable. FPL was unfairly attacked because it was the competition. Within the industry, FPL was not liked, especially in Nova Scotia, for the simple reason that Monroe was a strong-minded, independent individual who had succeeded, with the support and financial assistance of Joey Smallwood, in building a strong fishing industry in Newfoundland. FPL had a strong presence in the world market, particularly in the food-service industry in the US.

FPL was virtually excluded from the Kirby Report. I learned later that newly hired spokespeople of the Lake Group had told the Kirby task force that FPL had received preferential treatment in being assigned fish quotas for its trawlers. (When the government gave a $13 million bailout to the Lake Group in 1982, the bank insisted that the Group strengthen its management team: two men from Boston were hired as its spokespeople.) These false charges seemed to be Kirby's only information about FPL.

We weren't included in or able to influence the report—yet the government wanted to make FPL the centre of the newly restructured company. Had Kirby been anxious to get reliable data on the fisheries for the previous 10 years, he could not have found a better source than the six vice-presidents of FPL, who had lived through the agony of the resource problem from 1971 onward.

In the end, the foundation of Kirby's work was shown to be a shaky one. Less than a decade after the Kirby Report and its grand restructuring plans—all built upon the presumption of a resource that was on its way to recovery—a cod moratorium was declared.

If FPL had been left to run its business as a private company, as it had from 1941 to 1983, it could have been the one organization to step up, weather the storm, and eventually save the provincial fisheries. I believe the company would still be operational today and that the Newfoundland and Labrador fisheries would be better off and a major competitor in the seafood market.

FPL had a strong marketing company and secondary processing plant in Fishery Products Inc. Those assets, combined with an extremely experienced management group, could have attracted other investors (like CDC) with a vision for a long-term and successful fishing industry. We had proven ourselves to be an innovative and flexible company. I think we could have had the success Norway, Iceland, and other advanced fishing nations have, but we were not given the chance.

PART 4: ADVOCACY

But over and above all, we must exhibit both the will and the capacity to create conditions that will permit and encourage recovery of cod populations.
—Harris Report

Chapter 23

State of the resource 4:
The Harris Report, 1990

Two years before the 1992 announcement of the northern cod moratorium, the *Independent Review of the State of the Northern Cod Stock*,[61] by Dr. Leslie Harris, chair of the Northern Cod Review Board, was released. Unlike the political Kirby Report, the Harris Report was a science-based document, written by a man with deep roots in Newfoundland and a thorough understanding of Newfoundland and Labrador history.

Harris was from St. Joseph's, a fishing community in Placentia Bay. He worked as a teacher in various towns in Newfoundland and Labrador before becoming a professor at Memorial University and, eventually, the university's president from 1982 to 1990. He was sensitive to the challenges faced by scientists, attuned to the importance of accurate data, respectful of hard-working fishermen, and not afraid to point fingers.

Harris and his panel had a mandate to examine DFO's scientific reports and assessments since 1977—the data collected, the methodologies used in the collection and assessment of that data, and changes in the state of the resource—and offer a report on the state and size of the stock as of 1990. Harris was to recommend improvements in data collection and stock assessment "with a view to better forecasting the size, growth potential and behavior of the stock in the future" (11).

While researching and compiling his report, Harris observed that immediate action was required to save the northern cod—and that the weight of responsibility fell on the federal government. He

---

61   Leslie Harris, *Independent Review of the State of the Northern Cod Stock: Final Report* (Ottawa: Communications Directorate, DFO, 1990) (cited in text as *HR*).

explained the central theme of the report this way:

> The conservation of the northern cod stock(s) and their management as an infinitely renewable resource is a matter of the most vital interest to the coastal communities of Atlantic Canada who have traditionally depended upon them and whose future well-being is inextricably tied to their vitality. Furthermore, it is the constitutional responsibility of the Government of Canada to ensure the survival of the stocks and to provide for their proper management and for their protection. (149)

Of the 68 reports I have collected over the years, the Harris Report is one of a few worthwhile reports (the Walsh Report and those by Dr. Templeman are others). Almost all of the rest—reviews and reports from conferences, seminars, and commissions involving prominent sea lawyers, university representatives, and politicians of all stripes, many based on misinformation coming from DFO, the provincial governments, foreign fishing nations, or local industry players—I should burn.

Harris traced the history of Newfoundland's fisheries and fisheries management, stating precisely what had happened to cause the ongoing problems in the fisheries: the resource was mismanaged by Canada, overfished by foreign nations, and carelessly destroyed. Incomplete scientific data, and inaccurate reporting of fish landings, compounded by poor national and international management, presented major issues. This was exactly what I, and others around me, had been saying for years.

•••

For the hundred years leading up to 1950, Harris wrote, the average catch level of cod off Newfoundland and Labrador was about 250,000 tons, and appeared sustainable:

In general, the harvest level gradually moved upward as populations grew and fishing efforts increased. Nevertheless ... the overall historical record indicates that the stock(s) could sustain the fishing pressures imposed upon them without exhibiting any obvious sign of decreasing abundance. (1)

That changed. By the mid-1900s, inshore and offshore fishermen acquired higher-powered vessels (among them, longliners for inshore fishermen, otter trawls for the offshore) that enabled them to fish in deeper water, aided by electronic navigation and fish-finding equipment.

The increased fishing effort by the Canadian fleet, however, was nothing compared to what was coming from the other side of the ocean:

Then came the burgeoning of offshore technology, with West Germany in the vanguard and other European nations quickly following and the notorious assault upon the spawning aggregations on the northern banks during the late 1960s and 1970s. With catches reaching 800,000 tons in the peak year of 1968, the predictable result was a collapse of the stock with inshore landings falling to figures lower than any recorded in the previous centuries. (*HR*, 2)

When Canada declared its 200-mile management zone in 1977, many believed foreign overfishing would halt—or at least be reduced enough to allow groundfish stocks to recover. The extension of jurisdiction to 200 miles ushered in a new era of optimism for the fisheries. Even scientists were "[i]nfected like so many others by the post-1977 euphoria [and did] not appear to have appreciated the full implications for cod mortality of new technologies and new fishing practices employed by both domestic and foreign fishermen" (*HR*, 130).

Sure enough, in the years directly after 1977, catches increased, groundfish stocks seemed to be growing, and scientists were "lulled by false data signals and, to some extent, overconfident of the validity of their predictions" (*HR*, 2). TACs were increased steadily, from 135,000 tons in 1978 to 266,000 tons annually from 1984 to 1988—when the major restructuring of the fishing industry had taken place (*HR*, 9).

Harris credits DFO scientists for tackling the near-impossible task of assessing fish populations over broad expanses of ocean. It is only with the benefit of hindsight that he could say that the scientists failed to "recognize the statistical inadequacies in their bulk biomass model" and did not acknowledge "the high risk involved with state-of-stock advice based on relatively short and unreliable data series." Harris blamed these shortcomings not on the scientists themselves but on "weaknesses in scientific management and the peer review process" (2).

The collection of scientific data was also hampered by major variables, including the "misreporting of catches, bycatches, and discard rates and other significant inaccuracies in the commercial catch data" (*HR*, 2). This affected both the understanding and the overall health of the stock:

> The Panel heard repeated testimony that foreign vessel bycatch figures were almost invariably under-reported by as much as 25% and that discard rates … were far more significant than Department of Fisheries and Oceans calculations considered them to be. Not only is it imperative to reduce such waste to the absolute minimum that wise regulations and rigorous enforcement will permit, but we must also ensure that the information we record and use is as accurate as can be achieved. (133)

While incomplete data and the unfounded optimism of scientists and politicians were serious problems, Harris reserved his harshest criticism for foreign fishing fleets and the agencies that were supposed to regulate their activities.

Harris boldly stated: "As an agency for conservation … ICNAF was a total failure" (7). ICNAF's successor, NAFO, was no better: "it is totally devoid of 'teeth' … In practice, such nations as Spain and Portugal habitually ignore scientific advice, flaunt their defiance of conservational strategies, and limit their catches only by the capacity of their fishing fleets" (8). Harris was correct in highlighting ICNAF and NAFO nations' disregard for the recommendations of the scientific committee year after year. During the ICNAF and NAFO annual meetings I attended from the 1960s onward, I heard scientists warn that cod and other species were being critically overfished—only to be ignored as TACs were increased.

•••

The Harris Report reviewed the processes scientists used to assess stocks and recommend the amount of fish that could be taken. During the 1950s and 1960s, maximum sustainable yield (MSY) was the crucial number for fisheries management. MSY was a scientific model used to determine the amount of fish that could be safely taken out of the water while still leaving behind a healthy resource; it was used to establish TACs and set national fisheries allocations.

For many years the Newfoundland and Labrador stocks were supposedly fished at MSY. But the MSY model left no room for error. Even if fisheries scientists could guarantee that the data collected and delivered to them was correct, that they had full and complete knowledge of the true state of the resource, and that their calculations and analysis were 100 per cent correct, even then the MSY—fishing right to the maximum sustainable limit—model was risky.

With incomplete data being used to calculate MSY, the flaws in the model became even more apparent. Adding to the complexity, not only was the MSY questionable but fisheries management was also fraught with politics and socio-economic goals. Those types of goals, of course, are not subject to quantitative or scientific evaluation. As a result, Harris wrote, MSY "was easier to understand as a theoretical basis for management than it was to apply in the real world" (95-96).

The MSY model was followed by the introduction of Optimum Yield (OY), which was to allow for 15 per cent less fish being taken than with the MSY model. But the resource continued to decline, and OY was replaced after 1977 by another management strategy: $F_{0.1}$.

Adopted by Canadian scientists, $F_{0.1}$ was a calculation of fishing effort and mortality rate designed to allow annual fish landings of just less than 20 per cent of the biomass—a conservative and sustainable level of fish harvesting, by all estimates. It might have worked if the calculations for $F_{0.1}$ were based on accurate data and no overfishing occurred. As Harris discovered, fishing mortality rates between 1977 and 1988 had been at least double those projected in the $F_{0.1}$ strategy. As overfishing continued, no one seemed to fully understand the situation or exactly what was being taken out of the water:

> $F_{0.1}$ would have meant fishing at an instantaneous mortality rate of about 0.18. Instead fishing mortality was maintained at a level of at least 0.4 and possibly higher. At the same time, catches by foreign fleets outside the management zone consistently exceeded established quotas. Furthermore, the Panel believes that high discard rates and even high-grading of catches was a regular concomitant of the trawler fishery particularly in the earlier years of Canadian management and that underreporting of cod bycatches by both foreign and domestic fleets was a widely acknowledged practice. (*HR*, 130)

Not surprisingly, after an initial uptick after 1977, stocks trended downward. Harris reiterated: "recent catch levels simply cannot be maintained" (3). Fisheries management practices were simply not effective.

Harris proposed 29 recommendations, including "as a matter of urgency" an immediate reduction of fishing to a level of 0.3 and, as soon as possible, 0.2—in other words, half of what was being done at the time. He also called for a re-examination of fishing gear in order to reduce the number of young fish being caught and a limit on fishing during spawning season ("whatever management action is taken ... *the guiding principle must be the imperative necessity for an increase in the size of the spawning population*" [*HR*, 134, emphasis in original]). He recommended that Canada immediately "seek international agreement to permit its management of all fish stock indigenous to the Canadian Continental Shelf, and that extend beyond the two hundred mile economic zone" (152), urging unilateral action as required. Canada should also re-examine its policies toward foreign fisheries within the 200-mile limit "with the clear intention of eliminating any catch or bycatch of cod" (*HR*, 152).

Other recommendations dealt with science: Canada should invest in expanded data collection; develop a better understanding of cod spawning, bycatch, and stock trends; and create a more focused, coordinated approach to managing fish stocks. There were more—all good, sound recommendations about investing in scientific research, improving management and cooperation between the federal and provincial governments, reducing catch, and increasing the fight against foreign fishing.

The federal government accepted the Harris Report, in principle, and assigned an implementation task force and hundreds of millions of dollars to act on some of the recommendations. A few recommendations, however, were not acceptable to the government, including the immediate reduction of the TAC for 1990. It was "rejected by the [federal government] on 30 March 1990 because of the additional hardships it would produce in 1990 ..."[62] As always, the social and political impacts of changing the fisheries were put ahead

---

62   Department of Fisheries and Oceans, Ottawa, "Independent Review of the State of the Northern Cod Stocks (Harris Report): Response from the Government of Canada," May 7, 1990, 4.

of care of the stock.

The federal government also rejected the idea of establishing a joint board or commission between the federal and provincial governments to ensure more coordinated policies. Their response: such mechanisms were already in place and would continue. This was not so—Newfoundland had been pressing for joint fisheries management almost since the day of Confederation, and Ottawa had always refused, blind to the special requirements of fisheries of the size and complexity of Newfoundland's.

As for any unilateral action to control the continental shelf beyond 200 miles, Canada flatly refused; it would "continue to work through NAFO and existing mechanisms to provide for conservation of straddling stocks."[63] This response came even though Harris and his panel had clearly illustrated the deficiencies of NAFO.

Harris wrote accurately about the mismanagement of northern cod from 1955 to 1956 onward. His report also showed the truth of Dr. Wilfred Templeman's predictions from his 1966 *Marine Resources of Newfoundland* report about the decline of the cod fishery and other species.

The Harris Report is an important document. Had all of the recommendations been faithfully adopted, many advances in improving the health of the northern cod stocks would have been made. Even in 2013, the Harris Report holds many recommendations—for improved research and data collection and for bold action against foreign fishing within and beyond the 200-mile limit—that are worthy of consideration. Even if it had been given the attention it deserved, however, the Harris Report could not have prevented the closure of the cod fishery. The decline was too far advanced and the political will for decisive action absent.

---

63   Ibid., 5.

Chapter 24

The cod moratorium hits

The 1992 northern cod moratorium was inevitable. Anyone involved in the fisheries from the 1960s onward knew it was only a matter of timing.

At ICNAF's annual meetings the scientific council repeatedly urged commissioners to reduce TACs. Wilfred Templeman and other scientists at the Newfoundland Region of DFO spoke publicly about the impending collapse—many more aired concerns behind closed doors. Technologists and researchers on research vessels and scientists assessing stocks saw fewer and smaller fish. Fishermen dealt with the financial reality of the decline daily. The warnings were never acted on.

There were glimmers of hope, at times, along the way—good years, good months, good locations for fishing—but the signs had been undeniable: cod were in trouble. It's why we started SOFA in 1971; it's why many of us have been so frustrated by the lack of government action basically since Confederation and the onslaught of foreign overfishing. Not once did Canada take a firm stand and fight to defend its fisheries. There was no other possible outcome than total stock collapse.

When John Crosbie announced the closure of the northern cod fishery in July 1992, he stated that it was for two years. That projection was clearly unrealistic. It was a bold political statement to soften the blow felt across the province. Over 40,000 people instantly found themselves without work—imagine if he had announced a 25- or 35-year moratorium?

Just 43 years after Confederation, the world-famous fisheries on the continental shelf around Newfoundland and Labrador were gone.

The closure of the northern cod fishery (in NAFO divisions 2J3KL) was extended some months later to the adjacent cod stocks on St. Pierre Bank and in the Gulf of St. Lawrence, and the prolific 3NO stock on the southern Grand Banks. Flounder and other groundfisheries were also closed, resulting in more job losses for offshore fishermen and plant workers in once-thriving communities such as Trepassey, Marystown, and Port Union. The great tragedy is that foreign fishing on the Nose and Tail of the Grand Banks outside of Canada's jurisdiction did not stop at that time—and has not stopped as of 2013, unquestionably preventing the stocks' recovery.

Crosbie's 1992 announcement was met with outrage, anger, and fear. Although inevitable, his words forever changed Newfoundland and Labrador, a province that had so long identified with the cod fishery. Over the next decade, 80,000 people would move from Newfoundland, even as millions of dollars in government funding poured in for assistance and retraining. Throughout that time of confusion and uneasiness, realistic voices were periodically heard, but the greater public didn't pay much attention.

On January 3, 1994, the CBC evening news program *Here and Now* ran an interview with Carl Walters, a fisheries professor at the University of British Columbia, and CBC journalist Debbie Cooper. Difficult to accept at the time, Walters's predictions were accurate—and Crosbie's most definitely were not:

> **Cooper**: Dr. Walters, given everything that you've studied about the fishery here, how long do you think it will take for the cod stocks to recover enough to sustain a commercial fishery?
>
> **Walters**: Oh, I think the most optimistic estimate would be 15 years and if the foreign fishing isn't stopped and if there's some years of poor recruitment, it would be a lot longer, 30 years.
>
> **Cooper**: Thirty years?

Walters: Yeah, these projections of five to seven years are just nonsense. If you take the Department of Fisheries' own estimates of the stock and its recruitment it's a simple matter of arithmetic to project those forward and those projects don't show anything like full recovery.... What I really fear now is that maybe they're thinking about reopening the fishery again before the stock is fully recovered, like they did during the early '80s, and repeating that horrible mistake.

Cooper: Well, let's talk about what you think will happen if the fishery resumed in five to seven years. We've heard Richard Cashin say that recently. He expected that fishermen could go back to fishing in about seven years or so. What do you think would happen if that scenario was to happen.

Walters: It'd be a repeat of the 1980s.

Cooper: In what way?

Walters: Well, things would look good at first, it'd look like the stock was recovering but it wouldn't be very long at all before you'd be right back where you are today. The spawning stock of the northern cod needs to be allowed to build up to at least a million tonnes of fish. Right now, there's no way it's more than 10 per cent of that. It's going to need a good long rest....

Cooper: What do you think, when you assess everything that's happened, what do you think is the primary cause for the situation we're in now? What caused the collapse of the stocks?

Walters: Oh, it's the foreign fishing during the '60s and

'70s, basically destroyed the northern cod stock and it never had a chance to recover during the '80s.

Cooper: What do you think about the fact that there are foreign vessels off the Grand Banks now, outside the 200-mile limit?

Walters: If they aren't gotten rid of by one means or another, I think there's an excellent chance the northern cod stock will never recover....

Walters had it right. He wasn't the only person—scientist, industry veteran, or otherwise—who was skeptical about a fast recovery of the fish stocks. The truth was available, if not reflected in political speeches.

DFO and NAFO published statistics in 1995 (see Figure 4) confirming what Walters, I, and many others had been saying about the immensity of the overfishing problem on the stocks that straddled the 200-mile limit. NAFO member nations harvested approximately 10 times their allocated quota of groundfish between 1986 and 1994. Recovery was impossible while the groundfish were subjected to this level of overfishing

It was a serious mistake to have extended jurisdiction only to 200 miles, thereby leaving portions of the most prolific fishing grounds exposed to continuing uncontrolled fishing by NAFO fishing nations.

•••

A few months after the moratorium was declared, I received a call about a new organization called the Newfoundland and Labrador Inter-Church Coalition for Fishing Communities. Representatives from the five main denominations in the province (Roman Catholic, Anglican, United, Pentecostal, and Salvation Army) had formed an advocacy group.

Because the church leaders interacted directly with people

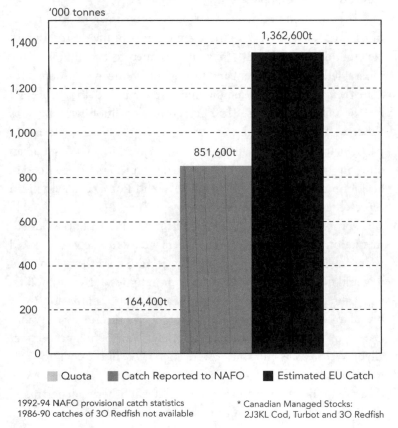

Total EU Quotas, Reported Catch, and Estimated Catch – NAFO and Canadian Managed Straddling Stocks* – 1986-1994

'000 tonnes

Quota	Catch Reported to NAFO	Estimated EU Catch

1,362,600t

851,600t

164,400t

1992-94 NAFO provisional catch statistics
1986-90 catches of 3O Redfish not available

* Canadian Managed Stocks:
2J3KL Cod, Turbot and 3O Redfish

Figure 4: The difference between total EU quota (164,400 tonnes), EU reported catch (851,600 tonnes), and estimated real catch (1,362,600 tonnes) and an example of deliberate misreporting and blatant damage of fish stocks, even after the moratorium. *Department of Fisheries and Aquaculture, Newfoundland and Labrador, 1995*

in every community in Newfoundland and Labrador, they had a deeper knowledge of the social effects of the closure of the fishery than anyone else, including the unions, federation of municipalities, and certainly the government. They represented the people of Newfoundland as nobody else could.

The coalition decided to confront European Union fishing nations which, they felt, were the main culprits in the destruction of Newfoundland's fisheries. They also planned to heavily lobby the Liberal federal government and Prime Minister Jean Chrétien to restore the fisheries and the employment opportunities they represent for coastal communities. The chairs of the coalition were Bishops Faber McDonald and Stewart Payne. McDonald had asked me to participate as a fisheries advisor, which I agreed to do. We set up an office in the Anglican Synod headquarters on King's Bridge Road in St. John's and worked closely with Reverend Ron Lee, an Anglican representative on the coalition.

For six months I advised the coalition and assembled documentation for them. The church leaders were extremely committed to raising awareness about the need to rebuild the fishery and what it would mean to the survival of the communities of Newfoundland and Labrador. They gave freely of their time for months and I was proud to be part of their efforts. We arranged a meeting with Walter Carter, provincial fisheries minister under Newfoundland premier Clyde Wells. Wells and Carter were supportive of the coalition's efforts and offered us resources, including a secretary and the time of an assistant deputy minister in the provincial fisheries department. These resources were invaluable as the coalition began its campaign.

It is a matter of record that the coalition also had the support of the federal fisheries minister, Brian Tobin. Both federal and provincial fisheries departments made financial contributions to the group, which enabled us to hire an assistant. School visits, community meetings, and outreach to interested organizations gathered support for the coalition and its efforts to convince the Canadian government to act. Carter brought attention to the inter-church coalition in the House of Assembly on November 30, 1992:

Mr. Speaker, I take this opportunity to commend the leaders of the Province's five major churches for taking a pro-active and public role in nurturing more responsible stewardship of fish resources....

As material circulated by the churches points out, "For the people of Newfoundland and Labrador, living in this fragile economy, the only ethical course of action is to undertake an energetic and dedicated effort to rebuild the fishery—stock by stock, and species by species."

That message, Mr. Speaker, echoes the much repeated clarion call of the Government of Newfoundland and Labrador for better management of our fish resources.

I point out that the five churches mentioned are circulating a petition calling on everyone to make the achievement of optimal sustainable levels on a stock by stock, species by species basis their highest priority for fisheries policy.

Mr. Speaker, the petition further calls for "the establishment of a form of joint management for the fishery, co-ordinated between the federal and provincial governments, which ensures a rational, non-political process, a process which strives for the full participation of the people of fishing communities in a transparent, accountable, decision-making process."[64]

The petition was our biggest public relations effort. We divided Newfoundland and Labrador into 29 districts and assigned a captain to each. We canvassed for signatures at malls and events across

---

64   House of Assembly Proceedings (Hansard), Forty-First General Assembly, Fourth Session, 41.74, November 30, 1992.

the province. It grew into a remarkable gathering of the people of the province. After many long hours, by March 1993 we had 112,000 names, 10,000 of which came from Labrador.

As we wanted to present the petition directly to the prime minister, we contacted Tobin's office to extend the invitation for Chrétien to come to St. John's. Tobin was not entirely encouraging. In fact, his response was: "Gus, who the hell do you think you are to ask the prime minister to come down?" Eventually he realized we were serious, and he supported us. We wanted to make the presentation to Chrétien on the helicopter deck of a coast guard vessel. That idea, however, wasn't acceptable.

About that time Chrétien was on a visit to Europe. One of his officials said he would stop down in the airport in Torbay on his way back to Ottawa to accept the petition. To that we said: "No way. He needs to come here to accept the petition properly, period."

The leaders of our coalition were in touch with five Quebec bishops who were schoolmates with Chrétien and remained tight with him. The bishops were asked to write the prime minister on the coalition's behalf, which they did. The letter basically said, "Jean, take your wife, Aline—don't go alone—and go to St. John's and accept the petition."

Three days later we received the response we were waiting for: Chrétien would come to the Confederation Building to meet with us. It was a big day. Every member of the House of Assembly and Member of Parliament from Newfoundland came to St. John's, many from outside the province as well. All the local and national media were there. There were about 500 people packed into the foyer. We presented the beautiful, leather-bound petition to Chrétien and the Canadian government, pleading them to take the necessary steps to rebuild the resource we had brought with us, in good faith, to Canada in 1949. Chrétien made a very eloquent speech and committed to presenting the petition to parliament.

He never did. Nothing came of the petition. It was a shame in light of the dedicated effort made by the coalition and all of the volunteers.

•••

The coalition continued its work, but turned its attention outside of Canada.

In 1994 we arranged with the Canadian federal fisheries representative in Brussels to make a presentation to the fisheries committee of the European Union. Four representatives of the coalition were to take part: Dr. Leslie Harris, a Catholic bishop from the fishing communities on Quebec's Gaspe coast, an Anglican minister from Fogo Island off Newfoundland's northeast coast, and me. Unfortunately, Harris had to cancel due to illness, but the remaining three proceeded to Brussels.

We were pleased to meet with all 35 members of the EU committee and their staff. For three hours we spoke about the negative impact of foreign overfishing on the social and economic lives of coastal communities in eastern Canada. The reaction was exactly what we hoped for: they got the message loud and clear.

At the end of the session, eight members of the EU committee, from fishing areas in Scotland, the north of England, and the Baltic Sea, stood up and described similar conditions in their communities. They saw the plight of their own fisheries and people reflected in our talk. This group asked the chair of the EU fisheries committee if money was available for them to travel to Newfoundland to see some of the places we had spoken about for themselves. When the chair agreed that he would find the money, we were elated. Hosting these visitors in Newfoundland and Labrador would be an opportunity to show them the effects of overfishing, a message they could report back to the EU.

We returned to Newfoundland and made a formal request to Premier Wells on behalf of the EU committee members. Wells immediately offered two helicopters for two or three days to show our visitors around. His only request was that we visit the Labrador coast, and the northeast, northwest, and south coasts of Newfoundland. He also wanted to meet with our guests himself. Wells, however, could not issue a formal invitation: it had to come from the federal government—specifically, from Fisheries Minister

John Crosbie. I sent details of the EU meetings and requested the invitation. Considering Crosbie's position, and the fact that the Newfoundland fisheries was in the state it was largely because of foreign overfishing, we felt the request was a mere formality. We expected an enthusiastic and positive response.

Silence. After several days, I called Crosbie's assistant, who promised to look into it. She called a few days later to say she was coming to St. John's to meet with me. At that meeting, she skirted around the issue for about 30 minutes before revealing that Crosbie was not willing to extend the invitation. Even though it would not cost the federal government, he would not agree. Everyone in the coalition was shocked. How could Canada possibly ignore this opportunity?

The only reason I could see was the strained relationship between Crosbie and Wells.

That visit could have made a difference. If the members of these fishing nations could have seen what was going on in communities like Fogo, Change Islands, Trepassey, or communities along the south and Labrador coasts, they would have witnessed the serious economic and social problems caused by foreign overfishing. They would have been more inclined to pressure EU fishing nations to halt their irresponsible fishing practices. Canada would have had allies to support efforts to rebuild the fisheries and our fishing communities. It would have meant our mission to the EU in Brussels had been well justified.

On another level, the situation was also personally embarrassing. I had to call the chair of the fisheries committee in Brussels and apologize. I said we had run into some trouble on our end—I didn't give any satisfactory answers because I didn't have any. Not surprisingly, he was befuddled. The coalition had gone to the EU to motivate them to control their fishing effort in our waters. We had made a major step in accomplishing that task, and they had responded positively. But when we came back to our own country and requested a gracious invitation, we were refused.

The issues between Wells and Crosbie were well known; perhaps it was fallout from the failed Meech Lake Accord.[65] I remember being asked to chair a meeting at Confederation Building about the fisheries, related to the coalition's work. Crosbie, representing Ottawa, was on one side of the meeting room and Wells and the province on the other. I would say there were 50 people in the room, all witness to the heated exchanges that took place between Wells and Crosbie. It was not pleasant.

A flavour of the relationship between these two can be gleaned from this excerpt from a lengthy 1990 letter from Crosbie to Wells, in response to Wells's criticism of the federal government's handling of Newfoundland's economic development struggles:

> ... It is difficult to understand why you think you should criticize, lecture and harass us with letters seeking to score political points at a time when there are serious problems in the fishing industry, we are working to find the solutions and when you say you want to work in cooperation with us.

> In your letter you suggest there is a lack of federal leadership, action and decisions on this issue. In your letter to the Prime Minister you suggest that the Government of Canada has not announced a response plan to the crisis caused by certain announced plant closures. You suggest management policies and systems have caused or allowed a resource decline along the whole of the Atlantic coast. These are all incorrect statements.[66]

How many other opportunities to deal with the problems in

---

65   The Meech Lake Accord was a package of proposed amendments to the Canadian constitution including the recognition of Quebec as a "distinct society." In 1990, Wells refused to endorse the Accord, a key reason the previous consensus unravelled, at great frustration to the federal government.

66   Hon. John C. Crosbie to Hon. Clyde K. Wells, February 14, 1990 (copy in author's personal files).

Newfoundland were lost due to squabbles between the premier and the federal fisheries minister, we'll never know. But this ended our first effort on behalf of the coalition to convey their message to the European community. It wasn't the last.

The coalition had support from their counterparts in other provinces who had contacts in the EU. Several European religious leaders, who were members of the Brussels parliament, arranged for me and a Toronto-based senior member of the United Church to make another presentation to influential members of the EU. It was the fall of 1994, months after our meeting with the EU fisheries committee.

By that time the EU had moved to Strasbourg, France, for their fall session. Our visit coincided with Kairos, an international gathering of advocates for stronger EU participation in environmental, economic, and social issues in various countries. The organizers of this social justice event insisted that we join in the opening ceremonies and tell this huge gathering about our mission. They gave us time to fully explain our problems and the need for action against overfishing. The audience was extremely supportive and passed a resolution urging the EU to take corrective measures. The church representatives followed up with EU officials and presented the resolution to their parliament.

Several Norwegians in attendance invited us to visit their country to talk further about the impact of overfishing. Norway was soon to vote on whether to enter the common market and the EU. Other Scandinavian countries, including Sweden and Denmark, had already joined and there was considerable support within Norway as well, including from Prime Minister Gro Harlem Brundtland.

While oil production was a key element of the Norwegian economy, the fisheries are too, particularly in the north, and it was among the northern population that resistance to joining the EU was strongest. Once a country joined the EU, the door was open to full participation in domestic fisheries by all EU nations. This didn't always work in a country's favour—the fisheries around the UK had been almost decimated by other countries following its entry into the common market. Norwegian fishermen were adamant that Norway not repeat the problems of England, Scotland, and other fishing countries.

Arrangements were made for me to visit several fishing communities in Norway. In each I outlined our experiences with EU countries fishing off Newfoundland and the impact of their uncontrolled fishing. My general theme, as picked up in the press, was "that no-one surpasses the EU's plunder of natural marine resources."[67] Representatives from other countries affected by overfishing practices were also invited to speak; the overall emphasis was on the need for a fishing nation to maintain full control over its renewable fisheries.

In the end the country voted to do just that, rejecting the invitation to join the EU and the common market.

•••

The case of Captain Curtis Mitchell

A healthy fishery can be a great contributor to the economy. It was in Newfoundland and Labrador, and it could be again. Here is an example of what just one fishing captain and his crew brought to the province over the course of his career.

Captain Curtis Mitchell is unusual in that he was on the deck of a fishing boat by age 16 and a trawler skipper with more than a dozen crew by 19. He captained nine different FPL and FPI vessels over his 42-year career. In each of his years on the sea, from 1948 to 1990, Mitchell made between 28 and 30 annual trips to the offshore (for a total of 1,212 trips), averaging about eight or nine days each. He and his crew caught a grand total of 276 million pounds of fish. Given an annual processing capacity of 30 million pounds, Mitchell and his crew provided the Burin processing plant with the equivalent of 9.21 years (50 weeks a year) of work. The fish Mitchell landed

---

67   A translation of the first line in a story about my presentations (Anna Heen, "EF-fiske gir oko-krise" [*Oslo Daily News*, September 1993]).

in effect permitted FP to pay a total of nearly $102 million in wages.

I contacted Memorial University's Economics Department about this exercise and asked about the spinoff effects of fish-plant work. I was told that, on average, 2.2 jobs are generated in the goods and services sector for each full-time plant job. Using this multiplier, it can be said that Curtis Mitchell and his crew contributed some $326 million to the economy of Newfoundland and Labrador.

I chose Mitchell for this exercise because of his longevity. That's not to say he was the only long-time captain; other captains and crews for FPL and other fishing companies performed at the same rate and contributed just as much. These people who fished year-round made a tremendous contribution to the economy and the social life of Newfoundland.

The fishery does not get the attention or have attract companies with big budgets the way other non-renewable resources like oil, gas, and mining do. It should. Not only is it potentially a renewable source of income, but it is also a source of food. Managed properly, the Newfoundland and Labrador fishery could be one of the biggest breadbaskets in the world.

Newfoundland and Labrador needs, but has never had, a premier who puts the fisheries first.[68] Beyond any other source of income or employment should be the fisheries because they are renewable and, if managed properly, could steadily fuel the province's economy. Every possible effort should be made by federal and provincial governments to develop legislation to ensure maximum safety, excellent working conditions, and income security for those dedicated and skilled participants in a renewable industry that is

---

68 In fairness to Premier Clyde Wells I should state that, in addition to supporting the Coalition of Churches, Wells supported Fisheries Minister Walter Carter in promoting better management of the industry. Carter appointed an industry advisory committee in 1990 to advise him monthly on matters related to fishery management; Dave Vardy was Deputy Minister and Les Dean was Assistant Deputy Minister at the time. I chaired the committee and can attest to the fact that the group felt they were communicating in a very effective manner. Carter's successor, Bud Hulan, dissolved the committee the first week he was in office without a word of explanation.

basic to our culture and way of life.

I've spent 50 years of my life intimately involved with the fisheries, in every aspect. I've seen the world of fisheries from the China Sea to Chile to Namibia to Murmansk and all points in between. It's given me perspective about our own particular problem and I know it well.

I look at Curtis Mitchell, his crew, and his many colleagues in the offshore sector and I know that not many others have made that kind of direct contribution to society or the economy. Perhaps this is at the root of the problem in this post-moratorium era—there are not many who recognize the importance and real value that healthy fisheries can bring to our province and its people.

Chapter 25

Since the moratorium:
a host of damning decisions

S ince the cod moratorium began, questionable decisions by politicians have only confirmed the government's abandonment of fisheries management.

Top on the list are decisions to slash fisheries science budgets, farm out federal monitoring responsibilities to non-governmental agencies (including the control of landed quotas and monitoring offshore vessels), export round fish (including undersized fish and bycatch species), and allow foreign-owned factory-freezer trawlers to fly Canadian flags and harvest Canadian quotas. Over it all hangs an ever-thickening shroud of secrecy.

•••

In the late 1950s, when I was manager of the Burin fish plant, I arranged a series of sessions for FPL's trawler skippers, first mates, and other key individuals involved in the harvesting of fish. The sessions, held in the FPL staff house, were led by federal fisheries scientists and they laid out, in layman's terms, the latest in fisheries research, including the general state of the stocks. They were held between Christmas Day and New Year's Day, the only time of the year captains and trawlermen and the scientists could get together. They gave up holiday time to listen to scientists speak, and they did so with great interest. We continued those sessions for years, and it benefitted everyone's understanding of the fish stocks. Nothing like that happens anymore.

Shortly after the moratorium was announced, I was involved in the creation of an organization called the Fisheries Crisis Alliance, spurred on by my work with the Coalition of Churches. It consisted

One of Dr. Templeman's assistants leads a session with FPL trawler skippers and other employees in Burin, c. 1954.

of former federal and provincial bureaucrats, fishermen, processors, fisheries scientists, clergymen, lawyers, representatives from Memorial University, and others, and I was appointed chair.

The Alliance's main objective was to rebuild our fisheries and its lobbying efforts directed at the federal government. As a group, we were not only familiar with the subject but also had experienced first-hand the impact of foreign fishing and federal fisheries mismanagement.

Fisheries scientists who had been employed by DFO recognized Ottawa's abandonment of its fisheries management responsibilities in the moratorium's wake. DFO was in the process of trimming its science research departments. Scientists and technologists who retired or moved to new jobs were not being replaced. The number of fisheries research vessels was also reduced and those that remained were poorly maintained, frequently breaking down at sea and having to be towed into port. Often they were left immobile because they lacked the fuel for routine surveys.

In 1995, Finance Minister Paul Martin substantially reduced the DFO science budget; and it was further reduced each year after that. In 1998, the Alliance brought the matter to the attention of the federal fisheries department. Dr. Sandy Sandeman and I made a presentation to the House of Commons Standing Committee on Fisheries and Oceans on February 5, 1998. Sandeman, a former DFO chief scientist for the Newfoundland Region, began with a call to action:

> The reason why, I think, much of fisheries regulation, the fisheries system, has failed in the past—and we should learn from our mistakes—is the lack of political will. This is where you gentlemen come in, to ensure that enforcement is done. During the days when I was there I don't think there was one instance where a larger fishing vessel, a trawler of the offshore fleet, lost its licence, with the many infractions that occurred throughout the years. All that's required is some teeth in that and the political will to do it. This is important.

He then discussed his primary concern of the time—cuts to research:

> I have made it my business to know the fisheries research situation in Newfoundland. I can say nothing but that it is absolutely grim. There are many things that I can tell you, but there are a few very striking statistics and I have to put these before you....
>
> In five years [1992-1997], the dollar resources devoted to traditional fisheries in St. John's, Newfoundland, have declined by about 40%. There have been small amounts coming back, but that's the basic decline. As of April 1997, the personnel had been reduced by 20%.... the most incredible statistic of all to me, which I didn't believe when I first discovered how bad it was—and I think everybody must be concerned—is that the research scientist group will be at

close to 50% of its strength by the summer of this year.

The cuts didn't stop. In 2003, Sandeman compiled a document for another meeting of the Standing Committee to illustrate the depth of the cuts to DFO's scientific capability in Newfoundland and Labrador. It included these points:

- The Newfoundland Region is responsible for the stock assessment research in an area that covers some 70 per cent of the total Atlantic shelf area and to do this it is only provided with 36 per cent of the full-time employees and 43 per cent of the total dollars spent on stock assessment research in the marine Atlantic zone of Canada.

- The full-time employees utilized in fisheries assessment research have shown a fairly regular decline of some 14.6 per cent during the period 1981 to 2000. Full-time employees devoted to groundfish have declined by 28.4 per cent.

- The dollars received by the region for assessment research have fluctuated considerably … The 2000 figure is $780,000 less than the average of the years 1981 to 1995.

- The expenditures for ships in the year 2000 was $3,500,000 less than it was in 1995 and $1,720,000 less than in 1981.[69]

Since then, more research vessels have been decommissioned or sold and staff reductions made, both scientists and technologists.
Even the DFO library in the regional headquarters in St. John's

---

69   Excerpts have been edited for clarity.

was shut down in 2011 without any notice—decades of research and valuable reports, once available to the public, have been boxed up and filed away, out of reach. I was told that these documents will eventually be moved to Nova Scotia, hundreds of miles from those who would find their contents most useful, and consolidated with other DFO library holdings.

Capelin, a small schooling fish and one of the more important base stocks in Newfoundland and Labrador, have not been adequately assessed since 1992. This situation applies to practically every other groundfish and pelagic species, including shrimp.

If the Newfoundland and Labrador fisheries are ever to recover, these scientists and the necessary resources must be reinstated.

•••

Most of the 80,000 people who left Newfoundland and Labrador as a result of the 1992 moratorium were residents of fishing communities who moved to Alberta and other parts of Canada and the US for work. There is little hope of these experienced fishermen and plant workers ever returning—especially now that the provincial government allows the export of unprocessed whole or "round" fish to other countries. This practice of exporting round fish shatters any hope of re-establishing a Newfoundland groundfish industry in three key ways.

First, it eliminates jobs in processing plants. It took over half a century to build a trained workforce of men and women who could process fish efficiently and to the standards of the seafood industry. By exporting round fish, the need for these positions is completely eliminated. Should the resource recover, and Newfoundlanders decide to re-enter the seafood market in a substantial way, there will be no existing knowledgeable personnel from which to draw. As well, Canadian companies are relinquishing their place in the American and European marketplace. With no processed fish to sell, competitors have stepped in to fill the gap. It will be difficult for Canada to get back in. Finally, 25 to 30 per cent of exported round fish are undersized, too young to reproduce; and cod, American plaice and other species under a moratorium are often bycatch. There is little hope for the rebuilding of the resource while this is occurring.

One excuse I get from government is that the seafood markets of the world demand unprocessed fish. There was always a market in China, Vietnam, and other Asian countries for small, unprocessed fish, to be sold to consumers in that form.

What happens more often, thanks to cheap labour in Asian processing plants, is that fish is being caught by Newfoundland and Labrador companies and exported for processing. By settling for low standards and low-end products it has become profitable for Newfoundland companies to do so. Back in 2006, FPI actually sent yellowtail flounder to China for primary processing (cleaning and filleting), which was then returned to the province for secondary processing (into the final product) and packaging. In 2013, it is not unusual to find Newfoundland-caught fish, which has been processed and packaged in China, for sale in Newfoundland supermarkets.

Surely the financial and environmental cost of shipping unprocessed fish to China and then returning that finished product to the North American market should prompt an investigation into the need for improved productivity, quality, and the potential loss of market access. Norway's and Iceland's more sophisticated processing operations should be a model for us. Jobs, food, market shares, and small fish that should be left in the water to grow and reproduce are being shipped out along with the round fish. The only benefit is a small financial return to the fish-harvesting company that sells the unprocessed quota.

The Progressive Conservative government of Newfoundland and Labrador set a new precedent in 2012 by allowing Ocean Choice International to export the majority of its yellowtail flounder quota. This has kicked the door wide open for other companies to participate in this destructive and lazy practice. There is no desire whatsoever to meet the challenge of improving productivity and production techniques.

The province made the deal in part based on the results of a report commissioned by the provincial Department of Fisheries and Aquaculture from financial consultants Deloitte and Touche. The report, a "Financial Assessment of Marystown Operation," released in late 2011, examined the losses experienced by Ocean Choice International at the Marystown fish plant. The Marystown groundfish operation lost millions each year ($1.2 million in 2008, $2.9 million in 2009, and $6.2 million in 2010), according to the report, due to fluctuating exchange rates, rising fuel costs, increases in overhead, and other factors. It also stated that losses could be slashed by exporting round fish: "Exported yellowtail provide a higher contribution margin to the operation when compared with in-plant processing." Reaching a break-even point at Marystown would "require 100% export with no onshore processing"—in other words, no use of the Marystown plant at all. Doing some processing at a plant with lower overhead (i.e., the plant in Fortune) would significantly reduce some costs.

That report seemed to give Ocean Choice International all the ammunition it needed to proceed with its campaign to export round yellowtail. The company made the case that the cost of continuing to process flounder at Marystown was prohibitively high. The government was eventually convinced.

As a result, the Marystown plant was closed, 25 per cent of the yellowtail was slated for processing in Fortune, and 75 per cent was given a green light for export in its round form. The FFAW was not in favour of the plan; however, the plant workers in Fortune, delighted by the prospect of full-time work, shut down the union's protest.

I take serious issue with the information upon which the report at the heart of this agreement is based. Ocean Choice International had been using the most expensive harvesting and processing procedures ever employed by a fish-processing company in the province, data about which was evaluated by Deloitte. This virtually assured the outcome of the analysis.

Starting in the 1940s, FPL had harvested yellowtail by conventional, smaller "wetfish" trawlers (using ice as a preservative), landing the fresh catch directly at the plant and immediately processing it into a primary product. It was then sent for secondary processing at our US plant to increase its final value. FPL had processed flounder at Marystown, Burin, and Trepassey plants using this procedure for 30 years. By contrast, Ocean Choice International used a large and expensive-to-operate freezer trawler, with a much larger crew, to harvest and freeze round fish on the Grand Banks. The frozen yellowtail were landed in Bay Roberts and stored for extended periods at considerable cost. Eventually, the frozen fish was loaded onboard a refrigerated carrier, trucked 200 miles to Marystown, unloaded, and thawed for processing. From start to finish, Ocean Choice International's yellowtail operation had to be expensive compared to landing iced fish directly at the plant for processing. No wonder it appeared more profitable to export the fish whole. Their method could be compared to using 10-ton tractor-trailer to do a job that could easily be performed by a half-ton pickup.

Had Ocean Choice International been serious about cutting costs and processing its catch in Newfoundland, its management could have employed a smaller, less expensive trawler, avoided extra transportation, freezing, and thawing costs, and adapted a smaller building within the Marystown operation to their needs. They also could have added value to the product through secondary processing. But, by all appearances, they wanted to export round fish—it was the easy option—and the Deloitte assessment helped them make their case.

There should have been thorough disclosure of all the facts about this analysis before a decision of such magnitude was made. Those who made the decision will go down in history as having committed a grave error which affected the future of many Newfoundland and Labrador communities.

•••

Many examples of Canada's resource mismanagement and destructive fisheries policies are unknown to the public because of a lack of transparency. There was a time when the Newfoundland office of DFO published a weekly report on the foreign vessels on the continental shelf. This publicly available notice of fishing activities stated the number, names, and nationalities of foreign vessels and the species being caught. It also recorded any regulatory infractions with the indication that punitive measures would be taken by the country of origin. This was important information and was referred to during annual ICNAF meetings. DFO has ceased making this information available to the Canadian industry and the public. I have filed a number of requests under the Freedom of Information Act to ask for foreign fishing surveillance reports; all have been denied. DFO seems to be taking whatever steps necessary to prevent public access to information on the conduct of foreign fishing on our doorstep. In major fishing ports in Europe, the local newspaper publishes daily reports on local and foreign fishing. Never in Canada.

Having worked in and observed the fishing industry for almost 60 years, I can say with some authority that things have worsened. A blanket of secrecy is now an integral part of Canadian government policy on all matters pertaining to the fisheries, particularly foreign activity in adjacent waters and the increasing influence of foreign ownership in the harvesting and processing sectors of the Canadian industry. Never has it been so difficult to get answers.

Canadians are aware that free-trade negotiations with the EU have been ongoing since at least 2010. The east-coast fishery is on the agenda, but neither Canadian fishing industry participants nor the general public has any idea of the details. In all likelihood we will learn more only if and when Ottawa announces the final agreement.

The Fisheries Community Alliance (formerly the Fisheries Crisis Alliance) was provided with an official questionnaire that the EU's free-trade negotiating committee gave EU fishing fleets. The questions were tabled during negotiations and were in specific reference to the fisheries adjacent to Canada. The list of over 20 questions included:

- Please indicate your area of business in fisheries (ship

owner, fishermen, importer, exporter, processor, etc.).

- Are you interested in establishing a commercial presence in the fisheries sector in Canada? Have you experienced any barriers to establishing a commercial presence in the past? If so, please specify.

The questions focused on the relationship of NAFO members with Canadian authorities and any problems they have had fishing off the coast of Canada. The obvious intent was to gather information so that any problems could be dealt with during the course of free trade discussions.

•••

In 2005, Prime Minister Stephen Harper pledged that a Harper Conservative government would establish custodial management of fisheries outside the 200-mile limit to better protect fish stocks. At a campaign stop in Petty Harbour, Newfoundland, he stated: "It is not just our responsibility to the fishermen of this country ... It is our responsibility to the planet to ensure that these resources are managed and regulated and used responsibly, not raped the way they're being now."[70] Harper indicated that his party would extend control within five years. Eight years later, Harper and his government have done no such thing.

It was widely believed that Canada's move to establish custodial management would occur at the 2007 NAFO annual meeting in Spain. During that meeting NAFO adopted a long-awaited document entitled *Amendment to the Convention on Future Multilateral Cooperation in the Northwest Atlantic Fisheries*.

Lo and behold, when the amendments were made public, we discovered that there was no reference to custodial management. Not only that but instead of the additional controls and regulatory

70   http://www.cbc.ca/story/canadavotes2006/national/2005/12/06/elxn-harper-nl.html, accessed July 8, 2013.

and punitive measures we expected, the amendments resulted in an overall loosening of the rules. For example, we expected the "objection procedure"—a clause that permitted European fishing fleets that were unhappy with their quota allocations to ignore the NAFO allocation all together and fish as they wished—to be eliminated. It was not. We hoped the useless "dispute mechanism" would be strengthened so that actual punitive measures could be applied. This was not dealt with. Worst of all, the new regulations provided an opening for NAFO fishing nations to re-enter the fisheries inside 200 miles under certain unstated conditions. These and other provisions in the proposed amendments were clearly against the best interests of our groundfish industry. We had been once again sold down the river by Canada's negotiators.

The Fisheries Community Alliance sought the advice of federal fisheries experts who had negotiated the original NAFO agreement in 1978, including former Canadian chief negotiator, Bob Applebaum; former head of the DFO science department, Scot Parsons; former fisheries representative for Canada in Brussels, Earl Wiseman; and a former deputy minister of Fisheries. The Alliance contacted Newfoundland's Premier Danny Williams, explained the seriousness of this development, and arranged to bring the four experts to St. John's for a seminar on the new NAFO regulations. Williams supported our efforts.

Arrangements were made to have government negotiators (the Canadian delegation had been led by federal Fisheries Minister Loyola Hearn; the Canadian commissioners were Earl McCurdy of the FFAW and Ray Andrews, a fisheries consultant) and representatives of the Alliance appear before the Standing Committees on Fisheries and Oceans of the House of Commons and the Senate. Having heard lengthy presentations from each side, both committees rejected the proposed negotiated amendments to NAFO regulations and indicated that a debate should take place in the House of Commons to be followed by a vote on the amendments by Members of Parliament.

The debate took place in 2009 and 289 federal members voted:

147 members opposed the amendments and 142 voted in favour of them. In spite of this, the morning after the vote Harper and Fisheries Minister Gail Shea ratified the amendments on behalf of Canada and informed NAFO officials accordingly. So much for democracy and protection of our valuable fisheries.

•••

When the groundfishery began to decline, many fishermen turned their attention and hopes to crab and shrimp. In the days after the cod moratorium, crab fishermen were the envy of many, pulling in good incomes and achieving Employment Insurance (EI) eligibility in a short season. Even though crab and inshore shrimp are seasonal fisheries, they could provide sufficient income to sustain many fishing communities, when combined with EI. If properly managed, these fisheries could be a permanent part of the total Newfoundland and Labrador fishing industry.

But it seems no lessons have been learned. Fisheries research has been totally ignored and a vast expansion in the licensing of crab and shrimp harvesters and processing plants has taken place since 1992. It was just like the 1970s, when politicians used their influence to increase the number of groundfish processing plants from 89 to 246—politicians lobbied for an increase in crab-harvesting licences for their constituents, putting far too much pressure on crab stocks. Crab, in particular, have been diminishing since 2005 or so and DFO has reduced the TACs and individual allocations accordingly. The declining crab resource has created labour unrest, driven by high-profile arguments about pricings schemes and licensing requirements. What was a lucrative industry in the 1990s is, in 2013, a toxic one.

Some crab fishermen and processors seem to want the public and government to believe that the recovery of the groundfishery, particularly cod, would result in further reduction of crab and shrimp stocks. While nothing could be further from the truth, I want to address this claim—some believe this unfounded concern for crab stocks is influencing DFO's groundfish rebuilding strategy, if there is indeed one.

Every cod gillnet fisherman on Newfoundland's northeast coast remembers when monofilament gillnets were introduced in early 1960s, when cod was in relative abundance. Back then, the lower section of gillnets, when hauled, was matted with crab. Crab were so abundant they were regarded as a nuisance by fishermen who had to remove them from practically every net. Any responsible fishermen on the northeast coast will confirm that both cod and crab were in abundance in those days. Crab were not being processed and were, in most cases, tossed overboard.

In 2009, a group of east-coast fishermen and companies had to pay $500,000 in fines after a DFO investigation found they had under-reported crab landings. Labrador Sea Products, Quinlan Brothers Ltd., and other individual processors were fined in the final court decision. In 2010, a crab fisherman from Fermeuse on Newfoundland's southern shore was fined $30,000 for misreporting his catch. There are more—and many have not been caught. Crab quotas have been greatly exceeded by certain fishermen and operations, thereby contributing to the diminishment of this resource. The dire state of the crab population is due to mismanagement by DFO and overfishing by greedy fishermen. It has little or nothing to do with any possible recovery of the cod fishery.

The same applies to the shrimp fishery. When FPL established a shrimp-processing plant in Port au Choix, there was abundant shrimp in the Gulf of St. Lawrence and on the Labrador coast in the Hawke and Cartwright Channels; there was also an abundance of cod in those areas. The Port au Choix fishermen landed large quantities of cod and shrimp on a daily basis for years. The species co-existed well. There is no proven relationship between shrimp and cod fisheries in terms of survival. Overfishing and over-licensing? These definitely had a negative effect.

•••

The factory-freezer trawler fleet has greatly expanded since 1992. From 1977 until 1992, these vessels were practically non-existent within the 200-mile limit.

Outside the 200-mile limit, of course, was a different story. Practically all NAFO and other foreign fishing nations used freezer trawlers or factory-freezer vessels because they were thousands of miles from home ports and fish could only be preserved by salting or freezing at sea. The Newfoundland trawlers, which were closer to home, were all "wet fish" trawlers: their cargo was preserved—but not fully frozen—for the eight or nine days at sea using flake ice.

Not long after the 1992 moratorium, the federal Liberal government of Jean Chrétien was elected. Two cabinet ministers, John Efford from Newfoundland and Geoff Regan from Nova Scotia, collaborated to find or manufacture a loophole in Fisheries and Transport regulations that permitted foreign-owned factory-freezer trawlers to be chartered by Canadian processors on a permanent basis. This was done, as so many things are in fisheries, as a favour by influential politicians. A business acquaintance of one of the ministers was a senior executive of a Nunavut fisheries development organization based on Baffin Island. The group was looking for a way to access the turbot in the area—there was no available landing port in the area and insufficient capital to purchase a factory-freezer trawler outright.

The solution was to allow the organization to charter vessels owned by another country. These vessels could be registered in Canada, fly a Canadian flag, and catch Canadian fish quotas. The catch was not required to be landed or processed in Canada; it was landed in a port in Greenland or Scandinavia for processing and shipment to market. Nothing in the agreement required that the crew of the factory-freezer trawler be Canadian. With this decision, a precedent was set. Newfoundland and Labrador is rapidly becoming a supplier of raw material, in the form of fish or other resources, to processors and manufacturers from Asia, the US, and Europe.

Prior to these changes in federal regulations, strict rules protected our fisheries from being harvested by foreign-owned vessels. For instance, if a fishing vessel was purchased by a Canadian company and later sold outside of Canada, the bill of sale had to include a provision that the new owner would not be permitted to return and fish Canadian waters. Since 2008 I have taken photographs of more than a dozen trawlers that once fished out of Newfoundland ports prior to the moratorium, were sold elsewhere, and have since returned. They had new names, of course, but the old ones are clearly visible.

As of early 2013, approximately 20 factory-freezer trawlers are operating in waters off Canada's east coast, from Nunavut to Newfoundland and Labrador and Nova Scotia. These vessels direct their efforts toward shrimp, turbot, yellowtail, and other fish. They operate inside the 200-mile limit, fish Canadian quotas, and fly Canadian flags—but are owned, in most cases, by foreign companies. These boats land thousands of tonnes of groundfish or shrimp in Newfoundland harbours such as Bay Roberts, Argentia, or St. Anthony, but only for immediate transshipment to markets in Europe or Asia. Some shrimp vessels head straight for Scandinavian ports for further processing and peeling of smaller shrimp or transshipping shell-on shrimp to Europe. The only financial benefits accruing to Canadian companies are the royalties paid to those Canadians chartering the foreign factory-freezer trawlers. Royalties amount to approximately 10 per cent of the marketed value of the catch. Little benefit trickles down to Newfoundland and Labrador communities.

Shrimp fishing grounds extend from the Grand Banks up to Baffin Island and into the Gulf of St. Lawrence. The shrimp stock outside 200 miles is ostensibly controlled and managed by NAFO. Two members of NAFO—the Faroe Islands and Greenland—have been banned from landing in Newfoundland and Labrador ports by the Government of Canada because they have consistently, according to NAFO statistics, overfished quotas. These countries pay an insignificant penalty but continue to overfish shrimp. NAFO does not apply any other punitive measures against those two countries despite repeated infractions. The shrimp fishery inside 200 miles is under the direct control of the DFO office in Ottawa (most fish stocks adjacent to the province are under the direction of the federal regional office in St. John's). There is no answer from DFO about why this anomaly exists.

Given this operational structure, it cannot be denied that foreigners and their factory-freezer fleets have returned to fish inside 200 miles as they did before the extension of jurisdiction. With the exception of seasonal operations by Newfoundland and Labrador longliners, the shrimp fishery is almost entirely conducted by foreign-owned vessels. It remains to be seen how long the shrimp fishery will last under these circumstances.

•••

In 2006 we changed the name of our group to the Fisheries Community Alliance to place more emphasis on the survival of fishing communities in Newfoundland and Labrador and the need to rebuild the fisheries to achieve that end. That year we met with the provincial Federation of Municipalities and asked them to introduce a resolution recommending that the Government of Canada take the necessary measures to rebuild the fisheries. The provincial body accepted the resolution; it was unanimously adopted by the Canadian Federation of Municipalities and presented to the federal government.

The Fisheries Community Alliance continues to advocate for rebuilding the fish stocks. The areas of greatest concern to our group are[71]

- The continued reduction of fishery science capability by Ottawa in the Newfoundland region.

- The increasing foreign infiltration into the Canadian fishing industry through the harvesting of Canadian quotas by foreign-owned factory-freezer trawlers that land directly in foreign countries or export unprocessed fish to them.

- The ongoing foreign overfishing on weakened strad-

---

71   Notes from author's personal files.

dling stocks adjacent to the 200-mile limit. This direct and by-catch fishery is conducted by a NAFO fleet heavily subsidized by the European Union.[72]

- The harvesting and exporting of very high percentages of undersized fish, too small to reproduce.

- The uncontrolled exploratory seismic blasting by oil companies on all areas of our continental shelf. Some restrictions should be in place, as they are on Norway's traditional fishing grounds.

- The abandonment of plans to rebuild the resource, such as the "Cod Action Plan" and the short-lived "Northern Cod Project." In 2013, there is no science-based rebuilding program.

- A lack of leadership or commitment at the political level, provincially and federally, to protect the common property resource that is the east-coast fishery.

Oil versus fish

The Newfoundland and Labrador government is far more interested in the short-term prospects of oil and gas than a potentially renewable fishery—that is obvious.

One of the clearest examples of this lies on the Grand Banks. The continental shelf once may have been home to the world's great-

---

72   The International Consortium of Investigative Journalists (ICIJ) carried out an in-depth investigation called "Looting of the Seas" in which they confirmed that the EU has subsidized Spanish overseas fishing operations by more than $8 billion (USD) in the last eight years. Other NAFO fishing nations of the EU have also received EU subsidization funds (www.icij.org).

est fishery; as far as the government is concerned, today it is the site of potential oil revenues. Oil exploration continues at a brisk pace, with little concern for how seismic blasting and drilling may affect fish stocks.

This is not a new issue. In the early 1970s when offshore exploration was being broached in Newfoundland, Norway was already moving forward with its own oil industry. I spent considerable time in Europe then and I was very interested in oil and gas developments. I visited the Institute of Marine Research in Norway on several occasions and discussed the relationship between oil and gas and the fisheries with the Norwegian experts. The Norwegian government had already introduced legislation to prevent seismic blasting in sensitive fishing areas; as well, after it had been discovered that oil and gas companies had left metal and other debris in the water, strict regulations about responsible operations and clean-up ensued. In this industry, Norway again showed itself to be a leader in responsible development.

Premier Smallwood heard that some people in Newfoundland's fishing industry were concerned about the potential conflicts between fisheries and oil exploration. In 1971, Smallwood travelled to New Orleans with some of his cabinet ministers to discuss matters of oil and gas. Rupert Prince, the province's deputy minister of fisheries, and I were invited. Prince and I must have visited 25 rigs in the Gulf of Mexico. One morning as our helicopter landed on yet another rig, we saw Smallwood already quite at home on the deck—with a pair of binoculars. He pointed to eight or 10 shrimp vessels on the horizon. "There you go, Gus," he said—his proof that the fish and oil industries could co-exist.

He didn't change our minds. I don't know the catch rates on those shrimp vessels but I do know that groundfish like haddock and cod are affected by seismic exploration.

In May 1992 an experiment was carried out by the Norwegian Fisheries Institute on North Cape Bank to determine if seismic shooting with air guns affects the catch availability of cod and haddock and how far from a seismic shooting area effects can possibly be felt. The experiment used fishing trials and acoustic mapping of the fish distribution before, during, and after the seismic shooting. The result? "Seismic shooting severely affected fish distribution, local abundance, and catch rates in the entire investigation area of 40 × 40 nautical miles. Trawl catches of cod and haddock and longline catches of haddock declined on average by about 50% (by mass) after shooting started ..."[73]

Norway has taken precautions to protect its fisheries against possible harm from the oil and gas industry. As of 2013, British Columbia severely restricts oil drilling off its coasts in order to protect the sensitive waters. In Newfoundland? If there are restrictions, I haven't heard of them. When oil and gas is eventually gone from the Norwegian coast, as it will be in Newfoundland and Labrador, they will have a fishery that is rated close to the top around the world—we will have nothing but a barren Grand Banks. More study is required to fully understand the effects of oil exploration and drilling activities on fish stocks. Action and regulation will be required, though I doubt very much if the provincial government will be willing to take such steps.

---

73   A. Engås, S. Løkkeborg, E. Ona, and A.V. Soldal, "Effects of Seismic Shooting on Local Abundance and Catch Rates of Cod (*Gadus morhua*) and Haddock (*Melanogrammus aeglefinus*)," *Canadian Journal of Fisheries and Aquatic Sciences*, 53 (1996), 2238-2249.

Chapter 26
Looking back and ahead

Along with other industry participants of my vintage, I have witnessed the rise and fall of the Newfoundland and Labrador fisheries over the past 60 years. And fallen they have (see Appendix 1).

There is every reason to believe that if the federal government made an honest commitment to rebuilding Newfoundland and Labrador's fish stocks, it could happen. Even though there have been steep reductions in DFO's science and research departments, there are still enough people and facilities to put in place a rebuilding program based on scientific advice (as opposed to one based on economy or politics). But I have grave doubts it will ever happen.

•••

Newfoundland and Labrador is hardly alone in its fisheries crisis. There are examples, however, to show what could have been. I have referred frequently to the fisheries in Norway and Iceland, and I do so with a combination of admiration and resentment. Why isn't Canada enjoying lucrative, healthy fisheries as these countries are? Why don't this country's politicians support participants in the industry or respect the value and potential of a sustainable fishing industry as the leaders of Norway and Iceland do?

Norway and Iceland manage their fisheries with long-term goals in mind. In Norway, a portion of funds generated from their oil and gas industries are used to strengthen the renewable fisheries. Both countries have solid fishing populations, people who depend on the resource and have been nurtured and supported within it. Their fisheries have been managed through well-funded science-based programs designed to provide a secure future. They demonstrate real leadership and vision.

Neither of these countries is a member of the EU; both declined to join the common market. The EU has benefitted the economy of many of its members and, in some ways, Iceland and Norway would have if they had joined. But they have rejected all invitations by EU members to join.

I saw first-hand why they didn't join: it was because of their fisheries and the need to protect them from the ravages of overfishing by foreign fleets. Those involved in the fishing industry did not want to join the common market; they had read the news reports about Spanish and Portuguese trawlers regularly entering EU ports and using them as if they owned them, changing crews and helping themselves to their adjacent resources.

The Norwegians voted not to join the EU in order to defend their resource rights. Twenty years later, Norway may have the most successfully managed fisheries in the world and the social and economic conditions existing in the country's fishing communities are just as healthy. In addition to having complete control over its own fisheries, Norway cooperates with Russia to jointly control the huge fishery in the Barents Sea, which lies between these countries. Due to proper fisheries management, quotas in the Barents Sea are on the increase:

> International Council for Exploration of the Sea on Friday recommended a more than 25 percent increase in the 2013 quota for North East Arctic cod in the Barents Sea.
>
> The council proposed a 2013 quota of 940,000 metric tons, which would be up from the 2012 quota of 740,000 metric tons. The 2013 quota is due to be set by the joint Norwegian-Russian Fisheries Commission in October.
>
> This would be the Barents Sea cod fishery's largest catch in 40 years, according to Norwegian Fisheries Minister Lisbeth Berg-Hansen, who attributed the pro-

posed increase to responsible fisheries management.

"Thanks to many years of good fisheries management and our continual work with Russia, we have succeeded in building up the world's largest cod stocks," she said.

Added Johan Kvalheim, director of the Norwegian Seafood Council for the UK and France: "The increasing cod quota in Norway is recognition that our ongoing commitment to sustainable fishing is working. It is excellent news, not just for the Norwegian economy and our fishermen, but for the millions of people who enjoy eating good quality seafood with a clear conscience."[74]

Another 5 per cent increase in quotas was recommended for 2014. It's infuriating. Canada should be able to boast about a "commitment to sustainable fishing" in the same way.

Norway, Iceland, and Russia are known for stopping foreign vessels that enter their waters to fish. I was in Tromso, Norway, in 2006 when a Spanish trawler was caught fishing illegally 5 miles inside the country's limit. The trawler was towed into port and charged. The captain and owners were heavily fined. If they did not pay, the Norwegian government reportedly threatened to charge the Spanish government about $1 million for accumulated infractions by Spanish vessels.

It is because of this kind of decisive action and Norway's cooperation with Russia that cod quotas in the Barents Sea have been increasing.

Cod quotas are increasing in Iceland as well. When their fish stocks showed signs of decline, their politicians took serious action. The country slashed quotas and fended off foreign fishing boats—the "cod wars" in the 1970s saw Icelanders cutting British trawler

---

74 SeafoodSource staff, "Increase Set for 2013 Barents Sea Cod Quota," SeafoodSource.com, June 8, 2012.

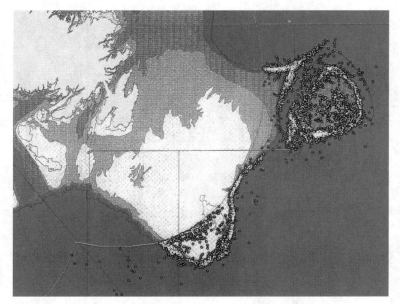

Figure 5: 1993 foreign fishing effort as represented by surveillance sightings. Each dot represents the sighting of a foreign fishing vessel which has spend at least one week fishing in the area in 1993. *DFO*

nets and British warships facing off against Icelandic patrol vessels. In 2013, Icelanders are reaping the rewards. Spawning cod are at the highest level in half a century; a scientific panel recommended a 10 per cent increase in Iceland's cod quota in 2013. Icelandic scientists report a higher proportion of older cod among their landings—better-quality fish which attract higher prices on the market.

Norway and Iceland manage and defend their fisheries; for decades they have paid attention to scientists and taken a long-term view of the potential wealth their fisheries can offer. Politicians make conscious and intelligent decisions to protect their resources. Fish companies successfully market their seafood as primary and secondarily processed products. Increasing quantities of chilled fillets are being sold in Europe and the US. Market prices for those premium products are high; as a result, those working in the fishing industry in these countries are among the highest paid in the world.

In Iceland and Norway, fish is considered part of the country's future. An economist in Norway would say "fish, oil, gas" all in the same breath. But not in Newfoundland and Labrador—it's "oil, iron, minerals." This is the difference. There is simply no political will to save Canada's fisheries.

There is simply no political will to save Canada's fisheries. The proof comes in images such as this surveillance photo (Figure 5) of the foreign fishing vessels clustered just outside 200 miles on the Nose and Tail of Grand Banks, catching as much as they could. This is from 1991, a year before Canada declared the moratorium on northern cod.

•••

It's been more than 25 years since I retired from FPI. In August 1988, four years after the creation of FPI, and 41 years after I had accepted Arthur Monroe's job offer, it was time for me to take that step. The previous four years had been tough, toiling beside Vic Young, determined to make FPI work. The privatization of FPI was complete and it seemed a natural time for me to make an exit.

It takes a long time to build a business that means something to the economy of the province. I was proud to be part of it and proud to have done so with Arthur and Denis Monroe. It was through Arthur's guidance and my great working relationship with Denis that I became so deeply involved in the fisheries. It is an industry that has meant so much to Newfoundland and Labrador, and I hope it will again in the future.

A dinner was hosted by Young and the board of FPI to celebrate both my 40 years in the industry and my (supposed) departure from it. I kept the many retirement messages that were sent to me for the occasion; to me they speak not to my own influence but to the importance of making and maintaining contacts and to the value of depth of experience and true commitment. FPL's relationships with hundreds of key contacts in the seafood industry, especially to our customers around the world, were successfully maintained because of the dedicated efforts of FPL management, production workers, trawler captains and crews, and the inshore fishermen selling their catch to FPL.

Since 1988 I've dabbled in business, travelled the world as a fisheries consultant, and, from time to time, enjoyed the leisure activities that retirement is supposed to provide.[75]

Above all, I consider myself a fisheries advocate—a fighter for the restoration of the once-great fishing resources of Newfoundland and Labrador. The Fisheries Community Alliance remains active, with about 15 members, most of whom wish to remain anonymous. I am the primary spokesperson. It is not peaceful work and I am constantly frustrated by federal and provincial politicians and angered by their decisions. Their short-sightedness and reluctance to commit to rebuilding sustainable fisheries in Newfoundland is frightening. They have no vision for it. This province was built on the fishery. Fish must still play an important role in our future—it is renewable, unlike oil and gas and minerals. But those in power are still bent on ruining any chance of a renaissance.

The FPI debacle still stings. The 1982 restructuring by the Canadian government dismantled FPL just as the company was finding its feet again.

Worse still, the 2001 takeover of FPI handed the reins of Newfoundland and Labrador's flagship seafood company to new management from Nova Scotia and Newfoundland. The new team promised prosperity for shareholders and a better future for the province's fisheries. Instead, six years later, the company and the industry was in ruins. FPI sold off its assets—Ocean Choice International purchased the groundfish operations and High Liner

---

75   I cannot leave out another important event from the 1980s. In 1982 I married Kay Diab of Lebanon. Thirty-one years later we are still hitting it off and enjoying life together. Kay had three children, all in their 20s, from a previous marriage, and I had my two boys. The two families came together in the best way possible. After my official retirement, Kay and I planned our great adventure—sailing our 35-foot boat, *La Reine Basque*, around Newfoundland in the summer of 1991. The circumnavigation took 42 days and we logged 1,172 nautical miles. I was able to revisit many of the communities I had worked with over the years and to see others for the first time. In sailing as in life, Kay is the ideal partner.

got the secondary processing plant in Burin and the prize: the US-based marketing arm.

It was a great day for many of our competitors. At long last, FPL/FPI was removed from the crowded seafood marketplace. This was accomplished with the assistance and the combined stupidity of provincial Liberal and Conservative governments.

On May 1, 2001, when the takeover of FPI was complete, Gerry Reid, the provincial minister of Fisheries and Aquaculture, read a statement in the House of Assembly:

> Now that a new board is in place at FPI, this government remains actively committed to ensuring the protection of the current FPI plants and the communities and workers which depend upon them. We are also committed to ensuring that all of the current plants are utilized to their fullest potential, irrespective of who sits on the board of directors today or in the future.[76]

So much for that.

•••

Arthur Monroe, Wilfred Templeman, and other mentors instilled in me that the key to success in the fishing industry is a healthy and well-managed resource. It's why I've always battled for competent, dedicated, and effective resource management. That is not to say I or FPL and FPI management were blameless.

I look back at my time as a heavy hitter in the fishing industry critically. There are things I, and the companies I worked for, should have done differently.

When the federal minister of fisheries offered a generous subsidy for the Canadian trawler fleet to fish the northern cod spawning grounds on Labrador's Hamilton Inlet Bank, we had no business going there. I knew it wasn't the right thing to do. We had limited

---

76   Department of Fisheries and Aquaculture news release, May 1, 2001.

knowledge of the Hamilton Inlet Bank fishery. We relied on the advice of Jim Cheater, a Twillingate native and the former captain of one of the UK's *Fairtry* factory freezers, to provide us with some details of the northern fishery. Cheater advised us to expect a high percentage of small fish, so we selected gear that might reduce the harvest of small fish. That fishery was hugely destructive and we and other Canadians enthusiastically participated.

We should have made a strong case to the Fishery Products board not to enter this cod fishery. We could have mounted a high-level public relations program across the nation to embarrass the federal government and, specifically, fisheries minister Romeo LeBlanc and his DFO bureaucrats for opening up the spawning ground for harvest. It would have caused a furor in the province and in the other fishing provinces and probably brought winter fishing off Labrador to a halt. Quite possibly we could have positively influenced future federal fisheries decisions.

We should have rebelled against provincial policies and closed fish plants instead of building new ones in the 1970s. We should have fought to keep SOFA alive and working to bring changes in federal and provincial policies.

While my colleagues and I spent a great deal of time and effort on the federal and international scene to restore, protect, and encourage fisheries management as they did in Norway and Iceland, I wonder what more we could have done.

The northern cod, flounder, redfish, and other species had been in noticeable decline since 1970, but we didn't stop fishing; we couldn't, and neither did our competitors on the east coast of Canada. We had customers to service and markets to maintain. And so the diminishing fisheries with its attendant financial difficulties continued as we entered the 1980s.

•••

In 1953, the Walsh Report on the state of the fisheries was submitted to the Smallwood government. It laid out, in great detail, the realities of the emerging fresh-frozen-fish industry in

Newfoundland and Labrador. The report was an in-depth assessment of the problems in the existing Newfoundland fisheries—the state of the fisheries, the challenges of quality and marketing, the lack of appropriate harvesting and processing facilities, the need for better transportation and communications, and the need for a better understanding of the resource. The Walsh Report was written at the time of Confederation, before foreign overfishing, before Ottawa's many management failures, before ICNAF and NAFO—before the destruction of the resource.

There were many issues to deal with back in 1950, but Newfoundland did have a healthy resource which, as the record showed, was sustainable at the level of harvesting at the time.

The Walsh Report should have been the authority for the development of the fishing industry in the province. It could have been of immense value to provincial and federal governments and for all those involved in modernizing the salt-fish industry and developing the new fresh-fish industry. It could have been used to educate the public about what was necessary to accomplish the job.

It wasn't. On one hand, the federal government realized by 1960 that the Newfoundland fishery was a valuable Canadian asset that could be used in international trade negotiations. On the other hand, the provincial government decided to ignore the value of the Walsh Report, opting to use the fishery as an employer of last resort. Thus ended any hope of that valuable report influencing the future Newfoundland and Labrador fisheries.

Newfoundland fishermen and fish processors felt the first nagging hints of the negative effects of increased fishing pressure in the mid-1960s. It was at that time Dr. Wilfred Templeman wrote *The Marine Resources of Newfoundland*, warning of the detrimental effects of foreign fishing and the importance of long-term planning. The inefficiencies in the inshore fishery were outlined, as were threats to some fish species.

In 1990, Dr. Leslie Harris submitted the *Independent Review of the State of the Northern Cod Stock*. He confirmed that practically all of Templeman's 1965 predictions and warnings had come to pass.

The Harris Report indicated that the scientific information to properly plan and sustainably manage the fisheries was available, and should be implemented. The comprehensive Harris Report stressed that we should all learn from the lessons of the past.

Unfortunately, it is more likely that the mistakes of the past will be repeated. Since 1992, pressure has been regularly applied by some fishermen, processors, and even politicians to reopen the fisheries in confined bays where there are small signs of recovery. Surely it's reasonable to expect some sign of recovery after a 21-year moratorium, yet common sense, as Harris pointed out, should convey to all that reopening a commercial fishery on an isolated bay stock is a recipe for another early closure. This is precisely what happened to the recovering cod stock on the St. Pierre Bank.

Five years after the 1992 moratorium was announced, the St. Pierre Bank cod fishery, traditionally a 60,000-tonne annual fishery, was reopened, with a quota of 20,000 tonnes. Scientists stressed that it had been opened far too early and that the quota was too high. Although some fishermen had asked for the fishery, others expressed hesitation—but politics prevailed.

Today the St. Pierre Bank fishery is in serious trouble, with an annual quota of about 8,000 tonnes. Some scientists and fishermen report that the annual catch consists of small fish and the stock is actually endangered. One thing is certain, the stock will never recover to historic levels unless this style of management changes.

The so-called "food" fishery is also political in that it is done purely for the residents of Newfoundland—certainly not for the benefit of the fish. The idea is to allow residents a small window of opportunity to catch a few fish a day for personal consumption. This could be acceptable, except that no one in the system has any idea how much fish is being caught. Most residents know that many participants make multiple trips to the grounds every day, catching far beyond their daily boat limit of 15 fish. It is so far out of control that scientists attempting to assess the state of the cod fishery will not include the unreliable food-fishery statistics in their calculations. This fact should be publicly reported by DFO's communications staff, and adequate surveillance measures applied.

The same problems apply to the sentinel fishery, which is under the control of the Fish, Food and Allied Workers. Even though this fishery is designed to expand knowledge of the stocks, no one knows for sure the amount of cod taken, and therefore the statistics are not included in scientific assessment calculations. Closer surveillance of both these fisheries is essential to determine precisely how much fish is being taken from a stock that is desperately trying to rebuild.

•••

I still have well-informed fisheries contacts, both domestic and foreign. I follow developments as closely and passionately as ever, and I speak up whenever I can. Even if few others will write letters or publicly comment, I (and other members of the Alliance) will continue to contact our provincial politicians and lobby them to demand that the federal government rebuild and sustainably manage our fisheries, as it is their responsibility. This position should be fully supported by the FFAW and every municipality, board of trade, chamber of commerce, and community organization. In the long term, the survival of most Newfoundland and Labrador communities depends on a thriving fishery.

For years, the provincial government has been focused on non-renewable resources such as oil, gas, and minerals. Fisheries are simply of no interest; they are too complex, too troubled, and not glamorous enough. There is no multi-billion royalty windfall. The federal government has long since backed away from its responsibility to manage the fisheries with hardly a word of protest from our elected politicians. This attitude must end.

Do the boom-and-bust histories of towns such as Buchans, Bell Island, and St. Lawrence mean nothing? Non-renewable resources can make a short-lived contribution to the local economy—but the fishery is renewable and should be nurtured and properly managed.

Norway has a $725 billion Heritage Fund and is directing the interest from that fund toward modernizing its renewable fishing industry to ensure future prosperity for its citizens. The provincial and federal governments of Canada have little interest in anything similar to that now, and this must change.

•••

Many politically influenced inquiries and reports have been written on various aspects of our fishing industry, but few have been worth the paper they're printed on, and fewer still have made the impact they could have, had the inquiries been conducted by competent and independent persons. The fisheries of Newfoundland and Labrador are at their lowest point ever. Citizens need to demand the rebuilding of the fishery to levels equal to those in 1949 when Newfoundland entered Confederation and entrusted the country's leaders to manage the resource with consideration and forethought.

Since the moratorium, there have been countless conferences and events, including Memorial University's "The Newfoundland Groundfish Fisheries: Defining the Reality" (led by Art May) in 1993 and the "Summit of the Sea" in 1997. What has come out of those discussions? No real, tangible results.

A judicial inquiry, led by an independent Chief Justice or other skilled leader and thinker, is a necessity. Great care should be exercised in the selection of the inquiry's committee. The committee should be free of all political ties; otherwise it would be a repetition of past useless and expensive processes. Those who still see and understand the importance of the fisheries—and there are many of us, even if we are not in elected seats—should lobby their politicians to instigate such an inquiry.

An appropriately structured judicial inquiry would present the people of Canada with the unvarnished truth of the state of the fisheries today and when, why, and how the current situation came to be. More importantly, after consultation with fishermen, processors, the public, federal and provincial governments, and especially the scientific community, the inquiry could offer conclusions and recommendations to rebuild the common property resource. The experience of advanced fishing nations such as Norway and Iceland can help set a course for the future that the Newfoundland and Labrador government can follow with confidence. Armed with a well-developed plan from the inquiry, the premier could approach Ottawa with confidence and the full support of the population.

A concrete starting point is required: a document that details the facts of Canada's fisheries mismanagement, a document the public can rally behind and get angry about. If we continue our current course, the fisheries will die. We cannot stand still. I believe a judicial inquiry, with the right leader and terms of reference (see Appendix 2), is that starting point.

•••

Between the declaration of the cod moratorium and 2013, little has happened to improve the future prospects of Newfoundland's fisheries. There is only a slow, sure readjustment of the people to the limited resource. Fifteen per cent of the province's population has left; since 1992 there has been a resigned adjustment to a diminishing situation.

There has been no recognition from government leaders of the need to rebuild the resource; the focus has been on managing its decline and the impact that it is having on communities. Time has shown that the federal government can't be depended upon to lead the charge; a robust effort on the part of the province is required to take up the cause and fight for it forcefully. Leadership is desperately needed.

After establishing an inquiry and setting a firm date for its conclusion, the premier should approach Ottawa and put forward specific proposals for the Canadian government to act on immediately. Cuts to the Newfoundland and Labrador office of DFO should be immediately halted. The morale of DFO scientists and technologists is at its lowest point; there are fears that what is left of fisheries management capability in this province will be transferred to Nova Scotia. This cannot happen. Fisheries research, science, and management should receive an immediate injection of cash, personnel, and responsibility. A senior representative of the federal government should be assigned to live in St. John's, develop a rapport with the provincial minister, and truly understand the fisheries. Discussions about an extension of jurisdiction to the edge of the continental shelf should begin.

It is difficult to believe that both levels of government, having presided over the demise of one of the great sources of food and one of the great renewable resources of the world, are now prepared to stand on the sidelines and accept that it is gone forever.

Surely the population of Newfoundland and Labrador and rest of Canada, when they are fully aware of the actions that brought us to this end, and by whom, will rise up and demand that our elected representatives take appropriate action to right the wrongs that have been done and rebuild the resource. That is my lasting hope.

APPENDIX 1
Recommended TACs versus Agreed TACs

A look at the TACs recommended for the 1974 fishery and those actually agreed upon shows that, in every case, the final TAC was equal to or higher than the recommendations of the ICNAF scientific committee. Even though the resource showed signs of weakness, the greater ICNAF membership pushed ahead, ignoring the advice of their own best scientists.

Not surprisingly, the official proceedings of ICNAF meetings in the early 1970s record heated discussions between Canadian commissioners and those representing foreign nations regarding the impact of setting TACs too high. Canada, outnumbered and overpowered, generally lost those debates.

The 2013 TAC is listed to illustrate the current situation, as it compares to that 40 years ago. The actual quantity of fish that was caught, including bycatch or discards, is likely much higher than any listed TAC. The columns show: species by stock and region; TAC recommended by the scientific council; final TAC agreed on by ICNAF members;[77] and the 2013 fish quotas, if any, in each region. All amounts are in metric tonnes.

---

77 Information for 1974 from *International Commission for the Northwest Atlantic Fisheries: Proceedings of the Third Special Meeting October 1973, [and] Fourth Special Meeting, January 1974, [and] 24th Annual Meeting June 1974* (Dartmouth, NS: 1974), 104-105.

Species by stock	Region	Recommended TAC (1974)	Agreed TAC (1974)	2013 TAC
Cod	2GH	20,000	20,000	0
Cod	2J3KL	650,000	650,000	0
Cod	3M	35,000	40,000	14,000
Cod	3NO	85,000	100,000	0
Cod	3PS	70,000	70,000	0
Cod	4RS	70,000	73,000	0
Redfish	2+3K	25,000	30,000	0
Redfish	3M	------	40,000	6,500
Redfish	3LNO	38,000	39,000	20,000
Redfish	3PS	23,000	25,000	0
Redfish	4RS	30,000	40,000	0
American plaice	2+3K	8,000	8,000	0
American plaice	3LNO	60,000	60,000	0
American plaice	3M	2,000	2,000	0
American plaice	3PS	10,000	11,000	0
Yellowtail	3LNO	40,000	40,000	17,000
Witch flounder	2J3KL	17,000	22,000	0
Witch flounder	3NO	10,000	10,000	0
Turbot	2J3KL	30,000	35,000	15,000
Capelin	(all areas)	250,000	258,000	Not Issued
Mackerel	(all areas)	251,000	304,000	Not issued
Squid	(all areas)	50,000	71,000	34,000

APPENDIX 2
Judicial Inquiry—Proposed Terms of Reference

A judicial inquiry into the history and future of Newfoundland and Labrador's fisheries should include the following considerations in its terms of reference. These are crucial issues that have had a major impact since Newfoundland's confederation with Canada, when the new province transferred fisheries management responsibilities to Ottawa.

1. **The federal/provincial relationship regarding fisheries management.** The Newfoundland and Labrador fisheries should be recognized as distinct from those of the other east-coast provinces; it cannot be effectively managed from Ottawa, 2,000 miles away. We'll never have joint provincial-federal management because Nova Scotia, New Brunswick, Prince Edward Island, and Quebec will not agree to it.

    But if a senior representative of the federal government, a deputy minister or assistant deputy minister, actually lived in St. John's and had a rapport with the provincial minister, he or she would see and understand the state of the resource and what needed to be done to properly manage the resource on an ongoing basis. We've never had that, although we have begged on bended knees for the creation of such a permanent position.

2. **The failings of NAFO.** NAFO is incapable of managing overlapping stocks and is the main cause of the non-recovery of the Grand Banks fishery. Canada must confront NAFO and the UN and insist on man-

agement of the total resources, giving due consideration to historic performances by traditional foreign fishing nations. Canada must take control of her entire continental shelf.

3. **The need for increased investment in fisheries research**. The federal regional science capability, in terms of research vessels and competent personnel, that was in place in Newfoundland and Labrador during the 1960s and 1970s must be restored and then increased to undertake the restoration of groundfish and pelagic stocks.

4. **Local management**. All sectors of fisheries management should be restored and returned to the regional headquarters of DFO in St. John's. Activities such as dockside grading, sentinel fisheries, surveillance, observation and monitoring, and other fisheries management tasks should be returned to government control and no longer contracted to outside companies.

5. **The impact of the offshore oil industry on the continental shelf on the fishing industry**. An in-depth investigation of seismic blasting on fish stocks and fish habitats conducted by Norway in 1992 demonstrated seismic blasting caused a major disruption of cod and haddock stocks on a well-known fishing bank. Tests involving a working seismic vessel and a modern fishing trawler for a two-week period showed those concentrated fish stocks were displaced as much as 18 to 20 kilometres from the site of the seismic activity due to seismic blasts. The trawler's cod and haddock catches were reduced by 70 per cent.

To my knowledge, seismic blasting is conducted without reference to fisheries impact. We have repeatedly presented the details of the Norwegian experience to the Canada-Newfoundland Labrador Offshore Petroleum Board, but we are told that unrestricted seismic explorations continue on all areas of the continental shelf, including on prime fishing areas.

6. **The pros and cons of various fishing methods.** Otter trawling, mid-water trawling, gillnets, Danish or Scottish seines, hook and line, and cod pots all have benefits and drawbacks. Opponents say otter trawling damages fish habitat, gillnets cause inferior quality, and hook and line is not productive enough for a viable fishery. Many fishermen say there are thousands of abandoned or "ghost" gillnets each year that continue to entangle fish. The newest technology in fishing gear being used around the world needs to be examined.

7. **The impact of the loss of Fishery Products International and its marketing organization to fishing interests outside Newfoundland and Labrador.** This has been a severe blow to the province's industry; there is interest in the creation of a marketing organization to replace it.

8. **The practice of exporting unprocessed fish.** Fewer and fewer fish are being processed in Newfoundland and Labrador. This must be reversed.

9. **The impact of free-trade negotiations between Canada and the European Union.** Newfoundland's fisheries will play a role in the negotiations, although little or nothing is known about the details. A shroud

of secrecy surrounds the talks.

10. **The management of the industry if and when the resource is restored**. Government policies must match processing capability and access to fisheries to maintain the viability of the processing, harvesting, and marketing sectors. The health of the resource must be the priority, not politics.

ACKNOWLEDGEMENTS

My Basque heritage, through my grandfather from St. Jean De Luz who fished the Grand Banks 175 years ago, has been a strong influence on me. So has my occupation—every day since the mid-1940s I have been involved with practically every aspect of the fishing industry provincially, nationally, and internationally. My advocacy for Canada's management of all fish stocks on the continental shelf is rooted in these experiences. This country should learn from the examples of sustainable, careful fisheries management advanced by the Norwegian and Icelandic governments.

Over the decades, it has been my privilege to work with many dedicated men and women in the harvesting, processing, marketing, and selling of seafood products around the world for such a long time. I offer deep appreciation to these associates and friends.

During the preparation and writing of this book, I have consulted many written sources as well as many experts who have been involved in provincial, national, and international fisheries. Far too many people have contributed and confirmed information on events covered in the book to list them all here—it would take many pages to complete the list. To them I am eternally grateful.

I owe personal notes of thanks to Ryan Cleary for his assistance in the early days of preparing to write this book and especially to my tireless and supportive writer, Stephanie Porter. Her patience, expertise, and all-around support during the project has been exemplary.

During my career I spent lengthy periods of time away from my family, and I had no desire to spend my retirement years in a confined space totally preoccupied with researching and writing. However, for well over a dozen years, my wife, Kay, and sons, Glenn and Grant, have insisted that I express my views on the Newfoundland and Labrador fishery in writing. This book would never have been written without their persistence and tenacity.